Poverty, Justice, and Western Political Thought

Poverty, Justice, and Western Political Thought

Sharon K. Vaughan

A division of
ROWMAN & LITTLEFIELD PUBLISHERS, INC.
Lanham • Boulder • New York • Toronto • Plymouth, UK

LEXINGTON BOOKS

A division of Rowman & Littlefield Publishers, Inc.
A wholly owned subsidiary of The Rowman & Littlefield Publishing Group, Inc.
4501 Forbes Boulevard, Suite 200
Lanham, MD 20706

Estover Road
Plymouth PL6 7PY
United Kingdom

British Library Cataloguing in Publication Information Available

Library of Congress Cataloging-in-Publication Data

Vaughan, Sharon K., 1956-
  Poverty, justice, and western political thought / Sharon K. Vaughan.
    p. cm.
  Includes bibliographical references and index.
  1. Poverty. 2. Justice. 3. Political science—Philosophy. I. Title.
  HC79.P6V38 2007
  362.501—dc22

                                                          2007033237

ISBN-13: 978-0-7391-2268-6 (hardcover : alk. paper)
ISBN-13: 978-0-7391-2269-3 (pbk. : alk. paper)
ISBN-13: 978-0-7391-3942-4 (electronic)

Printed in the United States of America

∞™ The paper used in this publication meets the minimum requirements of American
National Standard for Information Sciences—Permanence of Paper for Printed Library
Materials, ANSI/NISO Z39.48-1992.

**For
T. K. Seung**

Contents

Acknowledgments   ix

1   Introduction   1

2   Avoiding the Greatest Plague of All: Plato and Aristotle   9

3   Societal Responsibility and the Undeserving Poor: John Locke   45

4   The Noble Poor: Jean Jacques Rousseau and Adam Smith   63

5   Empirical Influences and the Complexities of Poverty: Alexis de Tocqueville and John Stuart Mill   105

6   Poverty as a Challenge to Capitalist Economies: G. W. Hegel and Karl Marx   139

7   Poverty and Justice: John Rawls and Robert Nozick   163

8   Conclusion   191

Appendix: List of Abbreviations   197

Bibliography   199

Index   209

About the Author   223

Acknowledgments

My research was supported in part by a grant from the University of Kentucky Center for Poverty Research. I thank Michael Brewer who worked as my research assistant. Michael made insightful comments, which helped me to sharpen and clarify many points. Fateen Bullock, Hamid Taqi, and Danté Taylor made helpful comments on individual chapters. James Vaughan and Anna Law not only read parts of the book, but they also provided support and encouragement throughout the project. I owe a great deal of gratitude to A. P. Martinich, T. K. Seung, and David Williams for their encouragement, insights, and most of all, for their scholarship that serves as an inspiration to me.

Chapter One

Introduction

The number of people who live in poverty has always far exceeded the number who do not. As a result, governments as well as individuals continually grapple with defining who the poor are, why they are poor, and what, if anything should be done to alleviate poverty. The normative question of how governments or individuals ought to treat the poor goes to the heart of the idea of justice and thus it is an essential element of political theory. Yet, there has been no formal study of the treatment of poverty in Western political thought. This is significant because the idea of justice surely encompasses caring about others who are in need. My goal is to reduce that gap in our knowledge by providing a systematic examination of the main arguments of some of the most prominent Western political theorists about the causes, effects, and solutions to the problem of poverty. I explore how their beliefs and treatments square with their ideas about a just state.

The chapters in this work include an analysis of Plato, Aristotle, Locke, Rousseau, Smith, Mill, Tocqueville, Hegel, Marx, Rawls, and Nozick on the subject of poverty in the context of their entire political theories. I chose these philosophers because they provide some of the most sophisticated and provocative insights and observations about the factors and circumstances that contribute to poverty. Their views encompass a wide variety of thoughtful explanations and possible solutions to the problem and thus, the diversity of their beliefs and arguments forces one to think about poverty and its relationship to a just state from different perspectives. Throughout the work, I explore their beliefs about the causes of, and possible solutions to the problem of poverty, and their evidence to support them as well as the consistency of their views. This study asks: what is the relationship between poverty and justice in the state? If one is to understand the relationship between the poor and the idea of a just state in the tradition of Western political thought, then she must be able to recognize how these

1

theorists' definitions, assumptions, and conclusions about poverty contribute to, or detract from the idea of justice. At the core of this work my claim is that the demands of justice necessarily entail that the political theorist engage with the problem of poverty with the goal being to suggest some thoughtful and reasonable approaches that might address the problem.

I show that without exception each theorist is concerned with fairness and justice in the state. Poverty is of interest to the majority of these philosophers since concern about those who live at the lowest level of economic achievement has direct implications for their beliefs about justice as well as their entire political theories. To be clear, I argue that mere concern is not enough since all the hand wringing in the world about the problem may lead to few, if any ideas about how to deal with it. Rather than having a gaping hole in one's political theory, one may be tempted to simply acknowledge, and perhaps even lament the fact that some members of society live in poverty. I do not mean to say that this interest is not genuine or that theorists cynically tip their hat to the poor to bring legitimacy to their works. Without a doubt, poverty has always been and will continue to be a fact in every society so one could legitimately ask: is it setting the bar too high for political theorists by saying that justice demands more than regret or lip service to the problem? My answer is no and this study substantiates the claim since I show how each of the political theories I explore demands that the theorist engage with the problem to some extent. One will see a correlation between the theorist's detail of attention toward addressing the problem of poverty and the coherence of his entire political theory. In most cases, one will find that the more robust and thoughtful treatments of poverty lend themselves to richer and more consistent theories. Finally, it is reasonable to ask that the Great tradition of Western political thought provide some ideas and proposals to alleviate poverty.

As mentioned earlier, the idea of justice goes to the heart of political theory. This is so because it concerns how individuals interact with each other and how societies arrange their institutions and processes. It has been associated with the Latin phrase *suum cuique tribuere*, which means to allocate to each his own. Not surprisingly, these theorists do not always agree about what justice demands regarding the poor. One might think that the treatment of poverty and justice depends so heavily on historical circumstances and economic systems that it is impossible to draw any conclusions about individual theorist's engagement with the problem. Certainly, understanding the historical context as well as the economic system is necessary to discern philosophers' arguments. There are other considerations, however, that may cause contemporaries to choose divergent conceptions of justice. Two twentieth-century philosophers, John Rawls and Robert Nozick, for example, provide distinctive conceptions of what constitutes a just state.

As a thematic work dealing with poverty much of the discussion focuses on the notion of distributive justice, which deals with how benefits and burdens are divided among individuals and groups in society. Samuel Fleischacker's *A Short History of Distributive Justice* makes a significant contribution to renewed philosophical analysis about Western philosophy's treatment of distributive justice.[1] His central thesis is that the term "redistributive justice" is a modern invention and when authors attribute this idea to Plato or Aristotle for example, they are bringing two issues, that is, distribution and justice, together that until two centuries ago at the most, have not been joined.[2] That is to say that the allocation of resources was not viewed as a matter of justice. I argue that his analyses of Plato, Aristotle, Smith, and Rousseau's political theories are not persuasive. Where appropriate, I engage with Fleischacker's arguments and analyses of these philosophers' views.

This leads to another issue this study explores and that is the roles that equality and desert play in understanding poverty and justice. These are re-occurring questions in Western political thought and thus, while the historical context certainly affects philosophers' answers, the moral and political considerations that each theorist uses to make these judgments are sometimes as revealing, if not more so, than their conclusions. I encourage readers to approach this work as a dialogue among some of the most provocative thinkers in Western political thought. This is an appropriate way to think about this study because often these theorists are indeed reacting or directly responding to the ideas, beliefs, and judgments of other political philosophers. This conversation is not limited to contemporaries. On the contrary, Rawls and Nozick, for example, are engaging with Kant and Locke's political theories. Likewise, Plato's warnings about the negative consequences for societies that do not aim to avoid or, at a minimum, severely limit the problem of poverty, are taken seriously by subsequent philosophers. One can hear echoes of Plato, Aristotle, and Rousseau when reading Marx, who directly confronts Smith's beliefs about poverty and its effects on human beings and society. These are only a few examples of how these political theorists call into question different philosophical ideas and judgments about the demands of justice toward the poor. This approach allows one to understand not only the individual philosopher's treatment of poverty as it relates to the just state, but it also reveals the ongoing relationship between justice and poverty in the tradition of Western political thought.

One of the most fundamental components of this study is my analysis of individual theorist's arguments and conclusions about the correct way to define and think about poverty. Since defining poverty is crucial, I want to be as clear as possible about it. I am not referring to an exact measure of income used by governments to designate one as being poor. Thus, I am not thinking of figures or standards such as poverty level, poverty index, or poverty threshold. When I use the word poor, I mean it in its broadest sense as those individuals who are at the lowest level of economic achievement.

Obviously, there are different types of poverty. One may speak about absolute poverty or poverty as deprivation, which means that one does not have the necessary items and conditions to lead a dignified or decent life. In this situation, one may lack the basics such as food, clothing, shelter, and access to medical care. Poverty may also be thought about as inequality. The term relative poverty is used to capture this idea. It means that some people in society have less, or perceive they have less income or material possessions than most others do in that society. This notion of relative poverty also applies when comparing different countries. One may observe that the poverty in Haiti, for example, is much more widespread and desperate than the poverty one finds in other countries in the same hemisphere. So one may ask the question, do the poor in the United States really have it that bad when compared to the poor in Haiti? Clearly, the idea of poverty is relative because rural poverty in Central America, or for that matter, in the United States is different from the urban poverty found in inner cities. This difference is significant because it is Adam Smith's belief that the poor in eighteenth-century England are much better off than the richest African King is.[3] While an individual in Manchester may have less material possessions than his or her neighbor, Smith thinks that since a free market economy promotes a higher and more comfortable standard of living, these inequalities are not significant. As I shall argue in chapter 4, this idea of relative poverty is central to his moral defense of capitalism. Following Rousseau and Hegel's beliefs, Marx challenges this claim because he believes there is a social nature that drives our individual needs and desires. While Marx dismisses the notion of "human nature," he does believe that human beings tend to measure their needs and desires by comparing them to others' situations. Marx actually provides the definition for relative poverty when he argues that poverty is socially defined and therefore to a great degree dependent on the social context.

Poverty as inequality is often a result of discrimination based upon gender, race, ethnicity, class, or religion. Thus, individuals who have been denied equal treatment and opportunities are more likely to be poor. Empirical data shows that larger percentages of the poor in the United States for example, are women, children, African Americans, Hispanic Americans, and Native Americans. Not to mention the long history and continuation of gender and racial prejudice and discrimination would be irresponsible. Not only do women and children throughout the world represent a larger percentage of the poor, but they are also subject to discriminatory policies, which penalize them because of stereotypes and prejudices.[4]

Besides defining the types of poverty, there are also different ways that one may view the causes for it. For example, Marxists refer to poverty as exploitation. Simply put, the ruling class profits from the poor as sources of cheap labor. In fact, Marx argues that capitalism depends on having enough poor people available at all times for exploitation. This is not to say that one has to be a Marxist to appeal to the idea of exploitation as a cause of poverty. Both Tocqueville and Mill thought that the English were exploiting the Irish, yet neither were Marxists.

Some theorists think of poverty as culture. In other words, there are particular attributes that poor people share, which means they lead a certain way of life that is passed on from generation to generation. Using this explanation, one might argue that even if the poor were provided with opportunities for decent employment or education, many of them would fail to take advantage of these favorable circumstances to get out of poverty. For example, Locke, Tocqueville, and Hegel, speak of poverty as culture and thus they ascribe certain traits to poor people. These traits may include the belief that poor people are "present oriented" and thus they are imprudent because they do not plan. This view sees the poor as a group that often lacks self-respect or motivation to better their situation. For all of these reasons they conclude that public assistance helps to create or contribute to a culture of poverty because individuals become dependent on government aid and continue to lose their self-respect and motivation to better their situations.

Finally, one can view impoverishment as a result of structural and institutional arrangements that promote discrimination against people and thus cause or, at a minimum, aggravate the problem of poverty. In short, this explanation encompasses how institutions and services in society are organized in ways that either discriminate against the poor or do little to help them get out of poverty. For example, empirical data shows that education is fundamental to overcoming poverty.[5] Since securing a decent education is so critical, access to schools with adequate resources and competent teachers is of great consequence. Schools located in poor districts often have fewer resources than schools in wealthier districts. It is also the case that women throughout the world are often denied access to education. This has major implications for reducing poverty since the more education a woman has the more likely it is that her children will also attend school. These are just two examples of how institutions, structures, and processes may aggravate or cause poverty.

In this study, I show how theorists' beliefs about the very definition of poverty and its causes have critical implications for their theories of a just society. Certainly, some philosophers' views, such as those of Mill, reflect all of these causes as well as others. In mentioning these ways of explaining poverty, I am not saying that these theories are exhaustive. There are myriad reasons for poverty and some are such that one has no control over them. For example, children have no choice about their parents or the situation into which they are born. When one starts asking who the poor are, many of the poor are young children. For example, in the United States 47.4 percent of families headed by women with children younger than five years old live in poverty.[6] Likewise, health problems can bring about exorbitant medical bills, which may drain an individual's financial resources and cause him or her to be unable to continue working. The loss of a job can be financially devastating. This is especially so for those who are not college educated and have worked in manufacturing or some other specialized industry that is downsizing. A large group is the working poor, who labor at low paying jobs with no health insurance. Many poor people live from paycheck to paycheck knowing that a health problem or a rent increase could cause them to become homeless. Keeping all of the different causes in mind, one can better appreciate the complexity of the problem.

The psychological dimension to poverty is often overlooked. The existential feeling of absolute helplessness or at a minimum, the sense of a lack of command over one's life can be debilitating. Moreover, the awareness that one has little control and hope for the future, may lead to severe depression. This is significant because while medical care for physical needs is often unavailable for the impoverished, mental health care is even more elusive. Some of the theorists, like Rousseau, capture the psychological component while others, like Locke, downplay any suffering, let alone the psychological aspect associated with poverty.

This psychological aspect relates to autonomy and freedom. What I mean by autonomy is that an individual has sovereignty over herself. This is the idea of positive freedom where one is self-determining. Philosophy often associates autonomy with an internal disposition, which means that one has control over her passions and desires. This is Plato's idea, for example, of autonomy or freedom. What I mean here is one's ability to be self-governing and to make decisions that are not externally imposed because of one's social class, race, gender, or ethnicity. The idea of rational autonomy is championed by Kant and Mill, and as such is connected to Modern political theory from the Enlightenment. Poverty affects an individual's autonomy because it limits her choices and life plans. Without a doubt, political theory is also concerned with negative freedom, that is, that one should be free of interference from others. In the following chapters, one shall see that the poor often have neither positive nor negative freedom, and thus they lose individual autonomy as well as freedom from external interference.

One of the thorniest issues in liberal theory is that of government assistance for the poor. On the one hand, liberalism is committed to the sanctity of private property and individual responsibility. By private property, I mean that one has the exclusive rights to a material good, such as land, to manage and use as one chooses and to exclude others from using it even if they may need it more. On the other hand, most liberals believe that it would be immoral to allow an individual to suffer, or possibly perish from lack of food or shelter. Yet, taking from the rich to give to the poor violates the sanctity of private property. One can easily see that the problem of poverty poses a dilemma or at a minimum reveals a fundamental tension in liberal theory. Locke, Smith, Tocqueville, Mill, Rawls, and Nozick are all liberal theorists, yet each one of them views the poor and the role of government aid differently.

Throughout the Western tradition of political thought, poverty has been a serious concern for almost all of these theorists albeit for different reasons. Plato, for example, believes that extreme wealth and poverty in the state jeopardize political stability, while Locke worries that public aid will only add to the problem while depleting the state's treasury. The former believes it will lead to civil war and revolution, while the latter thinks it is more of an individual moral problem. Without a doubt, the social and historical contexts between classical Athens and England on the eve of the Industrial Revolution present vastly different historical contexts. What they have in common, however, is that both Plato and Locke, and all the theorists for that matter, are dealing with the human condition and the roles that individual and societal responsibility play in creating and alleviating poverty. Each political theorist is also interested in justice. Not all theorists, such as Tocqueville for example, have a clearly articulated theory of justice, but I show that without exception, each philosopher aims toward creating a just situation in society. One of the virtues of this study is that it reveals each philosopher's views about justice even when he may not have articulated a complete theory of justice. By setting these theorists in a row, one gains insights about how their beliefs about human nature, morality, economic systems, and the demands of justice influence their understanding about who the poor are and why they are poor. This in turn helps to shape their ideas for what, if anything, society ought to do to alleviate the incidence of poverty. More importantly, it reveals answers to the principal question of this study: what is the relationship between poverty and justice in society?

By laying bare beliefs about the causes of poverty, one can clarify assumptions and conclusions made about poor people that effect today's discussions and public policies. One can learn from the history of philosophy because it provides examples that promote better understanding about commonly held assumptions and opinions about the poor and the problem of poverty. The role and power of ideas ought never to be underestimated since these theorists' ideas helped to shape, or at a minimum, affected the lives of countless individuals.

One may legitimately wonder why there is almost a two thousand year advance from Aristotle to John Locke. To make such a historical leap is dangerous, especially if one underestimates the significant differences in the political, economic, and social contexts in which theorists' ideas are put forth. I try to minimize this problem by paying close attention to these contexts in each chapter. This is why I include a transitional historical summary at the beginning of the Locke chapter. Given this transition and Locke's importance, chapter 3 is devoted exclusively to his political theory and treatment of poverty. Moreover, this work is not meant to be a comprehensive history of poverty in Western political thought. It does examine some of the most significant philosophers whose works are central to understanding the poor's relationship to the political community and the notion of justice in the Western tradition.

Certainly, views about poverty change through time. That being said, critical questions about how one defines poverty and its causes, and the role it plays in society are encountered and debated throughout the tradition of Western political thought. Each theorist's work is theoretical in the sense that he is attempting to address not just the problems of the moment, but also the dilemmas that many societies may encounter. Their work is also practical in the sense that these philosophers are concerned both with stating what the state ought to do about poverty and its relationship to a just state. I invite the reader to engage in this conversation by exploring some of the most significant Western theorists' beliefs and subsequent judgments about poverty and the just state.

NOTES

1. Samuel Fleischacker, *A Short History of Distributive Justice* (Cambridge: Harvard University Press, 2005). Hereafter referred to as *Short History*.

2. Ibid., 2.

3. Adam Smith, *An Inquiry into the Nature and Causes of The Wealth of Nations* (originally published, 1776), 2 vols. R. H. Campbell and A. Skinner, eds. (Indianapolis: Liberty Fund, 1981), 23–24, (hereafter cited as *WN*).

4. Diana M. DiNitto, *Social Welfare: Politics and Public Policy* (Boston: Allyn and Bacon, 2000), 360–96.

5. Ibid., 78–79.

6. U.S. Census Bureau, 2005 American Community Survey http://factfinder.census .gov/ (accessed July 15, 2007).

Chapter Two

Avoiding the Greatest Plague of All: Plato and Aristotle

Plato believes that a state where great disparities between the wealthy and poor exist is destined for civil war. In fact, he thinks gross inequalities ultimately destroy a society because it creates two cities, one rich and one poor. Aristotle agrees with Plato about the dangers of poverty. He, like Plato, believes that handouts to the poor do not solve the problem. Aristotle advocates providing the necessary tools and training so that poor individuals may become financially independent and productive members of society. The difference between the two philosophers is that Plato aims to construct a state that *avoids* the problem of poverty while Aristotle's political theory presupposes that to some degree, it will always be a problem. As a result, he aims to find pragmatic solutions that will limit it.

In this chapter, I explore Plato and Aristotle's treatment of poverty as well as their beliefs about the just state. The aim is to investigate what connection, if any, do Plato and Aristotle's ideas and conceptions about justice and the just state have to do with their treatments of poverty. One may remember from the previous chapter, Fleischacker's central thesis that the term "redistributive justice" is a modern invention and when authors attribute this idea to Plato or Aristotle for example, they are bringing two issues, that is, distribution and justice, together that until two centuries ago at the most, have not been joined. When appropriate, I engage Fleischacker's arguments and analyses of these philosophers' views. I argue that Fleischacker's claim is not substantiated since Plato and Aristotle support redistribution of resources from the wealthy to the poor. He is correct that both philosophers want to promote political stability. This explains only part of the reason that they support aid to the poor since I show that it has a direct connection to their views of the just society. Certainly, they never used the term redistributive justice; however, this is clearly what both undertake in their respective political theories. Providing government aid to the poor promotes justice and a just state is a stable state. I begin with Plato and then turn to Aristotle's treatment of poverty and the just state.

PLATO

One of the driving forces behind Plato's political theories is to design a state where there will be no poverty or excessive wealth. With the extensive amount of commentary on and analyses of Plato's writings, it is striking that few scholars have focused on Plato's fixation on eliminating poverty and controlling wealth in the state.[1] There are, however, some important exceptions. H. P. P. Lötter says that Plato's ideas about poverty and wealth play an integral role in the *Republic*'s main argument.[2] Moreover, he believes that Plato's views about poverty and wealth should challenge contemporary societies to acknowledge the link with justice and the negative consequences that excessive wealth and poverty have not only for individuals but also for societies.[3] Plato is especially critical of those who are preoccupied with making money because he believes that the love of profit making corrupts individuals and leads to internal factions in the state. He writes that a city divided between the wealthy and the poor ultimately destroys itself through civil war because it is based not on justice but ruled by the love of profit making.[4]

More than two decades ago, Alexander Fuks argued that Plato was preoccupied with the avoidance of extreme disparities in wealth and controlling poverty. These ideas are fundamental elements of Plato's political theory in both the *Republic* and the *Laws*.[5] More recently, Samuel Fleischacker has written about redistributive justice as it pertains to Plato. Fleischacker's central thesis is that scholars misunderstand and thus, misuse the term redistributive justice. If one looks at the accepted view of justice, it did not entitle the poor to more income or a better station of life until the eighteenth century. Thus, when scholars associate Plato with the idea of redistributive justice, they are wrong. There was no belief or argument from Plato, according to Fleischacker, that society had a moral obligation to end poverty, or that justice demanded a redistribution of wealth to benefit the poor during this time.[6]

Certainly, Plato never used the term "redistributive justice." One thing is certain however, Plato wanted to prevent poverty and excessive wealth in his plans for Kallipolis in the *Republic* and Magnesia in the *Laws*. As one explores Plato's treatment of poverty, it is evident his theory of justice in the *Republic* changes by the time he writes his last significant dialogue, the *Laws*. In both dialogues, justice is transcendent, thus it is eternal, unchanging, and universal. The difference is that in his last significant dialogue he uses a constitution and laws to construct a just state based not only on the transcendent idea of justice but also empirical facts.[7] What does not change is Plato's desire to construct a just state, which means avoiding the development of two groups, that is, the rich and poor. There is no doubt that his main concern in the *Republic* is to define the essential qualities of justice and to answer the question why one would choose to act in a just way. Justice, according to Plato is an intrinsic good because it is desirable in itself. It is also a consequential good because it is desirable for its results.[8] Preventing excessive wealth and poverty among the citizens is fundamental to his creation of a just state. In fact, this is the heart of Plato's state in the *Republic* and in the *Laws*. In the latter, he wanted to build this feature of the state into the constitution. As a matter of public policy, the poor would have the necessary means to provide for themselves. That may mean providing a plot of land for poor farmers or tools for destitute artisans so that they would be able to sustain themselves professionally. Thus a just state, according to Plato, would be a stable state because it is set up in such a way that it would prevent the emergence of poverty and riches. I examine Plato's treatment of poverty in both the *Republic* and the *Laws* in turn. After that, I revisit Fleischacker's claims about Plato and redistributive justice.

The *Republic*

T. K. Seung says the most difficult question in the *Republic* is: what motive does one have to be just?[9] Should one be just for the sake of its consequences or is being just a good in and of itself, that is, an intrinsic good? These questions frame the discussion when Plato articulates his theory of justice in Books 2, 3, and 4 of the *Republic*. Since individuals are not born alike, he says that different natures are better suited for different tasks or functions in the city.[10] He identifies three social classes in the city: the rulers, warriors, and artisans, respectively.[11] Plato refers to the rulers as guardians and the warrior as auxiliaries. The entire scheme is based on a "noble falsehood," which will be used to persuade citizens that while they are all brothers, some have gold mixed in them and they are the ones who are fit to rule.[12] The auxiliaries have silver mixed in while the farmers and other artisans have iron and bronze. While it is possible for a silver child to be born from gold parents and vice versa, it is critical for the good of the city to guard against the mixture of metals in future generations.[13] By keeping each rank separate by what is appropriate to their respective natures, Plato believes that each class performing its role and achieving excellence in it results in a just state. He says that wisdom is the excellence of the rulers, courage is the excellence of the warriors, and moderation spreads throughout the entire city.[14] These roles correspond to the four cardinal virtues, which are wisdom, courage, moderation, and justice.[15]

After constructing the just city, Plato introduces readers to his theory of human psychology. He says three parts compose the soul: the intellect, spirited, and appetitive.[16] One way to think about these is not literally as parts but as psychological attitudes. Intellect or reason rules the just individual. She finds courage and self-control in her spirited part. The appetitive part is where desires for things like food, drink, sex, and money reside. The just individual practices moderation or temperance concerning these desires. Like the city, an individual is just when each part of the soul performs its specific charge and achieves its virtue. Harmony in the individual is a necessary condition for justice.[17]

It follows that an individual who is ruled by the love of money or one who does not have the necessary tools to perform his craft cannot be just. In the same way, a city is not just when poverty is prevalent or when there are huge economic gaps between rich and poor since it violates the principle of moderation and creates disharmony. Moreover, as I shall show, Plato believes that this lack of moderation in the city has horrible consequences since it not only produces political instability but also causes unhappiness.[18] Seung persuasively asserts that Plato relies on the bond of brotherly love creating harmony in the city as well as in the individual.[19] This notion of brotherly love or *philia* means that members of the community have internalized the bonds that transcend blood kin and promote unity in the state.[20] His aim is to provide an environment absent of poverty and great wealth so that *philia* may flourish. Moreover, he claims that the reason a city is founded is that no one is entirely self-sufficient. People live together as partners and helpers so that all their needs may be met.[21] Certainly, Plato's theory of justice in the *Republic* is complex but this brief sketch provides the necessary background for exploring his treatment of poverty in it.

It is no accident that Plato addresses the issues of wealth and poverty at the beginning of the *Republic* in a conversation between Socrates and Cephalus. Socrates remarks that Cephalus has not been corrupted by the love of money because he inherited most of his wealth instead of earning it. Individuals who have made their money, according to Socrates, are preoccupied with it.[22] Cephalus says that money may be instrumental in making one's life less complicated. For example, wealth allows one to choose more easily not to cheat or to deceive someone because he or she must make a sacrifice to a god or repay money to another person.[23] While not glorifying poverty, Socrates says that great wealth does not lessen the burden on bad individuals or bring happiness to people who are not just. Thus, great wealth cannot bring peace to the unjust individual.[24] It is here that Socrates first connects poverty and wealth to the issue of justice.

Socrates explains in Book 4 why poverty and wealth are corrupting forces. Wealth corrupts the artisan because he becomes idle and careless.[25] Poverty prevents him from having the necessary tools he needs for his craft, which makes his work inferior and impairs his ability to teach his skills to others.[26] The city must avoid two things according to Socrates, "Both wealth and poverty. The former makes for luxury, idleness, and revolution; the latter for slavishness, bad work, and revolution as well."[27]

Plato's concern about the corrupting power of greed in the individual relates directly to his thoughts about justice in the state. The prohibition of moneymaking and bribery is a guiding principle for the construction of Kallipolis.[28] The only motivating factor for one to rule is the fear that someone worse would take the job.[29] Plato thinks that people should be unwilling to rule for the sake of money or honor.[30] "In a city of good men, if it came into being, the citizens would fight in order *not to rule*, just as they do now in order to rule."[31]

The conditions described by Plato paint a picture of the relationships between the poor and rich during his lifetime. As Edith Copeland pointed out, one who neglects to understand the historical and institutional settings of Plato's own time will fail to appreciate fully how the social, economic, and political ideals and conflicts of Athens influenced his work.[32] Not only were there new opportunities for wealth, but Athenians were also becoming skeptical about the idea of justice as the old societal distinctions were breaking down and government was becoming more corrupt.[33] Seung strongly emphasizes the importance of understanding Plato's historical context. He writes that the "ethos of acquisitive gratification" became the moral principle that shaped the imperialism and expansionism of Athens during this time.[34]

Aristophanes' play, *The Clouds*, illustrates the tensions between the old Athens, which was a rural culture and the new Athens of the Periclean era, which had an urban culture. He ridicules Athenians for their materialism, consumerism, and extravagance.[35] As the Athenian economy diversified, the population became more stratified. By the fourth century, the poor were doing most of the work as long as they could find employment. As unemployment became a more serious problem so did class conflict.[36] Thus, one must put Plato's work in the context of a time when traditional Athenian values were being replaced by an ethos of greed and power.[37]

M. I. Finley's account of Ancient Greece provides further evidence that persistent conflicts and power struggles between the rich and poor dominated ancient politics.[38] In fact, according to Plutarch, when the legendary lawmaker

Solon came to power in Athens, the times were worse than ever because the poor were completely indebted to the wealthy.[39] Solon, who was hesitant to enter politics, favored neither the wealthy nor the poor. Since both sides trusted him, the rich because he was wealthy and the poor because he was honest, he was able to reassure both groups that a peaceful and fair settlement could be reached.[40] He cancelled the poor's debts but softened the blow by calling it relief and made it law that no man could put himself into servitude as security for a loan.[41] He refused to redistribute the land but wanted to promote harmony by cultivating a large middle class in his state.[42] Solon's goal, according to Plutarch, was to have a state where no one was terribly wealthy or destitute.[43] There are numerous references to Solon running throughout Plato's dialogues.[44]

Plato also refers to Lycurgus, the legendary lawgiver of Sparta, in several dialogues.[45] Facing extreme inequalities in Sparta, Lycurgus orders the land and moveable property to be redistributed to promote greater equality.[46] To avoid the disparities in wealth he collects all the gold and silver. The new money is made out of iron so that hoarding will be less of an issue.[47] He wants to limit outside influences and the desires for luxuries. Finally, Lycurgus decrees that all Spartans should eat together in common, which resulted in the rich and poor sharing food and table.[48] Once all of these reforms were in place, he turned to education because he thought that once the young had internalized their loyalty to Sparta and to each other, they could avoid disaccord. It was his hope that Spartans would live in harmony and relate to each other as brothers and sisters and no one would lack life's necessities.[49] One cannot help but notice the conspicuous similarities among Plato's political theory and Plutarch's accounts of the reforms initiated by Solon and Lycurgus. How much the historical accounts about Solon or Lycurgus influenced Plato is uncertain, but one may safely assume that these stories reinforced his focus on the political problems and possible solutions for states divided between rich and poor.[50]

In the *Republic*, Plato eliminates property ownership and familial arrangements to promote unity and maintain the virtue found between the two upper classes, that is, the guardians and the auxiliaries.[51] It is an elitist and absolute communism because it only applies to the small number of individuals who have the best natures. For members of these two groups there will be no poverty or riches in their lives. This arrangement also allows him to separate political power from economic activity.[52] Since the guardians are charged with keeping wealth and poverty from slipping into Kallipolis, their economic arrangements are of paramount importance so that they may be true to their goal.[53]

Given that only a small number of people live under communist arrangements, Plato must ensure that the problem of poverty does not arise among the largest number of people in Kallipolis, that is, the producing class. This class includes farmers, artisans, wage earners, traders, wholesale and retail traders, and sailors to facilitate trade.[54] They have private property and families.[55] Plato does not provide much detail about how to avoid the problem of poverty and riches among the working class in the *Republic*. There is, however, some evidence that the economic activity and private property will be organized, controlled, and supervised because Socrates states that the guardians must guard against wealth and poverty from entering the city, implying that they should supervise and control it.[56]

Plato also suggests that a specific law is needed that would prohibit the state from enforcing voluntary contracts entered into by citizens. Those contracts will be made at the lenders' own risk to discourage behavior that is motivated for the sake of making money at others' expense.[57] He advocates population control for all three classes.[58] Since Plato emphasizes the need for structures in the state to promote unity, and states that each citizen must fulfill his or her own function, he surely must have intended to have some basic form of economic organization that applied to the working class.[59] It should be sufficiently evident that Plato's goal was to avoid the problem of poverty and wealth in Kallipolis and that such a goal required supervision and regulation of the largest class of citizens.

Plato's arrangements for Kallipolis in the *Republic* are based on some strong presuppositions about human nature. Not least among them is the fact that individuals are by nature somewhat greedy or at least predisposed to materialism. That is one reason why strict communism is prescribed for the two upper classes. Property ownership would almost certainly lead to corruption and to the decay of the upper classes.[60] Further, since the aim in the *Republic* is to build a community in which individuals treat others as blood kin, the upper classes must not have familial relations.[61] In this way, partial affection for blood kin cannot interfere with obtaining unity. Instead, friendship and love among the inhabitants constitute the prevailing bonds. Recalling the earlier discussion about Lycurgus, these arrangements are similar to what he instituted in Sparta.

Finally, one must keep in mind Plato's four cardinal virtues. The ideal city must be founded upon principles that promote moderation and harmony both in the individual and throughout the city. Disparities in wealth, and indeed, poverty would not do so and thus the city would be unjust.

His detailed examination of the history of different types of government illustrates that one of Plato's conclusions is that civil war constantly threatens the state when some citizens are excessively poor while others are rich. A great deal of the *Republic* is devoted to showing *how* and *why* this condition has been destructive to states. This examination of historical evidence drives home the point that when designing a state one should be determined to limit both extreme wealth and poverty by avoiding the economic framework that leads to these debilitating conditions. Through his analysis of aristocracy, timocracy, oligarchy, democracy, and tyranny, Plato shows how greed and divisions between poor and rich are prominent factors in all of the governments that eventually underwent revolutions. With the exception of aristocracy, which is rule of the wise, the defining issue is poverty versus riches. One can see how Plato's preoccupation with the latter relates to his theory of justice because moderation is one tenant of the internal and external harmony, which is necessary for the just individual as well as the just city. If the appetitive part rules the individual or the city, neither can be just.

Plato says that eventually, even aristocracy, which is the best constitution, decays over time because nothing can last forever.[62] Human nature is such that the leaders will make mistakes by marrying the wrong people and bringing children into the world that are neither good natured nor fortunate.[63] Bad marital choices introduce disharmony and inequality that in turn produce hostility and ultimately, civil war. Once there is disunion among the leaders, a struggle ensues between those pushing the state toward moneymaking and acquiring land, silver, gold, and more wealth versus those who see virtue as the goal of the state.[64] Eventually, a compromise is struck between the two groups. The agreement results in the creation of private property and the enslavement of some who were previously regarded as friends.[65]

A sharp division between poor and rich develops during a timocracy. It is described as a midpoint constitution between aristocracy and oligarchy where the citizens value material wealth.[66] The residents become obsessed with making money, which in turn creates economic class differences within the state. As a result, a class of poor emerges and the evil of poverty versus riches rears its ugly head.[67] As this state disintegrates, the rich become more and more powerful while the poor are powerless.

This leads to revolution. Post-revolution, an oligarchy is established as the new form of government. Class divisions between the wealthy and poor exist from the beginning in an oligarchy.[68] The wealthy few rule and economic polarization continues to increase. Socrates observes that a poor person may lose all possessions and thus he or she is reduced to being a helpless creature in the state.[69] Alexander Fuks points out that Plato took pains to describe the origins of pauperism and mammonism.[70] The mammonist is devoted to pursuing and accumulating material wealth. This has a debasing effect on the individual. Plato says that in an oligarchy some people are exceedingly wealthy while others are impoverished.[71] Thus, individuals who have neither land, money, nor occupations create a proletariat of paupers. Their poverty and absolute contempt for the rich become unifying factors. Plato believes that the poor develop a bond as they become aware of their own strength and the weaknesses of the ruling class. This process is similar to what Karl Marx would later describe as class-consciousness.

The poor's awareness and resentment of the rich ultimately results in a revolution that brings forth a democracy.[72] Socrates describes three classes of citizens who form society in this type of government.[73] The drones are the idle and spendthrifts who comprise the ruling political elite.[74] The second class is the wealthy, that is, those individuals who are preoccupied with making money.[75] Those who have few possessions and labor hard to make a living for themselves and their families make up the third, that is, the working class. The politicians and the working class constantly ask the wealthy for more money. These situations cause an internal struggle between the wealthy and working class that ultimately leads to a civil war between the poor and the property owners.[76]

The result of this struggle is tyranny. The tyrant knows that he derives his power from the poor and at first panders to their wishes. The redistribution of land and the cancellation of debts are two ways he appeases their demands.[77] Soon, however, the tyrant betrays the poor by becoming the source of internal oppression for all inhabitants of the city. The poor have provided the tyrant with the power to set them free from the oppression by the rich but now they have created a new source of oppression in the tyrant himself. In every case, the degradation and discord are a result of disparities between the wealthy and poor.

Through these historical examples, Plato demonstrates the dangers of class divisions. He shows that the only way to achieve a stable government is to constitute a government that prohibits the emergence of sharp disparities between rich and poor. This is why he restricts the use of private property and carefully organizes and controls economic activity in the *Republic*.

The *Laws*

An older and more mature Plato writes the *Laws*. As in the *Republic*, he maintains his belief that greed corrupts the individual as well as the state. He wants to prevent the same evils, that is, a class of poor and rich in the city, as he constructs his model city of Magnesia in the *Laws*. These evils were precluded by the economic arrangements in the *Republic*. It is greed, that insatiable desire for more and more wealth, which forces Plato to abandon his plans for the first-best state in the *Republic*. In a nostalgic statement, the Athenian

Stranger reaffirms Plato's belief that the communism for the two upper classes in the *Republic* is still the best arrangement, but human nature makes it impractical. Plato's reflection about the best state is worth quoting.

"You'll find the ideal society and state, the best code of laws, where the old saying 'friends' property is genuinely shared' is put into practice as widely as possible throughout the entire state. Now I don't know whether in fact this situation—a community of wives, children and all property—exists anywhere today, or will ever exist, but at any rate in such a state the notion of 'private property' will have been by hook or by crook completely eliminated from life. Everything possible will have been done to throw into a sort of common pool even what is by nature 'my own' like eyes and ears and hands, in the sense that to judge by appearance they all see and hear and act in concert. Everybody feels pleasure and pain at the same things, so that they all praise and blame with complete unanimity. To sum up, the laws in force impose the greatest possible unity on the state—and you'll never produce a better or truer criterion of a perfect law than that. It may be that gods or a number of the children of gods inhabit this kind of state: if so, the life they live there, observing these rules, is a happy one indeed. And so men need look no further for their ideal: they should keep this state in view and try to find one that most nearly resembles it. This is what we've put our hand to, and if in some way it could be realized, it would come very near immortality and be second only to the ideal."[78]

The combination of greed in the individual and the institution of private property make an unwieldy combination for one who is trying to construct the just state. Inculcating citizens with the virtue of moderation becomes more difficult, and thus Plato turns to a constitution with a preamble and detailed laws to restrain the destructive tendencies that create the problem of poverty in the first place. He does not abandon his beliefs about justice that were stated in the *Republic*. What he does abandon is the arrangements for obtaining justice. Moderation and harmony are still absolute necessary conditions for controlling the problems of poverty and great wealth. One central question in the *Laws* is: how can one create a political theory, which abandons the enforced communism among rulers and warriors, but still controls the inherent tendency of human nature toward greed?

Exposing the corrupting power of greed is a central theme in the *Laws*. Greedy individuals disregard the virtue of moderation in the individual and in the state.[79] The Athenian Stranger denounces the individual who is preoccupied with making money and accumulating private property.[80] He expands on his belief that virtue and great wealth are incompatible both for the individual and for the state.[81] The passion for great wealth, profit, and private property corrupts individuals and makes them unfit for citizenship.[82] The Athenian Stranger states that "all the gold upon the earth and all the gold beneath it does not compensate for lack of virtue."[83] In Book 11, he declares that he would prefer to have justice in his soul rather than money in his pocket because treasure for treasure, that is a better bargain and a better part of himself also.[84] The Platonic theme of virtue characterized by moderation and care for one's soul always trumps the pursuit of money and material greed.

That being said, how does Plato construct a state in the *Laws*, which will avoid the problems of greed and poverty? Fuks believes that Plato aims for a measure of socio-economic equality to be spread throughout the entire citizen body.[85] The laws limit foreign trade and outlaw buying on credit or lending money with interest.[86] The citizens use an internal coinage; gold and silver are retained by the state for the times when it is necessary for travel and commerce.[87] The number of inhabitants will be limited so that each may receive equal portions of land.[88] This allotment of land may not be mortgaged, sold, or donated, nor can it be reclaimed by the state.[89] Once allotted to the citizens, it remains in their possession until death, and then it will go to a single heir named in the will. These conditions sum up the landed property ownership in Magnesia for there are no other provisions for owning land. Contrary to his plan for the two upper classes in the *Republic*, private property ownership forms the basis for all citizen-families in the *Laws*.[90]

Each allotment includes a house for the family to live in and other buildings that may be necessary for farming the land. These initial land allotments provide a foundation to promote equality among the citizens of Magnesia. The Athenian Stranger says that the city must acknowledge different property classes so that offices, taxes, and grants may be arranged according to each citizen's financial worth.[91] All citizens start with the same allotment of land, and then depending on whether they grow richer or poorer, they will be transferred to the appropriate class.[92] Plato has the Athenian Stranger reiterate his absolute commitment to avoid "the greatest plague of all—civil war though civil disintegration would be a better term—extreme poverty and wealth must not be allowed to arise in any section of the citizen-body, because both lead to both these disasters."[93]

As a result of this commitment, strict limitations are established to control the accumulation of wealth as well as provisions to keep families from falling into poverty. As for wealth, landholders may acquire moveable property up to four times the value of a lot.[94] The poverty line is the ownership of moveable property that is equal to the value of the allotment. The family should have enough material goods to work the land they own.[95] In Book 6, the Athenian Stranger says, "in this state no one will go without the necessities of life."[96] Provisions are also made for the most vulnerable in society including orphans, the aged, and people with disabilities.[97] Thus, the levels of poverty and wealth are strictly controlled. This is true not only for the citizens, but also for the working force that is made up of foreigners. The amount of money that citizens can spend on events such as funerals and weddings is based on their class.[98]

All property, whether land or moveable, must be registered with the state. Monetary fines, as well as public condemnation designed to bring shame, are instituted to discourage noncompliance. The following passage makes clear how serious Plato is about monitoring the amount of goods one may own.

> "If anyone is found to possess anything in addition to the registered sum, the entire surplus should be confiscated by the state, and on top of that anyone who wants to should bring a charge against him—and an ugly, discreditable charge it will be, if the man is convicted of being enticed by the prospect of gain to hold the laws in contempt. The accuser, who may be anyone, should accordingly enter a charge of 'money-grubbing' against him, and prosecute in the court of the Law-Guardians themselves. If the defendant is found guilty, he must be excluded from the common resources of the state, and when a grant of some kind is made, he must go without and be limited to his holding; and for as long as he lives his conviction should be recorded for public inspection by all and sundry."[99]

Eligibility to hold political offices and to participate in civic affairs are not affected to any great degree by the inequalities of wealth found in the four classes.[100] On more than one occasion, the Athenian Stranger states his belief that no special distinction should be assigned to wealth.[101] Magnesia allows for equal distribution of private property and moveable property that may not be equal but that does have strict restrictions and limits on it. Fuks sums up Plato's goal in the *Laws* when he says, "The city resting upon this economic basis combines basic equality with controlled inequality."[102]

Moderating one's desires for wealth and material gain is not only necessary for a happy life, but is also essential to avoid the disintegration and destruction of the state. Poverty in Plato's state becomes a problem only when individuals want more than they actually need to live a comfortable, happy life. This relative poverty is a psychological state, which causes individuals to feel a sense of deprivation when they compare their situation with that of others. In future chapters, one will see how the idea of relative poverty plays an integral role in Western political thought. A rigorous education, according to Plato, will foster an appropriate sense among individuals about actual needs and unnecessary desires. It is through this education that individuals become better able to keep their desires in check.

To say that the economic structures in Kallipolis and Magnesia are contrary to a capitalist or free market economy is an understatement. Productivity for the purpose of achieving great monetary profits is prohibited through laws and policies that apply not only to the citizens but also to the state. These stringent laws are designed to educate citizens and harness the appetitive greed that Plato believes is part of human nature.

At the beginning of this chapter, I discussed Fleischacker's claim that the idea of redistributive justice is misunderstood and thus misused by scholars. The accepted view of justice, he argues, did not entitle the poor to more income or a better station of life until the eighteenth century. Thus, it would be incorrect, according to Fleischacker, for one to associate Plato with the idea of redistributive justice since there was no belief or argument from Plato about it. That is to say, Plato does not believe that society had a moral obligation to end poverty or that justice demanded a redistribution of wealth to benefit the poor during his time. According to Fleischacker, "Plato did not recommend his communal property arrangements for an entire society, nor did he see them as demanded by justice."[103] Later he says that Plato wanted to eradicate inequalities of wealth to ensure "social harmony" instead of justice.[104] Certainly, this last statement is correct to some degree, especially if one is talking about the *Republic*. While one could argue that Plato would never believe that a state where poor people, who were not having their basic needs met, could be a just state, one can grant Fleischacker's point that Plato's main goal was to reduce the chance of factions arising between rich and poor. This in turn creates social harmony among the inhabitants resulting in a more stable government. The problem with Fleishacker's claim is that it fails to engage with the *Laws*. If one grants that, the ideal of justice entails *suum cuique tribuere*—to allocate to each his due, than one would associate justice with the idea of desert. Thus distributive justice would be concerned with allocating resources based on desert. As a result, the question comes down to how a society determines what is due each person. One could argue that needs could be one way to calculate what is due to each person. Thus, what is due an individual would depend on his or her level of neediness. Certainly, Marx would agree with this, but would Plato?

I stated that in the *Laws* Plato wants to prevent poverty by making provisions in the constitution for the state of Magnesia. Thus as a matter of public policy, the poor would have the necessary means to provide for themselves. As a result, one of the policies that come from this is that no one will be allowed to fall below a certain level of poverty.[105] In Book 6, the Athenian Stranger says that "in this state no one will go without the necessities of life."[106] Finally, there are provisions made for orphans, the elderly, and people with disabilities so that they will not fall below a certain minimum standard.[107] Where is the money to come from to support these policies? It is going to come from taxes and other revenues from the state of Magnesia. This policy is redistributive since the wealthier citizens pay more taxes, which help to support the less fortunate.[108] Moreover, Plato bases the allocation of these resources on what is due each person and in this case, it is what is due each person based on his or her needs. It is important to note, however, that for those who are able to work, Plato's redistribution is designed to help them become self-sufficient. As I mentioned earlier, this may mean providing tools or land so that one can earn a living, or at a minimum provide for his subsistence. Thus, a just state would have a constitution and public policies that would not allow people to go without necessities. Fleischacker is wrong when he claims that in Plato, one does not find the idea "that government is obliged, in virtue of the justice that is due the poor, to try to eradicate poverty."[109] As a matter of pragmatics, Plato knows that the problem of poverty becomes far more difficult once it is entrenched. This is another reason why he wants to institutionalize policies to deal with it as it arises. Finally, if one accepts that Plato's theory of justice demands moderation and harmony as necessary conditions for the just individual and the just state, one can reasonably conclude that poverty would pose a real impediment to achieving justice. It is not surprising that Plato allows for some economic redistribution.

Reading Plato today, one notices that in his treatment of poverty he does not use invective language toward the poor. Being poor is nothing to be ashamed of, but it is nothing to be proud of either. The poor are not categorized as morally deficient, nor are they blamed for their sorry lot in life. Neither does he glorify being poor. Instead, Plato sets about trying to organize, educate, and legislate to *avoid* the problem altogether or at a minimum to limit drastically its occurrence. His beliefs about human nature force him to change his plans for the "ideal" state in the *Republic* and replace it with the second best in the *Laws*. While Plato calls Magnesia the second best, his aim was to prevent poverty from becoming a prominent feature of that state. Clearly, he believed that justice demanded that leaders, laws, and economic structures should do everything possible to prevent poverty. His intense desire to prevent or to restrict poverty severely is unique among Western political theorists. As we turn to Aristotle, one will see how he recognizes the problems associated with poverty but accepts that it will always be part of society. Since he assumes poverty will always be present in society, he directs his efforts toward controlling it instead of preventing it all together.

ARISTOTLE

Aristotle's political theory presupposes that even under the best constitution, there will be those who are less fortunate.[110] Like Plato, he believes that disparities in wealth may lead to one of the greatest divisions in society and thus, he thinks that controlling the problem of poverty is crucial to maintaining stability in the state.[111] To that end, he stresses several things that one must keep in mind when writing a constitution. First, property arrangements should be conducive to limiting class conflict. Second, since even the best state will undoubtedly have some poor people, a combination of private and government social services is necessary.[112] The main aim of charity and government support, however, should be directed toward helping the poor to become self-sufficient. Finally, he advocates population control.

I explore how on the one hand Aristotle's political theory holds great promise for the ethical treatment of the poor because his policies would enhance their abilities to live decent and possibly, flourishing lives. On the other hand, his elitist political theory excludes most members of society from citizenship. Therefore, what one finds in Aristotle's work is a combination of innovative ideas to help the poor and elitist attitudes that negatively affect them. The latter parts of his ethical and political theory are difficult for even the most ardent Aristotelians to defend. Yet, at the same time, Aristotle's treatment of poverty is pragmatic and hopeful because he realizes that no one can live a decent or happy life without meeting certain needs. As a result, there is a direct connection between the idea of a just state and trying to alleviate and limit poverty.

Aristotle spent twenty years at Plato's Academy. When one reads *Nicomachean Ethics* or *Politics*, however, one is struck by how different his approach to ethical and political theory is from that of his teacher. Plato's ideas are radical and sometimes shocking whereas Aristotle's ethical and political theories are rooted in the received opinions of his day.[113] Initially compiling common opinions about ethics and politics in the Greek polis, he extends his research and gathers additional information about social practices and governments from other states. From this collected information, he believes, philosophers should be able to gain knowledge about ethics and government. He wants to use information that mirrors everyday life situations so that one may know how individuals actually lived their lives, created constitutions, and organized politics. To use this information properly, however, one should understand the reasons behind the beliefs and practices and thus, empirical data must be accompanied by comparative analysis of different governments and constitutions.

Aristotle holds that one may have certain knowledge about living the virtuous life and constructing the best state. These normative judgments should be used to create a political structure organized to produce legislation, which would in turn create an environment for human flourishing or happiness. Happiness, *eudaimonia*, plays a central role in Aristotle's ethical theory. This means that the aim of government should be to create conditions so that individuals may flourish.[114] Since the purpose of the state is not just to allow people to live, but to live well, one might reasonably assume that the poor would benefit from living in an Aristotelian state. In many ways, the poor do fare well. Aristotle acknowledges that one cannot flourish without material necessities, such as proper nutrition. He states that no citizen "should be in need of sustenance" and that all citizens should be able to participate in common meals even if they are poor.[115] Moreover, he recognizes the need for clean air and water since they are fundamental for a state to have healthy citizens.[116]

That being said, one must be clear about who may achieve Aristotle's idea of happiness. In the opening passages of *Nicomachean Ethics*, he tells us that only those who have had a good or proper upbringing can become familiar with what is fine and just.[117] This sounds reasonable, but it is only the first of several conditions that makes it possible for one to live a virtuous life. Before discussing the necessary traits and circumstances conducive to virtuous living, one must understand that Aristotle believes that each human being has a purpose or function and this defines the individual's essential character.[118] Human flourishing is possible only when individuals live in harmony with their distinctive natures. Reason distinguishes human beings from other non-human animals but not all humans have equal capacities for being rational. Aristotle believes that women and most men are naturally inferior and they are reduced to playing instrumental roles in society. Their labor provides leisure time and thus, freedom for a few fortunate men to pursue virtuous lives and achieve true happiness.[119]

Not only are most human beings inferior to the select few, but also according to Aristotle, some human beings are natural slaves.[120] Moreover, any individual, such as an artisan who works for wages, is considered vulgar and useful only insofar as he allows superior men to have more leisure time.[121] The upshot is that most of the state's inhabitants, including all women, slaves, farmers, laborers, immigrants, and artisans are completely excluded from citizenship because they lack the capacity or the good fortune to participate in the Aristotelian life of excellence. Not surprisingly, the poor are members of these disenfranchised groups and thus, have even less control over their lives. Certainly, one must consider Aristotle's historical context because his views about women, slaves, and laborers are representative of the elite of his day who abhorred the uneducated poor and feared democracy. After all, democracy is essentially the rule of the poor according to Plato and Aristotle. The slaves and other poor members of the free population, who degrade themselves through their labor, are indispensable to the city's economy. Yet, they are ineligible for citizenship.

Richard Mulgan maintains that most mainstream Western political theorists do not focus on the limited number of men who are qualified for citizenship in Aristotle's political theory.[122] These parts of Aristotle's political theory "are set aside in the interests of sympathetically evaluating Greek theorizing about politics."[123] One of the best examples of this may be found in Martha Nussbaum's work. She argues that Aristotle believes that the goal of politics should be to distribute among individuals the conditions so that they may choose and live a good life.[124] This approach focuses on human capabilities.[125] Certainly, Nussbaum acknowledges his treatment of women, slaves, and laborers.[126] Nevertheless, as compelling a case as she makes for Aristotle, one must keep in mind the elite nature of his theory as well as the consequences for the choices that he makes.

Two political theorists, Susan Moller Okin and Jean Bethke Elshtain, focus on the treatment of women, as well as the issues of slavery and disenfranchisement of the working class, as prominent features in Aristotle's political theory.[127] I think to be sensible and intellectually honest one must ignore neither the historical context nor the essential aspects of Aristotle's political theory. Any other interpretation about his treatment of poverty would require one to read far too much between the lines or to ignore significant features of his political theory.[128] Since this study concerns Aristotle's treatment of poverty and its relationship to his idea of justice, it must do neither.

The Greek word for justice, *dikaiosynē*, connotes much more than what is legal because it also means what is morally right or fair. Aristotle's theory of justice has several parts to it. He has a general theory of justice based on viewing the state as a moral association among virtuous people. Justice in this sense for Aristotle means one must obey the laws but this notion of law applies to all virtuous actions.[129] For example, one should be brave in battle and one should be temperate and not commit adultery. He also has categories of special or particular justice based on the idea of equality among people who are free and equal. These are part of his general theory of justice and it is where one finds his discussion of distributive justice.[130]

Aristotle defines distributive justice as the proportionate or reciprocal equality of the contributions that an individual citizen makes toward enhancing the true purpose of the state. For example, as P has given to the state in the way of personal merit and contributions to its good, so P should receive from the state, in the way of offices and honor. If P's merits and contributions are equal to Q's, then they ought to receive equal amounts, and if they are unequal, then they ought to receive unequal amounts.[131] Aristotle is addressing how the polis correctly decides who should hold political office and who should be honored by the state. What does this mean for poor citizens? While he says that it would be dangerous to allow the poor to participate in the most important offices since they lack justice and practical reason, it would be wrong not to allow them to participate at all. He says, "For a state in which a large number of people are excluded from office and are poor must of necessity be full of enemies."[132] Thus, the poor should participate in deliberation and judgment.[133] This means they can vote in elections, serve on juries, and participate in the assembly. Aristotle's definition of distributive justice might strike one as being strange since contemporary theories of justice focus more on economic matters rather than civic affairs. When Aristotle declares that human beings are political animals he is saying that life in the polis is most advantageous for human well-being.[134] Political participation for citizens in ancient Greece was of the utmost importance. Indeed, Aristotle believes that engaged citizenship was a necessary condition for human flourishing. One could simply not live the good life without it. More than a century ago, John Burnet made this point most clear when he stated that in ancient Greece, "The citizen was a shareholder, not a taxpayer."[135]

Aristotle provides further clarification of his notion of distributive justice by discussing the distribution of flutes.[136] He makes it clear that "superiority in birth or wealth" should not be a factor in deciding who gets a flute.[137] Those who deserve to receive flutes are the individuals who merit them.[138] Given Aristotle's beliefs about human flourishing and his notion of distributive justice, is it reasonable to conclude that in the Aristotelian state every citizen merits a certain minimum standard of living as rational beings that are part of a social organization? It is indeed reasonable and the following exploration of his political theory shall substantiate this claim.

The golden mean is another fundamental idea in Aristotle's ethical and political theory.[139] To be clear, the mean is not simply the middle between two opposing forces, say bravery on the one hand and cowardice on the other hand. The mean is what is appropriate for the individual in the context of a given situation. For example, in times of war, one should lean more toward bravery and farther away from cowardice. As rational beings, individuals should choose the mean between excess and deficiency. This notion of choosing the mean is reflected in personal ethics as well as in the mixed constitution of the state, which is neither too democratic nor too aristocratic. Accordingly, too many poor people in a state would be unjust since the aim should be for a large middle class, where individuals are neither poor nor excessively wealthy. Since a virtuous person chooses the mean and politics should be aimed at the achieving it, excessive poverty in the state would be an unjust situation.

Property Ownership

Before embarking on a discussion of Aristotle's treatment of poverty, it is necessary to look briefly at his theory of property. He maintains that private property ownership is a *necessary* condition for the just state. In Book II of

Politics, Aristotle rejects communism for the guardians and auxiliaries in the *Republic* and criticizes equalization of property as an alternative. Here I examine his critique of these two property arrangements and then explore the system for property organization in his best state.

Aristotle has practical and theoretical reasons for rejecting communism in the *Republic*. His reasons may be summarized as the following:

- People are more likely to have conflicts in a communal situation than when they have their own families and property.[140]
- Communal arrangements deny individuals the pleasure of ownership.[141]
- Private property allows one to be able to help one's friends.[142]
- Communal arrangements take away the tasks of two virtues, that is, temperance and generosity (for example, temperance about having sex with different women and generosity with one's property).
- Communal arrangements may get rid of some evils but too many good things have to be given up, which makes it a bad arrangement.[143]
- Too much unity in a state is not a good thing. Instead of communal arrangements to promote friendship, the focus should be on education, habits, and laws.[144]
- If communal living and property arrangements were such good ideas, then one would find cities with those arrangements in their constitutions.[145]

Instead of eliminating the threat of factions in the state, Aristotle argues that Plato is actually creating fertile grounds for it by creating two states, one of the guardians and one consisting of the farmers and artisans.[146] He says that the guardians would be deprived of happiness because no one could be happy under those circumstances. When part of the city is unhappy, the whole cannot be happy.[147]

In spite of these concerns, R. F. Stalley argues that Aristotle's fundamental problem with communal arrangements is that he thinks differently from Plato about human nature. In brief, he says that Aristotle believes that communal living is contrary to nature. Even if Plato's ideal state in the *Republic* could be realized, Aristotle thinks that it would frustrate rather than promote the well-being of citizens.[148] At first glance, Stalley's argument is persuasive since it seems that Aristotle does believe that owning private property is natural and thus, one could not be happy without it. Yet, as I shall discuss later, Aristotle's commitment to private property ownership is confusing and weak. In light of this, Stalley's observation suggests that Aristotle's views about private property ownership are less than consistent.

Aristotle also dismisses the idea that the equalization of property ownership would solve the problem of poverty because he thinks people will always want more. He says that it is extremely difficult to know what amount of land is necessary and sufficient for human beings to live a temperate and generous life. While equalizing property may have certain advantages in preventing factions from arising, those advantages are outweighed by the accompanying civil discord. Many individuals would feel that they deserved more than equality and thus would revolt.[149] It is curious that Aristotle chooses the word *deserve* since it is not clear how the distribution of land has to do with desert. The land is not allotted as a reward or payment for labor nor is it distributed based on honor. In one of his many criticisms of Plato, Aristotle says that it is difficult to know what the appropriate allotment should be. He laments that Plato is too vague in his discussion about what one needs to live a temperate life. Not only is his formula too general, but also one may live a temperate life that is wretched. According to Aristotle, "A better definition is 'temperately and generously'; for when separated, the one will lead to poverty, the other to luxury. For these are the only choiceworthy states that bare on the use of property."[150]

It is important to pause here and mention that Aristotle introduces a frequently overlooked source of faction. He suggests that many feel a sense of entitlement to more than equal shares, whether there is a basis for this or not. Surely, he is right that some individuals will think for a variety of reasons that they should receive more than others will. For example, P thinks that he works harder than Q. As a result, P thinks that he should receive a larger allotment of land than Q because he will be able to use the additional land to produce more crops. P's beliefs may or may not be based on any evidence to support his claim. It could be that Q is a more efficient worker and thus he is able to accomplish in six hours what P accomplishes in nine. Aristotle says there will always be disagreements about who deserves what because people always desire more. These differences of opinions about desert lead to factions and political unrest because some people truly believe they are being treated unfairly. Moreover, one cannot underestimate human beings' propensity toward greed, and thus it is impossible to satisfy their wants because they will always desire more. Instead of focusing on equalizing property, Aristotle believes it is more important to educate citizens to be less greedy.[151]

Since Plato allows for moveable property that is worth five[152] times the landed property value in the *Laws*, Aristotle asks why one should not allow for more landed property.[153] He thinks that one should trust neither a system of *common* ownership nor a system of *equal* ownership. Instead of eliminating or equalizing private property, he advocates proper moral education, social customs, and legislation as necessary for individuals to internalize appropriate attitudes toward property. Moreover, those attitudes should be concerned with moderation.[154] It is ironic that in spite of Aristotle's criticisms of Phaleas and Plato's plans for equal allotments of property, he adopts the same policy in setting up his ideal state in Book VII of *Politics*.[155] Not only does Aristotle say that two allotments should be assigned to each citizen, but he also says that, "This not only accords with justice and equality, but ensures greater unanimity in the face of wars with neighbors."[156] While Aristotle does not mention desert, he associates the land allotments with justice.

Earlier, I discussed Fleischacker's work on distributive justice. I want to return to his argument because his discussion of Aristotle is relevant here.[157] As you may remember, Fleischacker thinks that scholars have misused the term redistributive justice. In brief, he states that it is incorrect to associate Plato or Aristotle with the idea of redistributive justice. Neither theorist provides any arguments, according to his account, that society had a moral obligation to end poverty or that justice demanded a redistribution of wealth to benefit the poor during this time.[158] He says that it would make no sense to Aristotle to tie the idea of need, independent of excellence, as the correct basis of a claim to a certain good.[159] Without a doubt, Fleischacker is correct that most of the time, Aristotle does connect justice with desert. There appears to be an exception, however, because Aristotle says that giving everyone two allotments is in accord with justice.[160] Moreover, this distribution is based to some extent on need. When Aristotle says that one must have enough land to lead a temperate and generous life, it appears he is saying that one should receive what one *needs* to lead that type of life. Thus, the distribution based on need is in accord with justice. One can join this idea of need and merit by returning to the example of the flute distribution discussed earlier. Human beings merit a certain minimum standard of living because they need it to be active participants in the polis, which in turn allows them to fulfill their function as rational human beings. Matters do not end there, because to some extent, the notion of need influences Aristotle's other ideas about property arrangements.

Aristotle discusses three options for property arrangements in the state.[161] As the chart shows, there are four possibilities but he never discusses the first arrangement, that is, both ownership and use could be private.[162] Instead, he discusses number two, which is private ownership with common use, number three, which is common ownership with private use of the land, and number four, which is common ownership with common use. In Book X, Chapter X, he explains why it is necessary for individuals to own private property and why he thinks private ownership with communal use (scenario two in the chart) is the best arrangement. He says,

> For while property should be in some way communal, in general it should be private. For when care for property is divided up, it leads not to those mutual accusations, but rather to greater care being given, as each will be attending to

what is his own. But where use is concerned, virtue will ensure that it is governed by the proverb "friends share everything in common."[163]

Production/Use

		Private	Common
	Private	**1** **Not an** **Option**	**2**
Ownership			
	Common	**3**	**4**

His choice is provocative because, as C. D. C. Reeve points out, Aristotle states in the *Rhetoric* that to own property, one must have the power to alienate or dispose of it through either gift or sale.[164] But in the *Politics*, Aristotle states that each qualified citizen, that is, each male head of household, in the ideal constitution should be given an *inalienable* allotment, which is equal with all the others.[165] If the lots were inalienable, then individuals would not be able to sell or give them away. He cannot mean that these citizens will have exclusive or private use of the land since its use is communal. Thus, one is left confused about what property ownership means to him.

Another complication arises from Aristotle's assumption that private property with communal use will encourage friendship among citizens. In the same way that he criticizes Plato's communal arrangements in the *Republic*, one can imagine that private ownership of property with communal use could create fertile grounds for disagreements. This is especially true if one accepts Aristotle's claim that people take better care of what they own and thus communal property would be neglected. It is not difficult to imagine that a property owner may become agitated if he thinks someone is not respecting his property. One might picture an overly protective property owner who supervises the use of his property so closely that those who use it feel harassed. It is also not too far a stretch to envision an individual who resents allowing others to use his property since he does not think they care for it properly. Finally, it is hard to determine how this arrangement will promote generosity since he seems to imply at times that communal land use would be required by legislation. At a minimum, it is surely a weakened notion of generosity.

At first, Aristotle's claim that private property ownership is a *necessary* condition for individuals to practice the virtue of generosity may seem strange. What he means, however, is that for one to practice the virtue of giving to others who have less or to support philanthropic activities, one should give freely some of his material resources when he is not required to do so by any principle of justice. It makes sense then that one must have some material resources or he could not be generous.[166] Terrence Irwin has argued, however, that Aristotle's proposition is problematic. It is a flawed argument, according to Irwin, because it would be the same as saying that we need "beggars because we value charity."[167] He also observes that Aristotle leaves room for philanthropy only by slighting the claims of justice since it requires some to be worse off than others. Aristotle's idea of generosity requires that some have more than they need while others have less. The question that arises is, could the inequality between the two have been removed by some other way that may better serve the interests of the one in need instead of making him reliable on the goodwill of another?[168] Irwin then alludes to Kant's observation that private property and inequality make philanthropy a possibility. While philanthropy is better than no philanthropy when inequality exists, Irwin wonders if it would not be best to remove the conditions that make philanthropy desirable.[169]

Nussbaum correctly points out that private property ownership is "provisional, subject to claims in need."[170] One of the reasons that Aristotle provides for communal use of property is that "no citizen should be in the need of sustenance."[171] And when Aristotle discusses poor relief, he mentions that communal use of property will help to alleviate poverty.[172] Again, it appears that Aristotle believes that need, not desert, accounts for at least part of the reason for his insistence that while one may own private property, the use of that property should be communal. Fred Miller, Jr., says that Nussbaum and others should not read too much into Aristotle's notion of communal use. Rather than any type of socialist program, Miller believes that owners have complete control over their property and communal use is subject to their discretion insofar as it is for "virtuous uses."[173] This means that the property owner would practice generosity by allowing communal use because there is no entitlement or legal reason for him to do so.[174] Miller is directly addressing Nussbaum and I think that somewhere between the two lies the most reasonable interpretation. Aristotle certainly does not say there is any entitlement, legal or otherwise, for the poor to use private property. It is clear that he is against the government confiscating private property for redistribution.[175] He does say, however, that it would be "a good thing" for property owners to give communal use of their property to the poor.[176] Thus, he is not a socialist but surely, there is a strong expectation that property owners will share their wealth and land with those who are less fortunate. While it may not be a legal requirement, anyone who wants to live a virtuous life and be part of the polis will allow others to use his property. After all, generosity is an Aristotelian virtue. His idea to use private property is just one of several that he has to aid the poor.

Measures to Limit Poverty

Along with having the appropriate property arrangements, Aristotle emphasizes the importance of population control as one component of limiting the incidence of poverty.

> "One might well think instead that it is the birth rate that should be limited, rather than property, so that no more than a certain number are born. (One should fix this number by looking to the chances that some of those born will not survive, and that others will be childless.) To leave the number unrestricted, as is done in most city-states, inevitably causes poverty among the citizens and poverty produces faction and crime."[177]

He considers possible causes for criminal acts and at one point he connects crime directly to poverty.[178] Later, he says that while some crimes are committed because people lack necessities, most are committed because criminals have desires that go beyond meeting their real needs.[179] Those desires drive them to commit crimes.[180] Aristotle agrees with Plato about the chief cause of poverty, namely, that greed renders individuals unable to distinguish between wants and needs. An insatiable appetite for the acquisition of material goods is the root cause for both crime and poverty. He also agrees with Plato that promoting friendship among citizens is desirable because it reduces factions and hostilities. In both cases, however, Aristotle claims that moral training, education, and legislation should be the primary solutions for the problem. Plato would undoubtedly agree since both the *Republic* and the *Laws* focus on how a state educates, legislates, and provides moral training to inculcate moderation among citizens.

Distributive Justice?

In Book III of *Politics*, Aristotle discusses distribution of goods, which chiefly concerns the distribution of political offices. His principal goal is to promote a good quality of life for citizens. He rejects the notions that societies form primarily for their own self-preservation, mutual defense, or economic interests. He provides an alternative:

> But suppose they do not do so only for the sake of life, but rather for the sake of living well, since otherwise there could be a city-state of *slaves* or animals,

where in fact there is not, because these share neither in *happiness* nor in a life guided by *deliberative choice*.[181]

Clearly, Aristotle thinks that states must encourage virtue among citizens so that the end result of living together is much more than an instrumental alliance. Indeed, he thinks it should be a collection of virtuous people who live happy lives.[182] He later says, "And a city state is the community of families and villages in a complete and self-sufficient life, which we say is living happily and *nobly*."[183] As discussed in the beginning of this chapter, Aristotle's notion of distributive justice is based upon the proportionate equality of the contributions that an individual citizen makes toward enhancing the true purpose of the state.

Besides, people resort to faction because of inequality not only of property but also of honors, although in opposite ways in each case: the many do so because of *inequality* in property; cultivated people because of honors, if they happen to be *equal*. Hence the saying, "Noble and base are held in a single honor."[184]

The significant difference between oligarchies and democracies, according to Aristotle, is the balance of power between the rich and the poor. Oligarchies are ruled by the wealthy few whereas poor majorities rule democracies.[185] These are the most common forms of government because the conflict between rich and poor dominates politics. Aristotle looks to the middle class to regulate the state by controlling the conflict between them because it enhances the inherent moderation of the constitution.[186] Thus, it is not surprising when he says that the best society places power in a large middle class.[187] Moderation demands that the rich should not be alienated through confiscation of their wealth and the poor should not be abused. Again, one is reminded of Solon, who believed that a large middle class was an integral part of the solution toward reducing societal conflict.[188]

Moderation also demands that measures be taken to improve the lives of those who are poor. To this end, Aristotle introduces a system of public and private social services that promotes moderation and well-being. He begins by analyzing the different ways that states have tried to solve the problem of poverty. For example, demagogues have made a habit of distributing surplus revenue among the people. He says that, "Helping the poor in this way, indeed, is like pouring water into the proverbial leaking jug."[189] There is a duty, however, to prevent excessive poverty because it is the chief defect of democracy. The appropriate measures would ensure a permanent level of prosperity and this would be in the interest of all classes.[190]

But the truly democratic man should see to it that the multitudes are not too poor (since this is a cause of the democracy's being a corrupt one). Measures

must be taken to ensure long-term prosperity. And, since this is also beneficial to the rich, whatever is left over from the revenues should be collected
together and distributed in lump sums to the poor, particularly if enough can
be accumulated for the acquisition of a plot of land, or failing that, for a start
in trade or farming. And if this cannot be done for all, distribution should instead be by turns on the basis of tribe or some other part. In the meantime the
rich should be taxed to provide pay for necessary meetings of the assembly,
while being released from useless sorts of public service.[191]

Aristotle's conception of social services includes constructive public assistance designed to enable men to set themselves up in life. This in practice
may be public block grants that enable the poor to buy a piece of property or
start a business in agriculture or commerce. It also demands private and voluntary social services from the notables, who are men of good feeling and
good sense. Each man, who undertakes the duty of helping the poor to find
occupations, should take charge of a group of men to help them make a start.
As mentioned earlier, Aristotle also thinks that the common use of private
property would benefit the poor. He believes that while poverty can never be
eliminated, individuals should not be destitute and that is where public assistance comes into play because it can provide opportunities for the indigent to
become more productive.

Miller downplays the significance of this by saying, "The rudimentary social safety net for the unfortunate which Aristotle admits is a far cry from the
modern egalitarian welfare state."[192] That is true but one should not ignore the
sophistication of his thinking about the poor. On the one hand, he realizes that
the state merely providing public aid alone may create a cycle of dependency.
On the other hand, all poor people should not be blamed or denigrated for
their lot in life. Thus he comes up with a social safety net as well as public
policies and programs that are aimed at not only preventing poverty, but also
toward helping the poor get out of poverty. He is clear that the community
must take responsibility for helping the poor. While Aristotle may not advocate for a welfare state, he did provide a sensible approach to attacking a difficult problem, and the responsibility for the problem falls not only on the
poor, but also on the wealthy.

Fortune

Happiness is enhanced by good fortune according to Aristotle. The upshot of
this is if an individual is fortunate to be born into a wealthy family, he will
have more opportunities to be virtuous. This is similar to Cephalus's statement in Book I of the *Republic*, when he said that wealth makes it easier for
one to be just. In addition, a wealthy individual has more possibilities and

control in his life, which may in turn allow for more happiness. On the other hand, if an individual is born into poverty, he may certainly be a virtuous person, but it will be more difficult for him to practice virtue and obtain happiness.[193]

Aristotle's idea of fortune means that it may harm or benefit individuals, but it is by definition beyond one's control. For example, A is a matter of fortune for B if and only if:

A harms or benefits B
B's decisions or desires do not control A.

Beauty, wealth, good birth, and good health are some of the examples used by Aristotle to describe external goods or goods of fortune.[194] While he makes it clear that good fortune is insufficient to make someone happy, he does believe that these external goods make it easier for one to share in the activities of goodness.[195]

John Cooper explores the role that fortune plays in Aristotle's notion of happiness, *eudaimonia*.[196] He says that Aristotle provides two different reasons to explain why happiness requires a sufficient amount of external goods. The first one is similar to his argument for private property because he believes that one needs a good deal of money to carry out some virtuous actions. The second reason is that if one lacks, for example good birth, then happiness is less than what it could be if the opposite were the case.[197] In addition, coming from a wealthy family gives individuals more life options.[198]

Cooper is correct in rejecting the notion that occasional good luck or misfortune are parts of these external goods. Aristotle means good fortune as a settled and permanent feature of someone's way of life. The main point that he is making is that external goods are not only intrinsically valuable, but they are also instrumentally beneficial because they allow the virtuous person to exercise his virtues and to continue to live a fully virtuous life.[199] Aristotle's claim has major implications for those who are born into poverty because through no fault of their own, their choices are limited and their abilities to live complete virtuous lives are compromised. Undoubtedly, he would have no qualms admitting this because children cannot choose their parents or a host of other morally arbitrary features, such as physical appearance, that surely contribute to individuals having more control and choices in their lives. To say that individuals may not live full virtuous lives, however, appears dubious. Certainly, the poor are confronted with numerous difficulties and challenges in their lives. It does not prevent them from being virtuous. Perhaps the difference lies in Aristotle's definition of virtue and that is why he thinks the wealthy have the advantage. Of course, some of the

greatest gifts to others are not monetary but involve the giving of one's time
and talents. It is also the case, however, that an individual who must work
two jobs or has other financial hardships may not be in a position to give her
time to philanthropic causes.

At the same time, one must be careful not to overstate his views about
virtue and external goods. In keeping with his emphasis on moderation, Aristotle tells us that while external goods may be instrumental to achieving happiness, too much of a good thing can also be harmful.[200] More importantly, he
says that, "For chance or luck produces goods external to the soul, but no one
is just or temperate as a result of luck or because of luck."[201] Also, he cautions
against thinking that good fortune is the same as happiness.[202] Finally, Aristotle repeatedly says that wealth alone does not make anyone virtuous. On the
contrary, one who is born into wealth may be arrogant and gravitate toward
other vices.[203] In fact, he says that the "acquisitive behavior" of the rich does
more to destroy the constitution than the behavior of the poor.[204]

While one may be appalled by his treatment of slaves and laborers, Aristotle has no tolerance for wealthier members of society abusing the poor. In
fact, he advocates heavier penalties being levied against the wealthy that do
violence to the poor than against those whose violence is directed toward
members of their own class.[205] Proper laws will help citizens internalize the
right attitudes toward the poor by moderating their behavior in society. As
mentioned earlier, Aristotle's idea about the right attitude is misleading since
in *Politics* the good life and true happiness are limited to a minority of citizens. Most of the inhabitants including slaves, women, farmers, laborers, immigrants, and artisans are excluded.

Aristotle investigates and uncovers what he believes to be the cause of
poverty. He thinks that human nature and its propensity toward greed predis-
pose civil society to be susceptible to the problem of poverty. Thus, societies
will always contend with it.

While Aristotle is critical of Plato's political theory, he adopts many of the
same ideas for preventing poverty. Both Plato and Aristotle believe that private property ownership must be regulated. Both look to establishing good
customs and habits through proper education and legislation in the state.
Moreover, both foster a community of friends. Perhaps their greatest agreement is about the devastating effects that poverty and riches will have on society because both think that if great disparities are left unchecked, the polarization between rich and poor will ultimately destroy the state.

When confronting the exclusion of women and natural slaves, Nussbaum
suggests that one might "separate Aristotle's philosophical principle here
from its unpleasant and unjust application."[206] This view has its merits because it appears that he wants to design a state where most, if not all, people

would flourish. For example, at the beginning of Chapter 11 in Book IV of *Politics* Aristotle poses the following question:

"What is the best constitution, and what is the best life for most city-states and most human beings, judging neither by a virtue that is beyond the reach of ordinary people, nor by a kind of education that requires natural gifts and resources that depend on luck, nor by the ideal constitution, but by a life that most people can share and a constitution in which most city-states can participate?"[207]

While Aristotle wants government to promote opportunities for human beings to lead decent, happy lives, he does not want to design a utopian state based on an ideal constitution. He also wants to limit the roles that good or bad luck play in human flourishing. In a later chapter, one shall see how this goal is similar to one that John Rawls will undertake many centuries later in *A Theory of Justice*. Like Aristotle, Rawls wants to level the playing field by eliminating arbitrary impediments that may negatively affect individuals' abilities to reach their potential and lead healthy, fulfilled lives.

As I stated at the beginning of this chapter, while much of Aristotle's treatment of poverty is laudable, one cannot ignore his exclusion of women, slaves, and laborers as citizens. Today, majorities of women throughout the world still do not have political rights and even when they do, they are at best second-class citizens who are marginalized economically and socially. While most people would outright reject Aristotle's ideas about slavery, it still exists in the forms of forced labor and prostitution. As a result, it is imperative to mention the shortcomings of his theory including the most disturbing ones, if one is to understand the assumptions and prejudices that continue to impact and harm human beings. Reoccurring ideas about the poor and poverty are based in broader normative systems, which directly influence political actors and policy-makers. The ancient world was no exception to this claim. That being said, Aristotle's political theory provides a pragmatic approach to alleviating poverty. Like Plato, his treatment is devoid of invective toward the poor.

Returning to the central question in this study, one can see that for Plato and Aristotle's political theories there are strong relationship between the idea of justice and limiting the incidence of poverty in the state. Justice requires creating an environment where human beings may flourish and find happiness. Part of that relies on moderation and choosing the mean between excesses as well as paying attention to the notion of merit. Aristotle believes that meeting certain human needs is fundamental to achieving these goals. As a result, his discussion of poverty is centered on pragmatic solutions that might help the poor better their situations and at the same time limit the growth of poverty in the state.

This chapter shows how Plato and Aristotle's political theories aimed to construct just states that would be stable. Both realized that poverty was an impediment to these mutual goals. It is noteworthy that neither philosopher dwells on the inherent shortcoming of poor people, but instead sets about to remedy the problem. In both cases, this involves the government's redistribution of resources through taxes dedicated to helping the poor. While neither uses the term "redistributive justice," it is incorrect to think that justice had nothing to do with this redistribution. I have shown that for Plato and Aristotle, justice demanded that resources be dedicated to help the poor.

In the next chapter we will leave the ancient world and the dialogue about who the poor are, why they are poor, and what, if any, role government should play in aiding them will change dramatically.

NOTES

1. There are some older articles that deal with aspects of Plato's treatment of poverty. See: C. Bradford Welles, "The Economic Background of Plato's Communism," *The Journal of Economic History* 8, suppl. *The Tasks of Economic History* (1948): 101–14; M. Wheeler, "Self Sufficiency and the Greek City," *Journal of the History of Ideas* 16 (June 1955): 416–20; E. Copeland, "The Institutional Setting of Plato's Republic," *International Journal of Ethics* 34, no.3, (April 1924): 228–42.

2. H. P. P. Lötter, "The Significance of Poverty and Wealth in Plato's Republic," *South African Journal of Philosophy* 22, no. 3 (2004): 189–206.

3. Ibid., 89.

4. Plato, "The Republic," in *Plato Complete Works*, ed. John Cooper and D. S. Hutchinson (Indianapolis, 1997), 422a, 547b–c, 552a. All references to the *Republic* refer to Stephanus notes.

5. A. Fuks, "Plato and the Social Question: The Problem of Poverty and Riches in the *Republic*," *Ancient Society* 8 (1977): 48–83; A. Fuks, "Plato and the Social Question: The Problem of Poverty and Riches in the *Laws*," *Ancient Society* 10 (1979): 69.

6. Samuel Fleischacker, *A Short History of Distributive Justice* (Cambridge: Harvard University Press, 2005), 1–16. Hereafter referred to as *Short History*.

7. T. K. Seung, *Plato Rediscovered: Human Value and Social Order* (Lanham, MD: Rowman & Littlefield, 1996), 233. Seung provides a thorough and convincing account of the development of Plato's notion of justice and theory of forms. In the *Laws*, Seung says that Plato's idea of justice in the real world "requires empirical knowledge."

8. *Republic*, 357d–358a.

9. Seung, *Plato Rediscovered*, 103.

10. *Republic*, 370a–c.

11. *Republic*, guardians, 374e–376c, 395b–d, artisans and farmers 389e, 401b–d; auxiliaries, 413c–414b.

12. Ibid., 414c

13. Ibid., 414d–416b.

14. Ibid., 432a–b, 433–34.

15. Ibid., 427d–e.

16. Ibid., 435c, 440e441a, 443d.

17. Ibid., 443e.

18. Plato makes the direct link between justice and happiness in *Gorgias* 478a–d and in the *Republic* when he discusses the miserable life of the tyrant.

19. Seung, *Plato Rediscovered*, 105–6.

20. For example, see *Republic*, 414e.

21. *Republic*, 369b–c.

22. Ibid., 330c.

23. Ibid., 331b.

24. Ibid., 330a

25. Ibid., 421c–d.

26. Ibid., 421e.

27. Ibid., 422a.

28. Ibid., 390d.

29. Ibid., 347c.

30. Ibid., 347b

31. Ibid., 347d.

32. Copeland, "Institutional Setting," 228.

33. Ibid., 229.

34. Seung, *Plato Rediscovered*, 5.

35. Aristophanes wrote *The Clouds* in 423 B.C. and historians date Plato's life from 428–347 B.C.

36. Copeland, "Institutional Setting," 234.

37. Seung, *Plato Rediscovered*, 6.

38. M. I. Finley, *Politics in the Ancient World* (Cambridge, 1983), 1–3, 11, 30–33, and 108–9.

39. Plutarch, *Plutarch's Lives* (New York, 2001), 114.

40. Ibid., 114.

41. Ibid., 116.

42. Ibid., 117.

43. Ibid., 117–118.

44. For examples in Plato: *Hippias Major*, 285e; *Timaeus*, 20e (Solon, the wisest), 21b, 22a; *Symposium*, 209d; *Laws*, 858e; *Republic*, 536d, 599e; *Phaedrus*, 278c, 258b; *Charmides*, 155a, 158a; *Laches*, 188b, 189a; *Lysis*, 212e; *Critias*, 110b, 113a and *Protagoras*, 343a.

45. *Laws*, 624a, 630d, 632d, 858e; *Symposium*, 209d; *Republic*, 1059d; *Phaedrus*, 258b; and *Epistle Four*, 320d.

46. *Plutarch's Lives*, 59.

47. Ibid., 60.

48. Ibid., 61.

49. Ibid., 74.

50. For a discussion about Solon's influences as well as Lycurgus' on Plato, see Glenn Morrow, *Plato's Cretan City* (Princeton: Princeton University Press, revised edition 1993) 78–88 and 56, n.47.

51. *Republic*, 462c–d and 464b.

52. Ibid., 521a.

53. Ibid., 421e.

54. Ibid., 370d–371e.

55. Ibid., 417a, and 419a.

56. Ibid., 421e.

57. Ibid., 556b.

58. Ibid., 372b–c, 423a–c, and 460a.

59. Fuks, "Plato and the Social Question, *Republic*," 78a.

60. *Republic*, 416d, 417a–b, 464c, and 543a–b.

61. Ibid., 463c.

62. Ibid., 546a.

63. Ibid., 546c–d.

64. Ibid., 547b.

65. Ibid., 547b.

66. Ibid., 547c.

67. Ibid., 544c, 548a–b, 551a.

68. Ibid., 50c–d, and 551d.

69. Ibid., 552a.

70. Fuks, "Plato and the Social Question, *Republic*," 58.

71. *Republic*, 552d–e, 553c–d.

72. Ibid., 556b–e.

73. Ibid., 564a–566e.

74. Ibid., 566a–b.

75. Ibid., 564e.

76. Ibid., 566d.

77. Ibid., 566d.

78. Plato, "Laws," in *Plato Complete Works*, ed. John Cooper and D. S. Hutchinson (Indianapolis, 1997), 739c–e. All references to *The Laws* refer to Stephanus notes.

79. See for example *Laws*, 869e–870b, 906b–e.

80. *Laws*, 736d–737b.

81. Ibid., 742e–743b.

82. Ibid., 831c–e.

83. Ibid., 728a.

84. Ibid., 913b.

85. A. Fuks, "Plato and the Social Question, *Laws*," 33–78, 38.

86. *Laws*, 705, 741e, 842d, 849, 919c–d, 849d, 850a.

87. Ibid., 742a–b.

88. Plato sets this number at 5,040 landholders, so there would be 5,040 families and for each individual family an allotment of land to support a citizen-family (*Laws*, 737c, 737e, 741b–c, 744d–e, 745a).

89. *Laws*, 740a–741e, 855a, and 928e–929a.

90. For a detailed discussion of these allotments and whether they should be called private property see Fuks, "Plato and the Social Question, *Laws*," 55–61.

91. *Laws*, 744b–c. To assure the equality of the initial allotment, Plato states that if the land allotted has poor soil, then that allotment should be larger to compensate for the poor quality of the soil (*Laws* 745c).

92. *Laws*, 744d.

93. Ibid., 744d–e.

94. Ibid., 744e.

95. Morrow, *Plato's Cretan City*, 131.

96. *Laws*, 774c.

97. Ibid., 761d, 766c.

98. Ibid., 959d.

99. Ibid., 754e–755a.

100. Ibid., 756c.

101. Ibid., 696b, 697b–c, 743d.

102. Fuks, "Plato and the Social Question, *Laws*," 64.

103. Fleischacker, *Short History*, 1.

104. Ibid., 42.

105. *Laws*, 744e.

106. Ibid., 774c.

107. Ibid., 766c, 761d.

108. Ibid., 744b–c.

109. Fleischacker, *Short History*, 42.

110. Aristotle, *Politics*, trans. C. D. C. Reeve (Indianapolis, 1998), 1289b30, 1291b8. All references to Aristotle's *Politics* are from this edition and refer to Bekker numbers.

111. Ibid., 1303b14.

112. Ibid., 1320a35–1320b15.

113. Richard Mulgan says that today most people read Aristotle's *Politics* immediately after Plato's *Republic*, thus one tends to overemphasize Aristotle's propensity for democracy. "Was Aristotle an Aristotelian Social Democrat?" *Ethics* 111 (October 2000): 83.

114. *Politics*, 1324a24–5, 1325a7.

115. Ibid., 1329b40–1330a8.

116. Ibid., 1330b8–12.

117. Aristotle, *Nicomachean Ethics*, trans. Terence Irwin (Indianapolis, 1985), 1095b5. All references to *Nicomachean Ethics* are from this edition and will be referred to as *Ethics*.

118. For a thorough discussion of Aristotle's functionalism see Susan Moller Okin's *Women in Western Political Thought* (Princeton, 1979), 73–96.

119. *Politics*, 1254b12–25, 1260a38–1260b6, 1278a1–25, 1328b38–1329a2.

120. Ibid., 1254b15–20.

121. Ibid., 1337b10.

122. Mulgan, "Was Aristotle an Aristotelian?," 83.

123. In this chapter, I refer specifically to three of Nussbaum's works. "Nature, Function, and Capability: Aristotle on Political Distribution" *Oxford Studies in Ancient Philosophy*, suppl. vol. (1988), 145–84, "Aristotelian Social Democracy," in *Liberalism and the Good*, R. Bruce Douglass et al. (New York: Routledge, 1990), 203–52, and "Aristotle, Politics, and Human Capabilities: A Response to Antony, Arneson, Charlesworth, and Mulgan," *Ethics* 11, no.1 (October 2000): 102–40.

124. Nussbaum, "Nature, Function and Capability," 145.

125. Ibid., 145.

126. Ibid., 158.

127. Mulgan, "Was Aristotle an Aristotelian?," 83; Okin, *Women in Western Political Thought*; Jean Bethke Elshtain, *Public Man, Private Woman* (Princeton: Princeton University Press, 1982).

128. A. P. Martinich provides a framework for interpretation that I have in mind here. "The Interpretation of Covenants," in *Leviathan, after 350 Years*, eds. Tom Sorell and Luc Foisneau (Oxford, 2004), 217–40.

129. *Ethics*, 1129b15–1130a.

130. Ibid., 1130a15.

131. *Politics*, 1281a3–8, and 1261a25–35. Aristotle provides an explanation of his notion of distributive justice also in *Nicomachean Ethics* in Book v.iii, which states that justice is proportionate equality.

132. Ibid., 1281b25–30.

133. Ibid., 1281b30–35.

134. Ibid., 1253a.

135. John Burnet, *The Ethics of Aristotle* (London: Methuen & Co., 1900), 212.

136. *Politics*, 1282b30.0

137. Ibid., 1283a.

138. Ibid., 1282b30.

139. *Ethics*, 1140a10–1104b.

140. *Politics*, 1263b14.

141. Ibid., 1263a40–1263b5.

142. Ibid., 1263b8–14.

143. Ibid., 1263b27–28.

144. Ibid., 1263b30–40.

145. Ibid., 1264a1.

146. Ibid., 1264a11–20.

147. Ibid., 264b16–25.

148. R. F. Stalley, "Aristotle's Criticism of Plato's Republic," in *A Companion to Aristotle's Politics*, eds. David Keyt and Fred Miller, Jr. (Oxford, 1991), 182–99.

149. *Politics*, 1267a37–1267b7.

150. Ibid., 1264a27–35.

151. Ibid., 1267a37–1267b7.

152. See Plato, *Laws*, 744e. Plato sets the limit at four times the landed property value and not five as Aristotle states.

153. *Politics*, 1265b20–24.

154. Ibid., 1263b35.

155. Ibid., 1330a14–18.

156. Ibid., 1330a14–17.

157. Fleischacker, *Short History*, 13–16.

158. Ibid., 13–16.

159. Ibid., 15.

160. *Politics*, 1330a15.

161. Ibid., 1263a1–9.

162. Ernest Barker discusses this omission, but he does not explain it. This is contained in Barker's translation of *Politics* (Oxford, 1958) 55, Note I.

163. *Politics*, 1263a26–30.

164. *Rhetoric*, 1361a21–22. Reeve raises questions about Aristotle's notion of private property ownership in his Introduction to *Politics*, lxxvii–lxxviii.

165. Aristotle, *Politics*, 1266b14–31, 1270a15–35, and 1330a14–18.

166. Terence Irwin, "Aristotle's Defense of Private Property" in *A Companion to Aristotle's Politics*, eds. David Keyt and Fred Miller, Jr. (Oxford, 1991), 213–14.

167. Ibid., 214.

168. Ibid., 212.

169. Ibid., 212.

170. Nussbaum, "Aristotelian Social Democracy," 205.

171. *Politics*, 1330a1.

172. *Politics*, 1320b90.

173. Fred Miller, Jr., *Nature, Justice and Rights in Aristotle's Politics* (Oxford, 1995), 330.

174. Ibid., 330–31.

175. *Politics*, 1320a–4.

176. Ibid., 1320b–9.

177. Ibid., 1265b5–1. Aristotle provides a similar critique of Plato's arrangements for community of property in 1263a 20–1264b6. At times Aristotle does not represent accurately Plato's actual argument in the *Republic*. For example, Aristotle claims that Plato does not deal with population control but he does in *Laws* 740b, 741b, 742c, 855a–b, and 856d–e. In addition, Aristotle confuses the communal ownership of land in the *Republic*. Plato does not advocate common ownership of land in the *Republic*. The farming class owns the land and the only element of communism is that of the Guardian class who make common use of the products from the land in return for their protection of the city.

178. *Politics*, 1265b9–11

179. Ibid., 1267a5.

180. Ibid., 1267a3–16.

181. Ibid., 1280a30.

182. Ibid., 1280b5–12.

183. Ibid., 1280b39.

184. Ibid., 1266b36–1267a.

185. Ibid., 1279b38–42.

186. Ibid., 1295a35–1296a21

187. Ibid., 1295b34–1296b10.

188. For example, Aristotle praises Solon for his wisdom in *Politics*, 1281b33 and 1273b33–1274a21.

189. *Politics*, 1320a30–31.

190. Ibid., 1320a33–35.

191. Ibid., 1320a35–1320b3.

192. Miller, *Nature, Justice and Rights*, 331.

193. *Politics*, 1294a15–20.

194. *Ethics*, 1099b.

195. *Politics*, 1323b40–1324a3.

196. John Cooper, "Aristotle on the Goods of Fortune," *The Philosophical Review* (April 1985): 173–97.

197. Ibid., 178–79.

198. Ibid., 188.

199. Ibid., 196.

200. *Politics*, 1123b5–11.

201. Ibid., 1323b26.

202. *Ethics*, 1153b22–23.

203. *Politics*, 1295b5–9.

204. Ibid., 1297a9–12.

205. Ibid., 1309a20

206. Nussbaum, "Nature, Function and Capability," 166.

207. *Politics*, 1295a25–30.

Chapter Three

Societal Responsibility and the Undeserving Poor: John Locke

At the outset of the study I stated that the aim was not to provide a comprehensive history of the treatment of poverty in the Western tradition but to engage some of the most significant and provocative theorists who wrote about the problem. This explains the gap in time between Aristotle and the modern world. Certainly, Cicero, Augustine, Aquinas, and others had interesting things to say about poverty. However, their treatments are not as extensive nor are they as critical to their political theories and notions of justice as the theorists chosen for this study. However, it is necessary to bring to the fore some of the crucial changes that had taken place in the interim so that one may properly understand Locke's treatment of poverty.

The teachings of Jesus Christ and the spread of Christianity profoundly affected the world and modern philosophers like John Locke. By 330 AD, the Roman Empire had adopted Christianity and by Locke's time the Reformation had taken place with Protestantism spreading throughout Europe. This is significant not only because Locke was a Christian but also because the plight of the poor and disenfranchised is foremost in Jesus's ethical teachings. One scholar claims that Jesus Christ's teachings about wealth and poverty approach fanaticism.[1] There are numerous quotations from the Christian scriptures about Jesus and his advocacy for the poor and contempt for the rich. For example, in the Sermon on the Mount as recorded by Luke, Jesus says, "Blessed be ye poor for yours is the Kingdom of God."[2] Perhaps, one of the most telling passages is when Jesus proclaims, "It is easier for a camel to pass through the eye of a needle than for someone rich to enter the kingdom of heaven."[3] Surely, the duty of charity toward the poor is a fundamental tenant of Catholic and Protestant teachings.

Christianity also provides the superhuman legislator, that is, God in Locke's natural law theory. Cicero was the first to articulate a theory of natural law. He says, "There is in fact a true law namely, right reason which is in accordance with nature, applies to all men, and is unchangeable and eternal."[4] The idea of natural law theory understood in the context of the Roman Empire deemphasized local and communal ties and created Roman Citizens. Since natural law is unchangeable, eternal, and applies to all human beings, it stands independent of human-made laws, which means that no government body can ever annul or alter it in any way. God is the author, interpreter, and sponsor of natural law.[5] Thomas Aquinas provides a sophisticated version of natural theory, which explains why he is known as "the natural law theorist." Locke bases his political and ethical theory on his construction of natural laws. He articulates substance to natural law and says that among these are life, liberty, and property. Locke's theory of justice rests on human-made laws acting in concert with natural laws. For example, since Locke believes that self-preservation is fundamental to natural law, which is God's law, positive law must promote self-preservation. One will see how his belief in God and natural law had profound consequences for his treatment of poverty.

Moreover, Locke's seventy-two years (1632–1704) coincided with other revolutionary changes in his native England. Those changes were not only political but also social. Perhaps the most significant was the beginning of industrialization and institutionalization of the free market economic system. The demise of medieval society brought with it social upheaval, massive unemployment, and destitution. Economic downturns, bad harvests resulting in food shortages, and wars also contributed to the rise of poverty. While industrialization and the transition to market economies created more jobs in the end, that development came with a heavy cost in human misery.[6] Mass poverty posed one of the English government's most formidable challenges during Locke's life.

The English government tried to address the problem of poverty with a series of Parliamentary Acts, which resulted in the Poor Law Act of 1598. The latter was significant because it stated that communities were not only morally, but also legally responsible for the poor. Up to the mid-seventeenth century, the government tried many different initiatives and policies for dealing with the poor with most being tied to broader social and political policies. After this and up until the late eighteenth century, local officials administered poor law matters. In spite of different approaches to dealing with the poor, there was great continuity in administering the poor law throughout the entire period.[7]

Locke is unique because he addressed the problem directly in his political role as a Commissioner on the Board of Trade in 1697.[8] As a result, his views about the causes, effects, and solutions to poverty are not a matter of speculation, but clearly stated in an official document that he authored. His conclusions about the causes of poverty do not agree with historical accounts of harvest failures, rising unemployment, and economic depression during this same period. As I explore Locke's beliefs about the poor, one will see how his convictions about their character shape his views about the causes and solutions to the problem of poverty. Locke was involved in English politics most of his adult life, and thus it is striking that he would have been unaware of the economic downturns since he had worked on other economic issues for the government during this time. While some of his proposals may sound shocking and cruel, they must be understood in their historical context. When seen in this light, most of his recommendations, while no less disturbing, are better understood as being in line with what had been the practice for many years. Moreover, the problem of settlement, which by law meant that the deserving and undeserving poor, including vagrants, were to be provided for in the parishes where they belonged, had become a pressing issue by the 1690s when Locke was making proposals for reforms to the poor laws.[9] In fact, it is not too strong to say the problem of settlement was spiraling out of control and the taxes specifically collected for poor relief were increasing.[10] I will revisit the issue of settlements later in the chapter. However, even if one considers the historical context, is it fair to say that one might expect a more nuanced and sensitive response from Locke, who was without a doubt, a brilliant political theorist? Did the increase in poor taxes and lawsuits between parishes and counties about settlement create political pressures and a sense of urgency that caused him to be less tolerant and understanding? Locke's beliefs about the poor had consequences because if one misunderstands the causes of poverty, then finding viable political solutions to the problem becomes difficult, if not impossible.

Another feature of Locke's treatment of poverty is that it exposes a fundamental tension within liberal theory. Mass poverty poses a threat to the basic principles of a market society because increased disparities in wealth magnify tensions in societies that are based on liberal maxims that include moral equality and democracy.[11] Liberals value freedom and equality. Poverty is a problem for them because freedom often, if not necessarily, results in inequality of wealth, and hence of comfort, honors, and happiness. Although some liberals may want to preserve or to reestablish equality, to do so means interfering with freedom or liberty. Locke, for example, believed in moral egalitarianism and a society that enhanced self-preservation. As a result, for his political theory to be intellectually and morally cohesive, he had to make some commitment to promote the preservation and welfare for all members in a liberal society. That meant, however, that the government had to undertake some redistribution of wealth to support the poor. Locke's political theory and ideas about justice are rooted in his Christianity and adherence to natural law theory where God is the

superhuman legislator. Self-preservation is fundamental to Locke's interpretation of natural law and thus his commitment to providing sustenance to the poor
follows from this belief. Can one be just without providing for the poor? More
importantly, what connection, if any, do Locke's ideas about justice have to do
with public aid for the poor? As one shall see, Locke's answers to these questions are not as predictable as one may suspect.

POLITICAL CONTEXT

To understand Locke's treatment of poverty one has to review briefly some
of the particularly tumultuous political events that were unfolding during his
life. He was only ten years old when the English Civil war began. This war
culminated with the beheading of Charles I in 1649. As a seventeen-year-old,
Locke was close enough to hear the crowd during the execution.[12] The Protestant rule of Oliver Cromwell as Lord Protector of England lasted for five
years, and after his death, the monarchy was reinstated in 1660 with Charles
II. In 1678, the Popish Plot, the rumor that a scheme was underway to assassinate Charles II and replace him with his Catholic brother, James, spread
anti-Catholic feelings throughout England. The Exclusion Controversy
(1689), which was an effort to ban the Catholic James from succession to the
throne, ended with the defeat of Locke's politically influential patron, the Earl
of Shaftesbury.

The 1683 Rye House Plot was a scheme to assassinate Charles II and put
his illegitimate Protestant son, the Duke of Monmouth on the throne. It failed
but it had significant consequences for Locke, mainly his exile to the Netherlands. The Catholic James II became King after the 1685 death of Charles II.
The Glorious Revolution of 1688 installed the Dutch Protestant, William of
Orange to be William I, King of England and the Catholic, James II, went into
exile. In 1689, the English Bill of Rights was approved. It barred any Catholic
from succeeding to the throne and increased Parliament's power while limiting the power of the Monarch. Shaftesbury died in exile and Locke returned
to England in 1689. The extent of Locke's involvement in the events from
1678 to 1683 is a matter of some controversy. Suffice to say that most Locke
scholars agree that he engaged in revolutionary activities and actively partic-
ipated in trying to get the Exclusionary Bill through Parliament.[13] Thus,
Locke had more political experience and expertise than the average political
theorist did.

Of course, Locke was no average political theorist and upon his return to
England in 1689, he had more political influence than ever.[14] This influence
led to several political appointments, culminating in his assignment in 1697

as a Commissioner on the Board of Trade. Locke presented a plan to this Board to deal with increased poverty in England. This Report, which is sometimes called "An Essay on the Poor Law," provides Locke's judgments about the causes of poverty, its impact, and finally, his policy proposals to deal with it.[15] I examine Locke's "Essay on the Poor Law" as well as his other works that elucidate his beliefs about the causes of, effects, and solutions for the problem of poverty and how they relate to his ideas about justice.

HUMAN NATURE AND THE POOR

Locke views poverty as a sign of individual moral corruption that drains the collective wealth of society. Poor people not only fail to contribute to the prosperity of the nation, but they also willingly take resources from those who work to get them. He believes that changing individuals first is necessary to solve the problem of poverty because they are responsible for their dire situations.[16] The irony is that Locke also believes that government is responsible for providing subsistence to people so that no one will perish from lack of food, shelter, or clothing. To allow someone to die from hunger or exposure would violate natural law and thus be unjust. That does not mean, however, that Locke enthusiastically endorses public aid or that he expresses much compassion toward the poor.

Locke's *Essay Concerning Human Understanding* provides some insight into his views about human nature. He believes that it is the responsibility of the individual to determine his or her own fate. Pleasure and pain are the ultimate cause of choices.[17] Thus, one may think of happiness for human beings as having that which pleases and avoiding that which may bring pain. Locke admits that what may bring pleasure to one person may bring pain to another.[18] Human beings have desires that are dictated by the "ordinary necessities of our lives," including hunger, thirst, heat, cold, and weariness. Individuals come to acquire what Locke calls "irregular desires" such as seeking honor, power, or riches by habits that come from fashion, example, and education, which custom makes natural to them.[19] J. B. Schneewind says that Locke's focus on pleasure and pain and our failure to choose what is good for us has important implications for his theory. For example, since human beings are sinners, they do not focus on the eternal consequences for their behavior on earth. Instead, they choose what relieves their uneasiness or what brings pleasure. That being said the idea of sanctions that involve pain could be effective in making individuals to either refrain or perform some given action. As a result, laws must be backed by harsh sanctions if they are to be effective.[20]

One reason that Locke provides for the cause of poverty is that poor people make bad judgments about what is in their best interests. Motivated by shortsighted notions of pleasure (for example, not having to work), they mistake what is evil for what is good.[21] Moreover, the poor are habituated to this way of life, thus necessitating punitive measures to change their ideas about good and evil. For example, if the English Poor Laws lack discomforting sanctions they will be ineffective. Locke uses the example of poverty twice to illustrate the misjudgments individuals make about what is pleasurable (that is, what is good) and what is painful (that is, what is evil) in the *Essay*. In the first example, he argues that an individual must feel the discomforts associated with poverty before he will improve his situation.

> But yet upon a stricter enquiry, I am forced to conclude, that *good*, the *greater good*, though apprehended and acknowledged to be so, does not determine the *will*, until our desire, raised proportionately to it, makes us *uneasy* in the want of it. Convince a Man never so much, that plenty has it advantages over poverty; make him see and own, that the handsome conveniencies of life are better than nasty penury: yet as long as he is content with the latter, and finds no *uneasiness* in it, he moves not; his *will* never is determin'd to any action, that shall bring him out of it.[22]

In the second example, Locke says that human beings must connect pleasure or pain as the consequences of a chosen action. He argues that if individuals could have the clear choice of working or starving set before them, there is no doubt that they would choose honest work. Locke says:

> Were the pains of honest Industry, and of starving with Hunger and Cold set together before us, no Body would be in doubt which to chuse.[23]

This helps to explain why he proposes such strong punitive measures for the poor. He wants individuals' good or bad choices and their subsequent good or bad consequences to be evident immediately. Thus if one is hungry, one would know that it is a direct result of his or her lack of honest industry.

MacPherson connects Locke's views about human nature and the poor to his Calvinism. He believes that Locke views the poor as inferiors. MacPherson says there is a similarity between Calvinism's view of the non-elect and Locke's views about the poor. While the Calvinist church included the entire population there was a difference made between the elect and non-elect. The latter, according to MacPherson were those who had no property, were never full members but they were subject to the church's rules and subsequent discipline for their violation.[24] John Dunn also relates Locke's beliefs about human nature to Calvinist social values.[25] He disagrees with

MacPherson that Locke viewed the poor as inferior. Dunn points out that Locke was raised in a Calvinist family and he embraced those values throughout his life because they reinforced the things that he believed were correct and thus provided him with security.[26] These beliefs forced him to think that each man had a calling. Dunn explains that according to Calvinism every human being arrives in the world in a particular social standing and with particular individual talents. Individuals have a duty to God to fulfill their proper roles. They come to know these roles, that is, their calling through careful reflection. All adults are responsible for figuring out what their proper callings are and then to fulfill them.[27] Thus, the non-industrious were sinning against God because they were not fulfilling the moral obligations required by the calling. Dunn admits that the Calvinistic idea of calling had a harsh side to it, especially for the poor. The "idle" poor had failed to heed their calling, and others had a moral responsibility to condemn them for no one owes them charity.[28]

THE REPORT

As I alluded to earlier, unlike other Western theorists, Locke authored an official government document about the causes, effects, and solutions to the problem of poverty. He wrote and subsequently presented the "Report to the Board of Trade to the Lords Justices 1697, Respecting the Relief and Unemployment of the Poor," more commonly known to scholars as "An Essay on the Poor Law" to the Board in October 1697. In Letter 2398, he referred to it as "my project about the better relief and employment of the poor."[29] His plan was to enforce the appropriate Elizabethan Poor Laws and amend them where necessary.

Locke begins the Report by saying that it is not the war, food shortages, or lack of employment that have caused the increased population of poor people.[30] On the contrary, he says that "the goodness of God has blessed these times with plenty."[31] According to Locke:

> The growth of the poor must therefore have some other cause, and it can be nothing else but the relaxation of discipline and corruption of manners; virtue and industry being as constant companions on the one side as vice and idleness are on the other.[32]

He argues that the failure to enforce the current English Poor Laws have also contributed to the current problem. These laws came from the Elizabethan legislation of 1598–1601, which required each parish to maintain the "impotent" and to provide work for the able-bodied.[33] In addition, he wants to limit the number of liquor stores and alehouses because these establish-ments also exacerbate the problem.[34]

Locke's aim is to suggest effective laws to reduce the burden of public sup-port and to make the poor useful to England. He stresses two main points: first, that the poor who can work must be forced to do so, and second, that laws should be enacted and enforced to compel them to work. Those who cannot work must be maintained. To that end, he proposes legislation in six policy areas:

1. The punishment of vagabonds;
2. The provision of work for the poor;
3. The establishment of working schools for poor children;
4. The schools' operations and oversight;
5. Poor guardians' authority and responsibilities toward the poor; and
6. The establishment of Poor Corporations.

To make sense of Locke's proposals, it is necessary to explore the poor guardians' duties since they figure prominently in all of his policy proposals. The taxpayers would choose the poor guardian for their parish. Once elected, he would have authority over the employment and relief of the poor. After one year of service, one-third of the poor guardians would resign, with that deter-mination being made by lot. After two years, another third would retire from the remaining two-thirds who were initially selected to serve, and so forth. After the first two years, poor guardians would serve three consecutive years and no longer. The poor guardian, along with a parish committee, would have to approve all poor relief prior to any distribution. These same guardians may also act as Justices of the Peace with power to issue passes to vagabonds and beggars. Additionally, they have the authority to send them to seaport towns or to correction houses. Individuals who receive government aid or make their living by begging would be required to have paperwork, that is, passes. These passes would allow them to leave their parish to travel. Locke urged the Board to require badges for all those who received poor relief.[35]

He also proposes grouping parishes together in the country while establish-ing "poor corporations" in towns. These subdivisions would collect poor taxes and administer services. Poor guardians, who would also be responsible for the punishment of vagrants and establishing "working schools," would manage these entities.[36] Locke advocates more centralized control of the poor at the ex-pense of local parishes. In fact, he argues that local people should be forbid-den by law to provide relief to individuals not wearing a poor badge or not of-ficially registered in the parish's poor book. His proposed regulations go even further to state that aid should be provided only at certain times during the day. At the same time, Locke says that neighbors are best equipped to judge the be-havior and needs of the poor in their parish.[37] This illustrates a tension in his proposals because on the one hand he is calling for more centralized government while on the other hand advocating limiting government's power and control. The latter policy would allow individual parishes more autonomy in making decisions about poor relief. Locke is strongly associated with the idea of limited government so it is surprising that he calls not only for more government administration, but also for also more centralized control.[38]

To reduce the number of "idle vagabonds," Locke says that new laws are necessary because some who receive aid pretend that they are unable to work and live only by begging or worse. These "begging drones" must be forced to work. Healthy males at least fourteen years of age but younger than fifty who are caught begging in maritime counties out of their own parish without a pass, should be seized and brought before a Justice of the Peace or a poor guardian. These men should then be sent to the next seaport town and kept at hard labor until a government ship comes close enough to pick them up.[39] They should serve three years under strict discipline at soldier's pay and be punished as deserters if they go ashore without leave or if they violate their leave policy. Any man, even if maimed or older than age fifty, who is caught begging without a pass in an inland county, should be sent to a house of correction for three years of hard labor. Locke wants Justices of the Peace to investigate the management of correction houses and check on the progress of those confined in them. If an individual has served his time, but the Justice or poor guardian judges him not reformed, then he should not be released until there is proof that he has changed for the better.[40] Locke reserves the most severe punishment for men who forge counterfeit passes. He says:

> That whoever shall counterfeit a pass shall lose his ears for that forgery the first time he is found guilty thereof, and the second time, that he shall be transported to the plantations, as in the case of felony.[41]

Throughout the Report, Locke is preoccupied with constricting the poor's ability to move freely throughout the country. His advocacy for mutilation for forging a pass demonstrates his intensity about it. The policy of parish confinement for old and young alike becomes a contentious one. Adam Smith and Alexis de Tocqueville will criticize this policy because it hinders the unemployed from finding work.

According to Locke, females should be treated differently. Young women fourteen and older who are found begging without a pass outside of their parish, but within five miles of it, should be returned to their parish and fined. The fine will be deducted from their poor relief or levied against their parents or master if they do not receive public aid. If an offender is further than five miles from her parish or if she is caught a second time for the same offense, she should be sent to the house of correction for three months of hard labor or until the Justice of the Peace has determined that she has been reformed. Boys or girls under fourteen who commit the same crime (if within five miles of their parish) should be sent to the closest working school, soundly whipped, kept at work until evening, and then sent home. If they live further away than five miles, they should be sent to the closest house of correction for six weeks and longer if necessary. Locke is confident these measures, if properly enforced, will suppress the number of idle vagabonds.

Another problem, according to Locke, is with individuals who pretend they want to work but complain that they cannot find employment. He says that in each parish, the poor guardian should ask residents to provide work at a reduced rate to people who say they cannot find work. He is certain that neighbors will provide employment opportunities unless those seeking work have "some defect in ability or honesty."[42] In that case, it is reasonable that the person should suffer the consequences. If no one voluntarily offers work, then the guardian will decide on a lower rate of pay and each individual without a job will work one day for each parish resident. If a resident declines to provide work for the poor, he will still have to pay the appointed wages. If anyone refuses to work and the parish is close to the ocean, he will be sent to a ship for three years of hard labor, otherwise he will be sent to a house of correction. In either case, his salary will be used for his subsistence and any surplus should be sent to his parish to help pay for the maintenance of his wife and children or other poor people if he is single.[43]

Locke believes there are two other groups that constitute the greatest drain on the government. The first is adults who do not have full strength but who are still able to work. The second is women with children who are married to day laborers. Since the latter have to care for their children, they cannot find jobs. Both groups receive public aid yet contribute nothing to society. Their potential for productive labor is wasted, causing a financial loss to the country. If the aged and women with children could be put to work in the textile or manufacturing industry, and paid as little as one pence a day, they could add as much as £130,000 to the English economy every year. In eight years England would be more than a million pounds wealthier.[44] These facts, according to Locke, point to what the proper policies for poor relief should be because the goal is to find them work and to make sure that "they do not live like drones upon the labor of others."[45]

Locke mentions a third group that needs attention, that is, the children of the working poor. Since these children are a burden, and the potential for their labor is lost to the public until they are twelve or fourteen years old, Locke advocates establishing compulsory working schools for children who are three years old but under fourteen years of age. This will accomplish two things. First, the mother will not have to care for them, which will allow her to find work. Second, the children will be better cared for and they can be taught a good work ethic. Locke says:

[F]rom infancy [children will] be inured to work, which is of no small consequence to the making of them sober and industrious all their lives after; and the
parish will be either eased of this burden or at least of the misuse in the present
management of it.[46]

In addition, children will be required to attend church because Locke says
that will provide them with a sense of religion and help to correct their bad
upbringing because presently they are "utter strangers both to religion and
morality as they are to industry."[47] Their labor will also more than pay for
their nourishment and education. Without their work, the parish pays as much
as fifty or sixty pounds for each child by the time he or she turns fourteen
years old. Locke says that the initial set-up costs for the workhouses will be
recouped quickly with a surplus.[48]

Local artisans in the parish should employ some of the boys in the workhouses as apprentices until they are twenty-three years old. Locke advocates that some men, who own property in the parish, may choose the boys
whom they wish to apprentice. Each property owner in the parish is
obliged to take at least one fourteen-year-old unemployed boy as his own
apprentice. No resident will be forced to take more than one boy at a time.
Adults who cannot find work may also come to the workhouses to learn to
work.

Those who are unable to work at all should be housed four or more in a
room and many more in one house. One fire should be sufficient to keep them
warm, and one attendant may care for all of them.[49] These group homes will
save money. Finally, Locke states at the end of the Report:

> "That, if any person die for want of due relief in any parish in which he ought
> to be relieved, the said parish be fined according to the circumstances of the fact
> and the heinousness of the crime."[50]

This statement, and a similar once at the beginning of the Report that says
that those who cannot work must be maintained, illustrate Locke's accept-
ance, although limited and harsh, of government's responsibility for the welfare of those who cannot provide or care for themselves. In his *Essays on the
Laws of Nature*, Locke ties this responsibility to natural law.[51] He states that
the law of nature demands that people provide food for those who are starving or relief to those who are in trouble. There is not a constant obligation to
do this; the obligation is only at a particular time and in a particular manner.[52]
According to Locke,

> We are not obliged to provide with shelter and to refresh with food any and
> every man, or at any time whatever, but only when a poor man's misfortune calls
> for our alms and our property supplies means for charity.[53]

In addition, Locke's *Two Treatises of Government* supplies further textual support for his beliefs about the poor's right to aid. He says that the preservation of mankind is the fundamental Law of Nature, that is, the will of God.[54] He also states that it is evident that God would never leave one man to the mercy of another to starve from lack of food. Thus, God gives the poor a right to the surplus of others' goods when their needs demand it.[55] Locke believes that God gave the world to mankind in common and while he thinks that man's labor turns common property into private property, he never abandons the idea that property should be understood as a right from God to preserve human life.[56] Finally, in an essay titled *Venditio*, Locke qualifies his statement that defends market determination of corn prices in times of scarcity. He says that if anyone "offends the common rule of charity" and extorts so much money that the people cannot purchase enough to keep from starving, that merchant is guilty of murder.[57] Thus, one finds in Locke a fundamental belief that no one should perish from want of subsistence because it would violate natural law and thus violate God's law.

Samuel Fleischacker argues that the natural law tradition never had anything to do with distributive justice.[58] In a long footnote, Fleischacker takes the historian Lynn Lees to task for claiming that English Poor Laws guaranteed the poor with a right to maintenance and thus created "social citizenship."[59] He states that one of the reasons that he believes Lees got it wrong:

> [E]ven if people under the poor law did see the relief granted them as a legal right, that does not tell us whether they believed that justice requires nations to set up systems of poor relief. It is crucial to distinguish between legal and moral rights. That something is recognized, as a legal right does not yet mean it is recognized as required by justice.[60]

As with Plato and Aristotle, Fleischacker is partially correct since Locke never uses the term "distributive justice" nor can one find it used in the natural law tradition. What Fleischacker fails to appreciate is that while those receiving the aid may not have believed that justice demanded it, Locke certainly did. As the textual evidence in the previous paragraph makes clear, he believed that natural law demanded relief for the poor. Surely, one can safely say that for Locke, aid for the poor had to be part of the law because it was a *moral duty* prescribed by God. As a result, it is not too far of a stretch to say that the moral duty gave way to a moral right, which in turn was codified into law. It is also safe to say that Locke would think that justice demands some type of public aid, which is a redistribution of resources because it involves collecting taxes from the wealthy and middle class to pay for poor relief.

CONCLUSION

Secondary literature focusing on Locke's Report is mostly limited to historians, who view Locke's policy proposals as being either progressive or in line with England's Elizabethan Poor Laws.[61] A. L. Beier is an exception because he thinks that even when one puts Locke's proposals in the proper historical context, they were harsh. This is especially true of his proposals for vagabonds.[62]

Political theorists including MacPherson, Dunn, Ashcraft, and James Tully mention the Report but do not provide any detailed analysis of it. Tully says that while Locke's ideas may be "severe and disruptive" that one must assess it relative to the seventeenth-century workhouse system.[63] This view is representative of most theorists' commentaries about Locke's treatment of poverty. As I discussed earlier, MacPherson and Dunn, for different reasons, attribute its harshness to Locke's Calvinistism and conservative attitude toward the poor. Ashcraft disagrees with them noting that the sharp criticism of Locke's Report is misplaced since it was used to defend the rights of the poor to relief during the eighteenth century.[64] Thomas Horne shares the latter view, pointing out that in spite of the Report's harsh measures, subsistence and education are provided for poor children as well as other measures to help the poor.[65]

While Locke's views may have been used to defend poor relief, one is still struck by his invective language toward the poor and his failure to consider major crop failures, economic downturns resulting in unemployment, and other contingencies that have nothing to do with their characters. Surely some individuals were lazy and lacked motivation to work, but to a large degree Locke was incorrect about the causes of poverty because he failed to consider structural or for that matter, any other possible cause. English society was undergoing a major transformation. High unemployment and growing numbers of poor were constant problems.[66] In addition, the decade in which Locke wrote this proposal was a time of intense economic depression. From 1690 to 1699, six out of ten harvests fell short of producing adequate amounts. Economic depression was a problem during the entire decade and the harvests of 1697 and 1699 were so bad that prices for wheat rose more than 50 percent. It was not just agriculture that was depressed but also manufacturing and trade. In fact, one historian, A. L. Beier says that it was the worse decade economically in more than 125 years.[67]

Rapid changes in the demographic depletion of villages, urban migration, price inflation, and the impoverishment of small towns led to enormous increases in the number of orphans, widows, sick, aged, and those with disabilities.[68] Traditionally, people received assistance from their families and neighbors with some help from local churches. Aid and welfare for the help-less, sick, and indigent changed dramatically during this time. As familial and small-town relationships broke down because of mass urban migration, those who needed help could no longer count on traditional resources. Urban poverty in an industrial center such as Manchester, for example, was wide-spread and it was no longer economically feasible for private individuals and churches to provide assistance to all those who needed help. Because of the increased demand and other changes in society, public bodies began to take charge of administering services to the needy.

In addition to unemployment and food scarcity, other unpredictable events such as the loss of a spouse, a natural disaster, or illness caused people to lose their financial means, making them unable to maintain their place, let alone flourish, in society. Locke does not address any of these possibilities. Nor does he acknowledge the terrible economic conditions in England that had begun in 1690. This is most surprising since the harvest of 1693, which was one of the worst in Locke's lifetime, happened only four years before he wrote the proposal for relief of the poor.

Locke's plan for more government control and increased bureaucratic ad-ministration of poor relief is a significant feature of the Report. It is surpris-ing since one associates Locke with championing the idea of limited govern-ment. His call for more government intervention and centralization illustrates his struggle to adjust to the changing face of poverty in England and the com-peting demands between his religious beliefs and his characterization of the poor. He thinks that local people know best how to judge who should receive relief and how to provide it. Yet, at the same time, the poor are multiplying, poor taxes are increasing, and the problem threatens to spin out of control. Moreover, while the poor guardians are elected officials, one should remem-ber that the poor could not participate in elections and the poor guardians have considerable discretionary, and one could even say arbitrary power. In his *Second Treatise of Government*, Locke argues passionately and convinc-ingly that arbitrary and discretionary government power is dangerous and leads to not only a loss of freedom but also injustice. It is clear in the Report, however, that he does not fear those abuses because he has confidence that once parishes are grouped properly and poor corporations formed in the cities, the poor guardians will act in unison to enforce the Poor Laws. Cen-tralized administration was necessary because Locke believed that the *correct* policies could curb the problem of poverty.

Locke's policies are based on his conviction that society would always be sufficiently productive so that the poor would never lack employment or sub-sistence as long as they were willing to work. His Calvinist values shape his views about the depravity of human beings and their propensity toward laziness and lack of virtue. Above all, Locke wants society to hold individuals personally responsible for their poverty. Thus, he believes that if the causes of poverty are properly understood, then the solutions should be evident to government officials.

At the beginning of this chapter, I posed two questions about Locke's treatment of poverty. First, does he believe that one can be just without providing for the poor? Second, what connection, if any, does he think justice has with providing public aid for the poor? It is clear that Locke thinks that government has a moral obligation, which translates into a legal obligation to provide aid to the poor. This requires redistribution because taxes are collected from citizens and redistributed to provide for the poor. This relates to that fundamental tension in liberal theory that I mentioned earlier. Mass poverty challenges the basic principles of a free market society especially since Locke is a Christian, who believes in natural law and God. While collecting poor taxes interferes with citizens' property, there is a fundamental commitment to promote self-preservation for all members of a liberal society. It also shows that no matter how strongly he suspected that most poor people did not really want to work and how committed he was to private property rights, his commitment to natural law and God's commandments were stronger. He had to answer the call for what justice demanded. Thus, Locke's theory of justice is complicated because not only does one see tensions between providing for the poor and liberal theory, but also for Locke, there is a tension between his belief in God's commandments and what one ought to do for the poor.

Locke's beliefs about the causes of poverty and their solutions received closer examination in the years following his death. While Adam Smith agrees with Locke that the productivity of a market society is a safeguard against absolute poverty, he rejects Locke's characterizations of the poor. Smith acknowledges the growth in the number of poor in Great Britain despite the nation's increased wealth. Unlike Locke, both he and Jean Jacques Rousseau recognize some of the contingencies that contribute to poverty, and thus, they present a more balanced approach to understanding poverty. Rousseau and Smith dramatically change the tone of the argument about the causes of poverty.

NOTES

1. Erwin R. Goodenough, "The Ethical Teaching of Jesus," *The Jewish Quarterly Review*, New Ser., Vol. 57, The Seventy-Fifth Anniversary Volume of the Jewish Quarterly Review. (1967), 265.

2. Luke 6:20.

3. Matthew 19:24.

4. Cicero, "The Republic," in *Readings in Classical Political Thought*, ed. Peter J. Steinberger (Indianapolis: Hackett Publishing Co., Inc., 2000), 455.

5. Ibid., 455.

6. Joseph Schumpeter, *History of Economic Analysis* (New York, 1954) 270–75.

7. Elizabeth Melling, ed. *Kentish Sources IV: The Poor* (Maidstone, England: Kent County Council, 1964) xiii–xiv, hereafter *Kentish Sources*.

8. John Locke, 1697. Reprinted as "An Essay on the Poor Law," in *Locke: Political Essays*, ed. Mark Goldie, 2nd ed. (Cambridge, 1999), 182–98. All notes in this chapter refer to this reprint and hereafter referred to as Report.

9. Melling, *Kentish Sources*, 55–58.

10. Gertrude Himmelfarb, *The Idea of Poverty: England in the Early Industrial Age* (New York: Alfred A. Knopf, 1984) 26.

11. Richard Ashcraft, "Liberalism and the Problem of Poverty," *Critical Review* vol. 6, no. 4 (1992): 493–516. Ashcraft says, "not only have the dimensions of the problem of poverty increased with the growth of democratic capitalist society, but also, viewed from an historical perspective, it is the problem of poverty that exposes the fundamental tensions at the heart of liberal political theory." Ashcraft (493).

12. John Locke, *Two Treatises of Government*, ed. Peter Laslett, 3rd ed. (Cambridge, 1999), 17. All references to the *First* and *Second Treatises* are from this edition and cited hereafter as *First Treatise* or *Second Treatise* with the appropriate section number.

13. *Two Treatises*, 31. Laslett says that Locke was much more involved than his earlier biographers had thought; Richard Ashcraft, "Liberalism and the Problem of Poverty," provides further evidence that Locke was indeed involved in several of the plots and thus if not committing treason, certainly came awful close to it.

14. *Two Treatises*, 37.

15. Report, 183–84.

16. John Locke, *An Essay Concerning Human Understanding*, ed. Peter Nidditch (Oxford, 1975), II.xxi.47: 263. All references to this work are from this edition and hereafter cited as *Essay* with the book, chapter, paragraph, and page number indicated.

17. *Essay*, II.xxi.47:263.

18. Ibid., I.xxi.55: 269.

19. Ibid., II.xxi.45: 261–62.

20. Ibid., II.xxi.41: 258–59. See also, J. B. Schneewind, "Locke's Moral Philosophy," in *The Cambridge Companion to Locke*, ed. Vere Chappell (Cambridge, 1994), 204.

21. What Locke describes here is similar to what Edward Banfield calls "present-orientedness." In short, he says that people who live in poverty are unable to plan for the future, to sacrifice immediate gratification in favor of long-term ones or to have the discipline to save and get ahead. Tocqueville makes this same observation as will be discussed later in this chapter. Edward Banfield, *The Unheavenly City* (Boston, 1968).

22. *Essay*, II.xxi.34: 253.

23. Ibid., II.xxi.58: 272.

24. C. B. MacPherson, *The Political Theory of Possessive Individualism* (Oxford, 1962), 227. MacPherson's footnote after this quotation refers readers to Christopher Hill, *Puritanism and Revolution* (1958), 228–29 for this view of English Calvinism.

25. John Dunn, *The Political Thought of John Locke* (Cambridge, 1969), 259.

26. Ibid., 259.

27. Ibid., 222–23.

28. Ibid., 227

29. John Locke, *Political Essays*, ed. Mark Goldie (Cambridge, 1999), 182.

30. Locke is referring to the war against France from 1689 to 1697.

31. Report, 184.

32. Ibid., 184.

33. The churchwardens increasingly relied upon an annual poor rate tax. England was the only country in Europe with a system of public aid for the poor financed through taxation. For more on this see M. J. Daunton, *Progress and Poverty* (Oxford: 1995), 447.

34. Report, 184. As I will discuss in the next chapter, Adam Smith disagrees with Locke about limiting the number of alehouses. "It is not the multitude of alehouses, to give the most suspicious example, that occasions a general disposition to drunkenness among the common people; but that disposition arising from other causes necessarily gives employment to a multitude of alehouses." In a later chapter, Smith denies that drunkenness is a problem among most workers. Adam Smith, *An Inquiry into the Nature and Causes of The Wealth of Nations (WN)*, ed. Edwin Cannan (Chicago, 1976), I.ii.5: 383; I: iv: 3: 517. All references to *Wealth of Nations* are from this edition and hereafter cited as *WN* with the volume, book, chapter, and page number indicated.

35. One historian reminds readers that Locke was not the first to advance the idea of requiring those who received poor relief to wear badges. A. L. Beier, "Utter Strangers to Industry, Morality and Religion: John Locke on the Poor," in *Eighteenth Century Life* 12, no. 3 (November 1988): 28–41, 37.

36. These working schools were primarily wool-spinning factories. Fifteen cities by Act of Parliament did establish corporations of the poor between 1696 and 1715. See Daunton, *Progress and Poverty*, 453.

37. Report, 197–98.

38. Classical Liberalism has been defined different ways but most scholars would agree that it is associated with the ideas of 1) limited government; 2) the rule of law; 3) avoidance of discretionary or arbitrary power; 4) the sanctity of private property; 5) the ability to make contracts; and 6) the idea that each individual is responsible for her own fate in society. For a more detailed discussion, see Alan Ryan, "Liberalism," in *A Companion to Contemporary Political Philosophy*, eds. Robert E. Goodin and Philip Petit, 2nd ed. (New York, 1995), 293.

39. Hard labor means "lump breaking," the breaking of stones for road building (Locke, Report, 185, n. 3).

40. Ibid., 186.

41. Ibid., 186.

42. Ibid., 188.

43. Ibid., 188.

44. In Locke's time one pound was equal to twenty shillings and a shilling was equal to twelve pence. Report, 183.

45. Ibid., 189.

46. Ibid., 190.

47. Ibid., 192.

48. Ibid., 192.

49. Ibid., 197.

50. Ibid., 198.

51. John Locke, Nine essays in Latin reprinted as *Essays on the Laws of Nature*, in *Locke: Political Essays*, ed. Mark Goldie, 2nd ed. (Cambridge, 1999), 79–133. All references in this chapter to this work are from this reprint and hereafter cited as *ELN*.

52. Ibid., 123.

53. Ibid., 123.

54. *Second Treatise*, sec. 135. See also sections 6, 159, 171, and 183.

55. *First Treatise*, 42.

56. Thomas, Horne, *Property Rights and Poverty: Political Arguments in Britain, 1605–1834* (Chapell Hill: University of North Carolina Press, 1990), 55; and *Second Treatise*, 26.

57. John Locke, "Venditio," reprinted in *Locke: Political Essays*, ed. Mark Goldie (Cambridge, 1997) 339–43 and 342.

58. Fleischacker, *Short History*, 18.

59. Ibid., 152n.88.

60. Ibid., 153n.88.

61. Four works devoted exclusively to Locke's Report include: M. G. Mason, "John Locke's Proposals for Work-House Schools," *Durham Research Review*, 4 (1962):8–16; E. J. Hundert, "The Making of Homo Faber: John Locke between Ideology and History," *Journal of the History of Ideas* 33 (1972):3–22; W. J. Sheasgreen, "John Locke and the Charity School Movement," *History of Education* 15 (1986): 63–79; and A. L. Beier, "Utter Strangers to Industry, Morality and Religion: John Locke on the Poor," *Eighteenth-Century Life* 12 (1988):28–41.

62. Beier, "Utter Strangers," 34.

63. James Tully, *An Approach to Political Philosophy Locke in Context* (Cambridge, 1993), 66.

64. Ashcraft, "Liberalism and the Problem of Poverty," 507.

65. Horne, *Property Rights and Poverty*, 64–65.

66. Michael Walzer, *The Revolution of the Saints* (Cambridge, 1965), 199–202.

67. Beier, "Utter Strangers to Industry," 32. England was able to avoid widespread famine because poor people ate barley, oats, and sometimes rye and horse corn. The prices of these grains did fluctuate during the decade of the 1690s. For example, the price of oats increased as much as 36 percent and the cost of barley increased by 50 percent. See Andrew Appleby's "Grain Prices and Subsistence Crises in England and France, 1590–1740," *Journal of Economic History* 39, no.12 (1979):877–79.

68. Lawrence Stone, *The Family, Sex and Marriage In England 1500–1800* (New York, 1979), 106–7.

Chapter Four

The Noble Poor: Jean-Jacques Rousseau and Adam Smith

Jean-Jacques Rousseau and Adam Smith lived and wrote during the age of Enlightenment, political revolution, and the beginning of the Industrial Revolution. Although the enlarged edition of Bernard Mandeville's *The Fable of the Bees: Or Private Vices, Publick Benefits* was first published in 1723, this work influenced the discourse on poverty throughout the much of the eighteenth century.[1] In brief, Mandeville argues that immoral or evil behavior benefits the economy. For example, vanity drives individuals to purchase unnecessary goods and bad behavior, such as getting drunk on alcohol supports the liquor industry. He says that avarice, gluttony, competition, waste, and conspicuous consumption form the moral foundations for a healthy economy. Not only are these "vices" beneficial but also what one generally thinks to be a virtue is really a pretence for vice. He believes that religious devotion, for example, is often used to impress others and thus the most religious are often nothing but hypocrites. If there were a society of true Christians, according to Mandeville, it would be a poor society and one that could hardly defend itself. He never intended his work to be a criticism of commercial society, because Mandeville admired it.

Smith confronts Mandeville's argument because his aim is to show that while human beings may be vain and self-interested, there is a difference between immoral and moral behavior. Human beings know this difference because of their capacity for sympathy, which allows them to identify with others' well-being. The upshot of this is that Smith believes one can be moral and thus, virtuous in modern commercial society. Moreover, self-interest compels individuals toward productivity, which in turn benefits all society.

While Smith rejects Mandeville's claims, one might suspect that Rousseau would be more sympathetic to his arguments since on more than one occasion, he blames civil society for eroding the natural goodness of humankind. Like

Mandeville, he believes that with the onset of private property and commercial society, most human beings live under the tyranny of opinion, caring more about what others think of their appearances and possessions than about their humanity. Therefore, like Mandeville, Rousseau thinks that appearances are often deceiving since appearing virtuous is more important than actually being virtuous. The compassion or sympathy that Smith relies upon had declined significantly since the onset of civilization because of corruption. While Rousseau may agree with Mandeville about the state of affairs, he certainly does not approve or admire it. He rejects both Mandeville and Smith's conclusions because he longs for a simpler life, where individuals could be genuinely virtuous, self-sufficient, and above all, free. Rousseau knew there was no turning back. As a result, he searches for a way that human beings can live together without all the trappings of materialism, greed, selfishness, and poverty.

With this background, it may seem curious, or even odd that Rousseau, known for his provocative *Discourses*, which indicted the rich and elevated the poor, shared similar views about the poor and the problem of poverty with Smith, who is most often associated with conservative liberalism and *laissez-faire* policies. In this chapter, I explore their treatments of poverty and show that Rousseau and Smith do indeed share similar beliefs about the poor as well as how society treats them. Both men have positive views about human nature and this applies no less to the poor. In fact, one could argue that Rousseau as well as Smith admire the noble character of those who live in poverty. They agree that with the advent of private property came inequality, yet they also think that owning private property is one of the most fundamental of all individual rights. Both theorists advocate progressive taxation and sumptuary taxes.[2] They share the belief that poverty is a relative concept, and that the poor living in industrial societies are rather well off when compared to those living in pre-industrial ones. Indeed, this is the moral justification that Smith uses to reconcile the inevitable inequalities that arise in societies based on market economies. For Rousseau, it points to yet another reason why money and luxuries are so damaging to human beings and civil society. Finally, they write about poverty and its effects on individuals with great sensitivity and understanding.

I show that despite all these agreements, Rousseau and Smith had different ideas about the effects of poverty both on the individual and on society. Most critical to their treatment of poverty is that they have different conceptions of justice. Because of this they make dissimilar judgments about how a just society ought to treat the poor and what steps, if any, government should take to solve the problem of poverty. I begin with Rousseau's treatment of poverty and then turn to Smith's works to investigate the details and nuances of each theorist's treatment of poverty all the while keeping in mind the principal question of this study: what are Rousseau and Smith's judgments about the relationship between poverty and justice in the state?

ROUSSEAU

On December 20, 1776, a premature obituary for Rousseau appeared in the Paris newspaper, *Courrier d'Avignon*. In eulogizing him, the second line notes that, "He lived in poverty; he died in misery; and the strangeness of his fate accompanied him all the way to the tomb."[3] While he had not died, it is telling that in his own day the philosopher, who spent his life writing about equality, was remembered for his poverty. Rousseau writes about poverty with a sensitivity and understanding that surpasses most other political theorists. He identifies the contingent factors that contribute to poverty as well as the injustices that the poor must endure. He says that it is his imagination that allows him to identify with the poor and feel their anguish.[4] Perhaps his imagination was part of the explanation, but he also had profound insights about poverty because he knew what it felt like to be dependent on others.[5] He had firsthand experience feeling powerless and enduring injustices because of poverty. Indeed, throughout his *Confessions*, Rousseau tells his readers about the humiliation he felt because he was without resources and forced to rely on others for charity.[6]

Not only was he sympathetic toward those who were destitute, but he was also painfully aware that because of the accident of birth and other contingent factors, like the loss of a parent or a job, individuals could be born into poverty or become impoverished because of circumstances beyond their control. After all, Rousseau's mother died nine days after giving birth to him. His father, who had not inherited enough money or land to sustain his family, depended on his trade as a watchmaker to support his children.[7] Rousseau refers to the "accident whose consequences have affected my life ever since," when he writes about his father being exiled from Geneva.[8] Because of his father's departure, Rousseau's life changed dramatically when he was left with his uncle and later apprenticed to a disagreeable man with violent tendencies.[9] At sixteen, he was on his own without any means to support himself.[10] As an incredibly gifted young man, he realized at an early age that intelligence or merit would not always be enough to change one's unfortunate situation. During his years in Paris, he was surrounded by individuals, such as Voltaire, who were wealthy and while Rousseau achieved notoriety during his life, he never had financial security. His last work before his death shows that he never forgot the humiliation or the unfairness that often accompanies poverty.[11]

Rousseau never desired great wealth because he thought it unhealthy and most of all, unnecessary for one to be happy. In the *Reveries*, he devotes the

"Eighth Walk" to a discussion about why he prefers poverty to prosperity.[12] He had no pleasant memories about the times when he was prosperous. Wealth cannot make one happy. His statement that, "joy is more a friend of pennies than of large gold coins" typifies his attitude toward wealth because he thought that it was nature and the simple pleasures in life that brought happiness.[13] Money is a means to an end and surely not an end in itself. The end in itself was freedom. Wealth is important insofar as it allows individuals to have more control of their destiny thus giving them more freedom to do what they desire. Indeed, Rousseau's political theory reflects his preoccupation with freedom as well as equality.

There is another aspect to Rousseau's life that allowed him to view society differently from his contemporaries. As Patrick Coleman has observed, Rousseau was always an outsider. He never had any formal education and whether it was his religion, his political beliefs, or his social status, he was always different from those around him.[14]

This "outsider" status provided Rousseau, to some degree, the independence he so deeply wanted. Just as important for his political theory, however, it gave him the ability to observe and challenge conventional beliefs. Often, it takes an outsider to penetrate the received opinions and practices of the day. Moreover, Rousseau was able to do just that in his political and economic writings.

One would be remiss not to mention that in spite of his sensitivity and compassion for the poor, Rousseau sent each of his five infant children to a foundling home in Paris. He never clearly states why he did this; however, he justifies his actions several different ways, none of which seem authentic. On one occasion, he rationalizes that the children would be better cared for given his poverty and inability to provide for them. Another time, he appeals to Plato's ideas about the rearing of children in the *Republic*.[15] When remembering the birth of his third child in *Confessions*, he says that it was a common practice in Paris to place children in foundling homes. Moreover, he says that it was a sensible solution, which was best for his children.[16] In his biography of Rousseau, Leo Damrosch points out that during this time it was indeed a common practice for illegitimate babies to be taken to foundling homes and thousands of babies were abandoned every year in Paris.[17] The odds were extremely high that these children would never reach maturity, however, since Cranston says that the mortality rate at the Paris foundling home was as high as 68 percent in 1741.[18] Likewise, Damrosch says that the great majority of these passages begin with Rousseau's regrets and admissions that he neglected his duties as a father and then end with anger because perhaps, an acquaintance wanted to discuss it with him.[19] He abruptly concludes one discussion by saying, "I promised a confession, not a justification;

and so I will say no more on this point."[20] It is not, however, his last word on the subject because later in Book IX of *Confessions* and in *Reveries* he returns to the subject. In both of these instances, he says that he did not want Thérèse Le Vasseur's family to rear his children.[21] Without a doubt, this aspect of Rousseau's personal life is almost incomprehensible given that he wrote about humanity with great compassion coupled with the fact that his own father abandoned him at a young age. Rousseau himself acknowledges a disconnect between his benevolence and compassion toward his fellow human beings and the complete abandonment of his own children.[22] Clearly, he felt guilt and shame about it since he tries to explain his decisions on several occasions and he wants to keep it a secret.[23]

In spite of his personal failures, Rousseau stands next to Plato as a brilliant political philosopher. His political theory provides insights about poverty and reveals that it plays an important role in his philosophical works. Rousseau knew that material equality was impossible; however, he believed that it was incumbent on government to level the playing field to some degree through policies such as progressive and sumptuary taxes. Justice demands equal treatment under the law for the impoverished as well as for the wealthy and this was surely one of his goals in *On the Social Contract*.

Samuel Fleischacker would certainly agree with the last statement, however, that is where agreement about Rousseau's treatment of poverty ends. Fleischacker argues that Rousseau was not concerned with the plight of poor people per se. His concern for the poor extended only insofar as it related to corruption in the state, which in turn had a debilitating effect on civic virtue.[24] That is to say, that poverty troubles Rousseau only insofar as it affects citizenship or politics.[25] Moreover, Fleischacker says that one who believes otherwise has been seduced by Rousseau's exemplary rhetoric.[26] Citing one passage from the *Discourse on Political Economy*, he says that it is the only extended place where Rousseau dwells on the suffering of the poor.[27] Finally, he argues that concerning property rights, Rousseau is more of a libertarian than Smith.[28] Is Fleischacker correct? Is Rousseau's treatment of poverty solely concerned with the role equality plays in politics? Are his insights about what it is like to be poor just imaginative rhetoric? The answer is no on all accounts. Fleischacker exaggerates when he says that Rousseau's work is exclusively concerned with poverty only as it relates to politics, and that his rhetoric about the poor is just that, mere rhetoric. These claims seem to require an interpretation that rejects Rousseau's own words.[29] One should be cautious when discounting Rousseau's own words on the subject in favor of an interpretation that lacks sufficient textual support. In addition, Fleischacker is setting up a false dichotomy because Rousseau's concerns about political equality are tied to his concerns for the poor and thus, the two are not mutually exclusive. That is to say that clearly Rousseau was concerned about the negative effects that poverty would have on instilling civic virtues in citizens, however, he was also painfully aware of what effects poverty had on an individual's life. He understood and wrote about the loss of freedom and the sadness associated with the life of the poor individual. One could argue that his sensitivity to the poor's loss of autonomy and freedom informed his attention to equality and political rights for them. As I shall show, there is strong evidence in Rousseau's treatment of poverty that supports the claim that he had a profound understanding of the plight of the poor and as a result, great empathy for their predicaments. It is also doubtful that Rousseau was more libertarian about property rights than Smith since the latter never would have endorsed Rousseau's plan for completely eliminating taxes for the poor, using taxes to provide aid to the poor, or having government-funded scholarships for the least advantaged. I cannot pretend to offer a psychological account about Rousseau's intentions or motives in his treatment of poverty. It will be instructive, however, to turn to Rousseau's own words, which provide evidence contrary to Fleischacker's claims.

Before moving on to consider Rousseau's treatment of poverty, it is necessary to discuss his ideas about justice. The difficulty here is that Rousseau never really defines justice. Scholars such as Robert Wokler, George Kateb, and John Rawls equate his notion of justice to his idea of the general will.[30] For example, Kateb says, "The essential fact is that the aim of the general will is justice."[31] David Wooten suggests that one might think of the general will as being similar to John Rawls' "veil of ignorance."[32] Rawls asks what sort of society one would want to establish if an individual did not know what his or her position would be in that society. This lack of information includes knowledge about one's race, gender, physical disabilities, or intellectual capacities. In this situation, intuitively most of us would choose a society that would benefit virtually all members since it would be in our best interest to do so. In the same way, Wooten says, Rousseau is trying to get citizens to think about creating a community where the common good is considered the aggregate will of all. Thus, the government would pursue programs and policies that would benefit the common good.[33]

Equality is a necessary condition for the general will to work. By equality, Rousseau does not mean to say that everyone should have exactly equal amounts of material wealth or power. He explains,

> Regarding equality, we need not mean by this word that degrees of power and wealth are to be absolutely the same, but rather that, with regard to power, it should transcend all violence and never be exercised by virtue of rank and laws; and, with regard to wealth, no citizen should be so rich as to be capable of buy-

ing another citizen, and none so poor that he is forced to sell himself. This presupposes moderation in goods and credit on the part of the great, and moderation in avarice and covetousness on the part of the lowly.[34]

He elaborates further in a footnote to the above quotation by saying, "Bring the extremes as close together as possible. Tolerate neither rich men nor beggars. These two estates, which are naturally inseparable, are equally fatal to the common good."[35] Moreover, he claims that one cannot have liberty without equality. "If one inquires into precisely wherein the greatest good of all exists, which should be the purpose of every system of legislation, one will find that it boils down to two principal objects, *liberty* and *equality*."[36] Rousseau's aim is to unite citizens because of their common interests so that they may enjoy the same rights. He says it is "an admirable accord between interest and justice" because it is equitable to all.[37] When listing the qualities that this type of government presupposes, he says, "Next, a high degree of equality in ranks and fortunes, without which equality in rights and authority cannot exist for long."[38] From this discussion, one can reasonably associate Rousseau's notion of justice with the general will, which aims to secure freedom and equality for all citizens.[39] Finally, David Williams argues that like Plato, Rousseau does not have a determinate definition for justice.[40] Rather he has an indeterminate one, which means that it is abstract and thus laws are enacted to give it substance. Williams makes a convincing argument and this helps to explain some of the difficulty defining Rousseau's notion of justice as opposed to Smith's, which as we shall see is determinate.[41]

The First *Discourse*

With the publications of Rousseau's *Discourse on Inequality* and *Discourse on Political Economy*, there can be little doubt that 1755 was a momentous year for political philosophy. Some scholars view the latter work as a partial answer to one of the main questions posed by the former one.[42] That question is; how might one establish a legitimate government in a world full of corruption? To understand the development of Rousseau's political thought and his views about poverty, one must return to his sharp critique of society in 1750 when he won the prize at the Academy of Dijon. That year the question—"has the establishment of the sciences and the arts served to purify or to corrupt manners and morals?"—received an emphatic reply from Rousseau.[43] Commonly referred to as the First *Discourse*, his answer provides a damning critique of the luxuries and conspicuous consumption that abounds in modern society. Moreover, he links these vices to corruption. He concludes that the advancement of the arts and science has always contributed to the corruption of morals and manners.[44] Although he mentions inequality only once, he places the blame for its beginnings on "the distinction of talents and the degradation of virtues."[45] As a result of these superficial distinctions, Rousseau says that men are no longer valued for their moral integrity but merely for their talents.[46] Individuals constantly have greater needs and increased desires for more and more luxuries. This is an indication of how morally degraded people have become since most of these so-called needs and desires are for the sake of appearances. He uses the example of wealthy men, who wear fine clothes for appearances all the while concealing their lack of physical fitness. This is telling since it is the common man, the field-worker, who is healthy and fit underneath his plain clothes. Not only are appearances deceiving, but they also lead individuals to value the wrong things, such as fine clothes, while ignoring their natural selves and the values that matter.[47] At one point, Rousseau praises King Cyrus, who was poor and humble but rose to greatness.[48] Therefore, in the First *Discourse*, one already sees that Rousseau regards the poor as more virtuous than the rich. It is the affluent who waste their time pursuing worthless projects in the arts and sciences while abandoning practical endeavors that could benefit society.

The Second *Discourse*

Given Rousseau's critique in the *First Discourse*, it is not at all surprising that he felt compelled in 1755 to answer another question posed by the Academy in Dijon. He thought that the question "what is the origin of inequality among men, and is it authorized by the natural law" was too interesting and useful for him not to answer it.[49] At the same time, Rousseau says that it is one of the most difficult questions in political theory.[50] Political theory owes a great debt of gratitude to the Academy for posing this question because Rousseau's answer provides one of the most thought-provoking works in political philosophy. Formally called the *Discourse on the Origin and Foundations of Inequality Among Men*, it is more commonly referred to as the Second *Discourse*.

This work is remarkable for several reasons, but not least among them is how Rousseau provides formidable challenges to both Hobbes and Locke. Both appealed to the idea of a "state of nature" as a pre-political state, that is, a state without government or rule of law. According to Hobbes, the state of nature was "the war of all against all."[51] Thus, he believed since there were no laws, each person would be entitled to do whatever he, or she desired. This includes taking someone's life. In fact, preemptive strikes on others are not only permitted, but they are smart because one can never be sure who is going to try to take his property, or even worse, his life. There is no such thing as right, wrong, justice, or injustice in the state of nature.[52] Hobbes tells us that life in this pre-political state would be "solitary, poor, nasty, brutish, and short."[53] Since human beings fear death and would like to lead a more comfortable life, they enter into a social compact to get them out of it.[54] While Locke paints a somewhat rosier picture of the state of nature at the beginning of his *Second Treatise of Government*, the conditions deteriorate as he gets closer to offering his version of the social contract as the way out of it.[55] Locke believes that individuals will want to protect their life, liberty, and estate. Thus, he wants to put a fence around certain inalienable rights so individuals will consent to a social contract to leave this pre-political state to secure these rights.[56]

Rousseau believes that both Hobbes and Locke are wrong about their views of human nature. Instead of describing the first human being, which he calls savage man or natural man, he says, they are in fact describing civil man.[57] At the heart of their mistakes, according to him, is their ignorance about human nature.[58] Rousseau says that all of the philosophers speaking, "continually of need, avarice, oppression, desires, and pride, have transferred to the state of nature the ideas they [that is, human beings] acquired in society."[59] This claim is critical since he asserts that all of these negative qualities, such as jealousy and greed, come from the corruptive forces of civil society. Certainly, they are not natural to human beings.[60] Rather, man is naturally good and thus all the evil qualities that have been ascribed to natural man are false.[61] This critique applies to Mandeville's claims as well as those of Hobbes and Locke. As I shall show in chapter 6, this idea about the effects of society and culture will become central to Karl Marx's political theory.

Putting aside science books, he observes that all human beings share two qualities, which are distinct from wisdom or reason. First, individuals are passionately interested about their well-being and self-preservation. Second, all human beings have a "natural repugnance" to seeing any sentient being perish or suffer.[62] In the case of the latter, reason or wisdom plays no role since human beings naturally feel compassion toward other sentient beings. This "inner impulse" as Rousseau calls it, prevents humankind from doing harm to other human and non-human animals. Of course, if one legitimately felt that his or her own preservation was at risk, he or she would do whatever was necessary to survive.[63] While the bad habits and education fostered by civil society have debased this sentiment, Rousseau believes that human beings still have the capacity to feel some pity since the natural impulse has not been totally destroyed.[64]

Just as there are two natural sentiments, there are also two types of inequality. First, there is natural inequality, which comes from differences in intelligence, strength, health, and other physical attributes. Second, there is artificial inequality, which may also be called moral or political inequality.[65] The latter comes from convention and culture in societies. There is nothing that can be done about the first type of inequalities, however, the second type, that is, the artificial inequalities, are not determined by nature and they affect human beings because they cause some to become wealthier and more honored in society. Most importantly, these artificial inequalities result in some men oppressing others. Rousseau's aim in the Second *Discourse* is to explain the origins of these artificial inequalities, but in order to do that one must first discern what is originally natural to man from what man has created for him. As a result, one must go back in time before civilization to learn about or rediscover natural or savage man.[66] Preceding the work of Charles Darwin's *The Origin of Species* by nearly a century, Rousseau takes his readers on a remarkable anthropological and philosophical journey to discover original man.

He suggests that human beings developed from primitive bipeds into the highly developed individuals of modernity. Since natural man was simple and focused on satisfying immediate needs such as hunger or thirst, he lacked curiosity and foresight. All his needs were satisfied.[67] He was healthy and robust unlike men in modern society where the wealthy are overfed with rich, unhealthy foods, and the poor are underfed. In addition, some individuals are idle while others are overworked. No diseases, anxieties, excesses, and sadness that one sees in the modern world were present in the state of nature, he says, because civilization generates these afflictions.[68] Rousseau compares modern man to domesticated animals since both are subservient and have lost their abilities to survive in their natural habitats. While modern man affords himself more luxuries than domesticated animals, those comforts only serve to further his deterioration.[69] According to Rousseau, however, one thing that non-human animals do share with human beings is that both are naturally lazy.[70]

There are several important traits that separate human beings from non-human animals.[71] Human beings are not driven by instinct in the same way that animals are but instead have free will.[72] Further, human beings have the "faculty of self-perfection," which, according to Rousseau, is the source of all men's subsequent misfortunes.[73] This latter quality forces men to abandon their simple, natural life. As human beings evolved through the centuries, their lives became more complicated and their needs more numerous. Natural man was free and innocent whereas modern man is dependent and corrupt.[74] Indeed, Rousseau says that the state of nature was a place of peace and individuals were self-sufficient.[75] This self-sufficiency meant that savage man was free "from the chains of dependence," which stands in stark contrast to modern man, who is held down by the "bonds of servitude."[76] Men were not evil nor were they constantly in fear of death. Just as important to Rousseau's argument is the fact that neither Hobbes, Locke, nor Mandeville considered the one natural asset common to all human beings, that is, pity.[77] Moreover, it is reason and not inherent evil that alienates individuals from that natural feeling because it causes egocentrism and further reflection only serves to reinforce it.[78]

Rousseau makes a provocative assertion when he says that the poor, more so than others in modern society, have retained their natural sense of compassion. In the Second *Discourse*, Rousseau uses the example of the poor women separating the fighting men so no one will get hurt.[79] Cranston states that in the unfinished manuscript *Discours sure les richesses*, Rousseau says, "The poor man is sensitive to the evils of poverty precisely because he is poor himself; but once he is rich, why should he continue to have the same feelings?"[80] Surely, Rousseau was speaking from his own experiences, which is why he understood and cared about the poor's plight. Contrary to Fleischacker's claim that his concern is solely about civic virtue, Rousseau's sensitivity toward the poor points to his recognition of the difficulties they face as well as concern for equality.

Rousseau says that the advent of private property brought with it the beginning of civil society.[81] This followed years of enlightenment during which time man's vanity and egocentrism increased. As he established his superiority over non-human animals, man became concerned with his individuality.[82] The first "revolution" that led to inequality happened when families started to build huts, which introduced private property and conflict soon followed. Through the years, he thinks that human beings' needs became greater because they wanted more conveniences, and with these conveniences came more dependence along with less freedom. Rousseau provides some provocative insights about the human condition during his discussion of modern conveniences. He says that depriving one of all the modern conveniences creates greater unhappiness than the happiness that one derives from possessing them.[83] It is far more than dependence, however, that Rousseau is discussing here. He is also pointing out that the more possessions one acquires the more one becomes burdened by them. At the same time, one's true needs become entangled with one's desires until the two are indistinguishable.

The ideas of merit and beauty accompany these new needs. Affection and passion develop between the sexes and with them comes jealousy. As more and more people live closer together and have occasion to socialize, competition grows among individuals and families. Individuals make judgments about who is the prettiest, the strongest, the smartest, etc. Rousseau says that this is the first step toward inequality.[84] However, it was the creation of metallurgy and agriculture that produces the greatest revolution. Paid labor was necessary to mine the iron as well as to smelt and forge it. These workers had to be fed, but there were fewer farmers to produce the food while the number who needed food did not decrease. Individuals had different talents and thus some did the work while others took advantage of their labor. The former earned a lot of money while the latter earned barely enough to live. The rich depended on the poor for their labor, the poor depended on the rich for employment and help, and then as one may imagine, along with increased inequalities, human beings lost their freedom and independence.

As the inequalities solidified, neither the rich nor the poor were happy. Instead, greed, distrust, ambition, and wickedness ruled individuals. Echoing Plato's warnings about civil wars between rich and poor, Rousseau says it was a time of perpetual conflict resulting in a state of war. With everyone miserable, the rich came up with a plan to control and use the poor to their advantage. This plan was none other than the idea of convincing the poor to consent to a social contract. On the surface, the idea seems reasonable since the establishment of government would be preferable to anarchy. What the poor did not understand, however, is that this arrangement would give new powers to the wealthy, which would enslave them even more. The upshot of the social contract, according to Rousseau, is that the poor sold themselves into servitude and misery. Institutions were created, laws were passed, and private property became sacrosanct. Thus, inequality became institutionalized in society.

Notice that once again, Rousseau turns Hobbes and Locke's political theories upside down. Both Hobbes and Locke praise the social contract as the best, if not only, solution to protect one's life and possessions. Individuals may have to sacrifice part of their liberty to preserve some, but it was far more advantageous to do so than to face the uncertainties of anarchy in the state of nature. And this does sound attractive, but Rousseau says that few men were able to foresee the abuses accompanying this contract, and the few who did foresee them used them to their advantage.[85] Any idea of natural law was gone and convention replaced the natural sentiment of compassion.

As the number of societies increased, more and more barriers separated humankind throughout the world. Individuals' natural capacities to feel benevolence toward their fellow human beings were gone. Rousseau is writing about the universality of humankind. That is to say, one would be able to recognize and to relate to the suffering of others, no matter what their race, religion, social class, or country of origin might be. While a picture of a starving refugee in Sudan may temporarily move one, legal conventions, military, and economic power govern most relations among human beings. Rousseau believes that only a few "cosmopolitan souls" retain their natural compassion in spite of the many barriers erected between societies.[86] Moreover, he criticizes the ethnocentricity of the Europeans because he says they "know no other men but the Europeans alone."[87] As a result, Rousseau says that "ridiculous prejudices" abound because even for the educated, the study of man means only the study of men like them.[88]

Fleischacker claims that in the Second *Discourse*, Rousseau's description of the state of nature is a paradise and that "he separated his dream of presocial man from the practical proposals that he made to human beings in society."[89] One must not overlook, however, the importance of Rousseau's description of human nature, which has critical implications for his treatment of poverty. Since human beings are naturally good, this means that the poor are not innately bad or innately different from the rich. A philosopher's view about human nature may have profound consequences about his or her beliefs about the poor. In the last chapter, I explored how Locke's negative view of human nature resulted in a strong distrust and even contempt for the poor. As one turns to Rousseau's *Discourse on Political Economy*, one will see that he believes that to a large degree, individuals become what their governments make them.

Discourse on Political Economy

While the Second *Discourse* seeks to explain the origins of inequalities, it is the *Discourse on Political Economy* where Rousseau proposes solutions to inequalities in civil society.[90] Rousseau says that the first and most important maxim of government is for it to provide for the good of its citizens through the general will.[91] As mentioned earlier, the general will means that governments should pursue policies that benefit all citizens. The difficult questions, he says, are first, how to recognize the general will, and second, how to maintain public liberty while granting authority to the government.[92] It is here where Rousseau lays bare one of the most difficult questions in political philosophy, especially liberal theory, when he asks, "And how can the public needs be attended to without altering the private property of those who are forced to contribute to it?"[93] Protection of private property, according to Rousseau, is sacrosanct but without support, a state cannot exist.[94] Yet one must explain, and indeed, defend the idea of taking an individual's property to maintain the state because one of the fundamental reasons that societies exist is to protect private property. Indeed, the foundation of the social contract is to guarantee the protection and enjoyment of private property.[95] One may remember that Locke struggled with this same problem. Locke's beliefs in God and natural law provided a solution to this dilemma. Thus, Locke reconciled his commitment to private property and taxing some to provide for the poor because he thought that it would violate God's law to allow anyone to perish from lack of subsistence. In contrast to Locke, Rousseau says that the solution to this quandary is to recognize that the general will is the "first principle of political economy and the fundamental rule of government."[96] Since the general will is concerned with the common good, extreme disparities in wealth will be avoided in a properly run state.[97] In fact, Rousseau wants to promote economic equality with a large middle class forming the bulk of the state.[98] Foreshadowing Marx and disagreeing with Locke, Rousseau believes that to a large degree, individuals are what their governments make them.[99] The poor are not innately different from the rich; and the purpose of societal laws goes beyond ensuring justice and liberty because he says, "It is this healthy tool of the will of all which reestablishes as a civil right the natural equality among men."[100]

Since Rousseau's conception of the general will requires citizens to love their country and their fellow countrymen, he thinks that the welfare of all citizens, especially those who are poor, will be everyone's concern in the state.[101] One may remember that Lycurgus wanted all Spartans to live together as brothers and sisters. Plato wanted the same in the *Republic*. Given Rousseau's respect for Plato and his intimate familiarity with *Plutarch's Lives* and thus of Lycurgus, it is not surprising that he focuses on creating a community of brotherly love where the homeland is the common mother of all.[102] Thus if one citizen suffers from poverty, then all suffer. The state protects each member and there is a political and moral obligation to care for the poor. His idea of the state as a mother suggests care, security, as well as comfort and affection.

Again, echoing Plato's warnings about the harmful effects of large gaps between the rich and poor, Rousseau says that it is the "greatest evil" when there are poor people to defend and wealthy ones to restrain.[103] It is absolutely necessary but incredibly difficult to provide equal justice for all; however, he believes that it is the state's role to protect the poor from the tyranny of the rich. Laws alone cannot prevent conflict since the poor break them and the rich escape them. This leads Rousseau to conclude that one of the most critical issues for any government is to prevent extreme inequalities of fortune.

Of course, like Plato and Aristotle, Rousseau wants to prevent this because he knows once there is a division between rich and poor the state will deteriorate. He provides a list of conditions, which are some of the most likely causes for inequalities in modern societies. This includes unequal geographic distribution, which causes crowding in some areas while others are under populated. The arts of pleasure and pure industry are favored over useful and demanding crafts and agriculture sacrificed to commerce. Of course, there are the problems of corruption and bad administration of state funds, which causes bribery and private interests taking precedence over public ones.[104]

Notice that Rousseau, like Plato and Aristotle, takes a pragmatic approach toward understanding the problem. He believes that when some or all of these conditions come about, citizens are indifferent to the common good, corruption becomes rampant, and government is weakened. A wise administration focuses on preventing these conditions from taking root while at the same time "instilling good mores, respect for the laws, love of country, and the vitality of the general will."[105]

As in Plato's *Republic*, public education plays a vital role in preparing children for citizenship. If children are reared in equality, they will value impartiality and feel oneness with each other.[106] Of course, he favors a small geographic state with a limited population for several reasons but not least among them are to avoid areas of wealth and poverty in the same country.[107]

Like Aristotle, Rousseau recognizes the role that fortune plays in life. In government, however, it is wisdom and not fortune that brings happiness to the state.[108] The general will requires government to provide subsistence for its citizens. While he reaffirms the sanctity of private property, he says it is simply a fact that citizens must support their government. Rousseau's idea of good government promotes equality, simplicity, and self-sufficiency.[109] Toward that end, government should prevent needs rather than increasing revenues. This avoids unnecessary taxation, encourages simplicity, and promotes wise management of government resources.[110] To avoid the advent of uneven distribution of income and wealth, he proposes sumptuary laws and progressive taxation policies.[111] At first, he calls for taxing citizens proportionately to their incomes and assets.[112] This is not his last word on taxes, however, because later in the work he says that the poor, who can barely afford life's necessities, should not pay any taxes. This would result in a larger percentage of revenue coming from the rich and less from the poor, which means he proposes a progressive tax policy.[113] Rousseau dismisses the idea that the poor will not work since they do not have to pay taxes. Indeed, he believes the opposite to be true since taxing products of labor results in poor farmers, for example, having little, if any, incentive to plant all their fields.[114] As we shall sees later in this chapter, Smith would never eliminate taxes for the poor and rely on the wealthy to support the state. In light of this, one is perplexed how Fleischacker characterizes Rousseau as more libertarian than Smith about property rights.

Since the wealthy enjoy most of the benefits and advantages from society, it is only just for them to pay more.[115] Rousseau anticipates the cries of injustice from the wealthy so he forcefully defends his policies. First, he says that the state must provide protection for their properties and it is the rich, who fill the most lucrative government positions. As for sumptuary taxes, he argues that superfluous luxury items do not benefit society. The main reason individuals desire them is to distinguish themselves from the poor. In addition, he advocates taxing imported luxury items as well as exported goods that are scarce in the state. These duties will help to provide poor relief and to limit the growth of income disparities.[116] As for the rich, Rousseau believes they will continue to purchase extravagant material goods because they would rather go hungry than live without them.[117] He paints a picture of privilege that extends throughout modern societies, which includes the justice system. In short, the rich man lives a luxurious, pampered life where he is shown deference and respect without ever earning it. The poor man's life is quite different since the greater his needs, the more contempt society has for him. Opportunities are nonexistent since doors are slammed in his face. He takes the jobs that others avoid and the poor bear the burden in military service. Contrary to the respect that the rich receive, the poor are treated with disdain. Moreover, when a poor man suffers a loss, it is far more problematic for him to recover. It takes money to make money and thus the poor are not in a position to better their situation. Finally, Rousseau sums up his thoughts in the following passage:

> You need me, for I am rich and you are poor. Let us come to an agreement between our selves. I will permit you to have the honor of serving me, provided you give what little you have for the trouble I will be taking to command you.[118]

Much like modern day proponents for family-owned farms in the United States, Rousseau painstakingly presents the plight of the farmer to his readers. Most importantly, he says farmers receive the smallest returns.[119] Criticizing the practice of taxing farmers' properties and goods, he points out that while farmers may not sell their products, they always pay taxes on them. Moreover, while the urban areas get richer, the rural areas become poorer.[120]

At this point, it is appropriate to return once again to Fleischacker's argument noted at the beginning of this chapter. One may recall his claim that Rousseau's concern for the poor was limited to his preoccupation with their preparedness for citizenship and politics instead of true compassion for the poor that motivated his treatment of poverty. In addition, he claims that nowhere did Rousseau write about "the unfairness of capitalist systems to the poor so strikingly," as Smith did.[121] One can see that the *Discourse on Political Economy* provides significant evidence contrary to these claims. The passage, quoted above, is about the unfairness and exploitation of the poor by the rich. Though the passage is short, Rousseau's point is clear and as a result, this passage succinctly sums up his main argument. It is no accident that Rousseau concludes his *Discourse on Political Economy* with a defense of the poor and an indictment of the rich.

Corsica and Poland

Rousseau wrote two practical works, the *Constitutional Project for Corsica* (drafted in 1765) and *The Government of Poland* (1772) to advise the two respective governments.[122] Many of his policy suggestions from the *Discourse on Political Economy* are included in these works. While both are certainly practical in the sense that he was providing advice to existing countries about their respective constitutions and governments, they may strike one as more utopian than practical. This is certainly true of his advice to Corsica since his preoccupation with the avoidance of currency, foreign trade, and commerce is similar to Plato's ideas in the *Republic*.

Rousseau argues that since Corsica is poor, the government should concentrate on creating a stable environment where simplicity and self-sufficiency can flourish.[123] As a result, he believes that a wise government will be one that is most favorable to agriculture. He argues that farmers are the backbone of any successful country because human beings cannot survive without food.[124] For a nation's population to depend on outsiders for their nutritional needs is foolhardy and dangerous. The farmer is the archetype of simplicity and self-sufficiency.

Equality, according to Rousseau, should be the fundamental law for Corsica. All men should have equal rights by birth and any distinctions should come from merit rather than inheritance.[125] This is especially true for those who work in agriculture since Rousseau wants them to be content and to feel neither inferior nor envious of city dwellers.[126]

As alluded to earlier, Rousseau has a strong aversion to the use of money and any state economy that focuses exclusively on acquiring wealth. Indeed, he makes the claim that money creates poverty. Using Switzerland as an example, he argues that an increased circulation of money brought about inequalities in resources and fortunes.[127] Before the onset of this standard of value, the Swiss people may have been poor but they were never needy. Not only did their lust for money make them feel poor, but it also had a corrupting influence that destroyed their independence and unity. After all, money is really a token of inequality and Corsica should strive to eliminate and to avoid it completely in the future.[128] For Rousseau poverty was a relative concept especially relating to money. He makes this claim twice, once in the piece on Corsica, and again in *The Government of Poland*.[129] In the Corsican case, he believes their history illustrates that the people who could not raise enough money to pay their taxes were made to feel poor. He proposes a system of barter and in-kind contributions where citizens may restrict their use of money.[130] It is in this spirit that he advises them to limit trade and commerce because he says, "Everyone should make a living and no one should grow rich."[131] With the aim of encouraging Corsicans not to pursue luxuries, he advocates a sumptuary tax, which should be more severe for government leaders.[132]

Fear and hope motivate human beings, however, Rousseau does not believe that the fear of poverty causes one to be industrious. On the contrary, it is the hope that an individual has to live well that makes one work hard.[133] Smith certainly agrees with Rousseau when he says that is one of the reasons that capitalism is such a productive economic system. In some disconnected fragments at the end of the Corsica piece, Rousseau makes two provocative assertions. First, he says, "People will be industrious when work is honored; and it always depends on the government to make it so."[134] Second, he states that human beings are naturally lazy, which is an observation that he made in the Second *Discourse*. This time, however, he adds that individuals will have a passion for work in a well-governed society. When human beings lapse into laziness and discouragement, it is a result of society's failure to give proper respect and honor for their labor. With this insight to human nature, Rousseau puts the responsibility squarely on the government and society to motivate workers. This is in line with his beliefs about the primacy of historical contingency and social constructs to shape human beings' characters.

In *the Government of Poland*, Rousseau emphasizes many of the same themes from his earlier works. For example, he says that the government should root out luxuries. He admits that inequalities will always persist in societies, but he argues that education is paramount to alleviating poverty and reducing these inequalities. One of his specific policy proposals is that the government should provide educational scholarships for the least advantaged.[135] Moreover, he argues that the government must prepare individuals for democracy and this is why educating Polish citizens is so crucial to constructing a successful and stable state. Rousseau appeals to natural law to justify enfranchisement of the poor.[136] Poland's goal should be for the state to have neither beggars nor millionaires or to put it another way, no luxury nor indigence.[137] Finally, as in the plan for Corsica, he stresses the importance of not basing the country's economic system on money and praises the merits of simplicity and self-sufficiency.[138]

Like Plato's plan in the *Republic*, which emphasizes education, Rousseau wants to create a community of civic virtue with brotherly love where individuals have true partial affection for their fellow citizens. As a result, the general will, which promotes the common good, will never allow citizens to suffer from lack of subsistence. He relies on public education to promote equality among the citizens because above all he wants to avoid huge disparities in properties and wealth since these lead to instability and suffering.

Rousseau never wavered from his beliefs that poverty should not disqualify one from being a citizen. Nor did he think that others should condescendingly look down upon the poor. One can trace many of his beliefs about the poor back to his positive view of human nature and his longing for simpler times when human beings were self-sufficient and free. So one can see that the First *Discourse* not only brought him fame, but it also set the tone for his treatment of poverty throughout his political works.

While Rousseau believes that most individuals have a diminished capacity for fellow-feeling in the modern world, on some occasions he has not given up hope that it is lost forever while other times he is extremely pessimistic. As noted in the beginning of the chapter, this becomes evident in *The Social Contract*. Judith Shklar says that for Rousseau "Justice, unlike pity, makes the weak independent."[139] Rousseau believes that the poor's membership as citizens of a polity provides them strength in both body and mind. Rousseau also wants to remind his readers about the universality of humankind. He wants human beings to be able to recognize and relate to the suffering of others. His aim is to create a society where everyone feels a strong commitment to the general will.

Contrary to Fleischacker's claims, Rousseau's writings provide overwhelming evidence that he sympathized and cared about the poor as individual human beings. After all, one of the best ways to empower the poor is to make sure they have equal political rights so that they not only have a stake in their government, but they would also have the ability to influence the politics that affect their lives. As we saw at the beginning of this chapter, the aim of the general will was justice. Equality was a necessary condition for the general will. Rousseau's insights and treatment of poverty greatly influenced Marx, who, like Rousseau, never had a great deal of money nor financial stability. Before Marx, however, this study investigates Smith. I will show that he shared similar views with Rousseau about poverty and poor people. The difference, however, is that Smith does not believe in government aid for the poor and unlike Rousseau he is not as concerned about disparities in wealth in capitalist societies.

ADAM SMITH

Adam Smith, whose name for many years was synonymous with *laissez-faire* capitalism and conservative liberalism, has undergone somewhat of a transformation in recent years. In the last thirty years, scholarship has consistently focused on Smith's beliefs about poverty, his concern for the poor, and the optimism that penetrates his works.[140] With the publication of Emma Rothschild's

book in 2001, Alan Kroger writing in *The New York Times* referred to "The real
Adam Smith" as a complex thinker, meaning that one could not simply com-
partmentalize him as a "narrow, unyielding defender of unfettered free enterprise."[141] Moreover, Rothschild, along with other authors such as Himmelfarb
and Fleischacker, makes plain how Smith recognized the difficulties faced by
the poor, and that caricatures of him as an ideologue who opposed any government regulation are wrong.[142] To be sure, Rothschild does not try to make a case
that Smith's beliefs were in accord with those of the political right. What she
does do, however, is to encourage individuals to read Smith's writings so they
may go beyond clichés to discover the complexities and nuances of his work.[143]
Samuel Fleischacker and Daniel Rauhut are two recent authors who laud
Smith's compassion and liberal policies toward the poor. As mentioned earlier,
Fleischacker argues that Smith, not Rousseau, was a genuine advocate for the
poor because he was the first to draw widespread attention to the effects that
poverty had on their personal lives.[144] This was in contrast to Rousseau, who,
according to Fleischacker, was concerned about poverty only insofar as it affected politics.[145] Daniel Rauhut argues that Smith was truly a patron for the
poor. He says that in a "contextual" reading of Smith, one can see that he thinks
"government activity is needed in the provision of public goods, such as infra-
structure, education, health care, poor relief, etc., and that the government is
needed to supplement the market."[146]

While one can surely agree that Smith was not the narrow ideologue
who ignored poverty or the poor's difficulties, these last two descriptions
of Smith's policies toward the poor have caused the pendulum to swing too
far to the right after years of being stuck on the far left. That is to say, that
both Fleischacker and Rauhut overstate features of Smith's treatment of
poverty. In the case of the latter, there is no textual support offered to substantiate his claims. That Smith was concerned about the poor should not
be that astonishing since he was a moral philosopher as well as a political
economist. Moreover, sympathy plays a crucial role in his ethical and political theories. Therefore, it is not surprising that he wrote with compassion about the poor and that he had insights similar to Rousseau's about the
daily challenges that confronted them. That being said, one would be wise
to take Rothschild's advice and return to Smith's writings to examine his
treatment of poverty.

As with Rousseau, before moving on to his treatment of poverty, one must
understand Smith's account of justice. His notion of justice is connected to his
psychological theory of the impartial spectator. How does one come to approve or disapprove of a moral agent's actions or one's own actions? Smith
says that when one sympathizes with an agent's motive for a given action, one
approves of that action. Moreover, one also sympathizes with the individual

or individuals affected by that action.[147] This involves three individuals, that is, the spectator, the actor, and the recipient. The recipient may feel gratitude or resentment for a given action. If the spectator views the recipient's gratitude as appropriate then the action is judged meritorious. If the spectator thinks that the recipient's resentment is proper than the act is demeritorious. Merit rests upon the sympathy with gratitude for the benefit. To be clear, Smith's notion of merit is concerned with the intent or motive and not with its consequences.[148] His use of the word "sympathy" connotes not only fellow feeling but also the appropriateness of the response expressed under the circumstances. He says that the propriety or impropriety of a given response rests on whether or not an individual's response is in harmony with the spectator's reaction.[149] One might relate this to Aristotle's idea of the mean.[150] Actions are praiseworthy or blameworthy relative to the appropriateness of one's response given the situation.[151] For example, if P falls down and skins her knee, Q will feel sympathy for P if P's response to her minor injury is appropriate. If P screams and cries for hours about a small scratch on her leg, Q will feel little sympathy for P. The previous examples rely on an actual recipient's response. Smith is concerned with the spectator's judgment of what is appropriate and not what the actual individual feels.

In the case of judging one's own actions, he thinks that one should imagine what an impartial and benevolent spectator would think about his or her actions. Smith recognizes that human beings desire approval and feel satisfied when they receive love and admiration. He explains it in the following passage. "But in order to obtain this satisfaction, we must become the impartial spectators of our own character and conduct. We must endeavor to view them [our actions] with the eyes of other people or as other people are likely to view them."[152] Smith believes that individuals know when they are deserving of approval. When one is not truly worthy of the approval, her conscience is aware of this and thus, her satisfaction is incomplete.[153]

Smith's bases his definition of justice on the sympathy for the resentment one feels for harm. That is to say, a spectator would judge an action unjust based on her sympathetic response to a recipient's resentment of an act. An unjust act is demeritorious and deserving of punishment. Resentment, according to Smith, is the "safeguard of justice."[154] The following passage provides his definition of justice.

> There, is, however, another virtue, of which the observance is not left to the freedom of our own wills, which may be extorted by force, and of which the violation exposes to resentment, and consequently to punishment. This virtue is justice: the violation of justice is injury: it does real and positive hurt to some particular persons, from motives which are naturally disapproved of.[155]

Daniel Levine ties Smith's notion of justice to his conception of the duties of the capitalist state.[156] The state has three main duties, according to Smith: first, to protect the state from violence and foreign invasion; second, administering justice so that every citizens is protected from injustice and oppression; and third, constructing and maintaining certain public works and institutions that benefit society.[157] Levine succinctly states Smith's view of justice because government's main role is "protecting from injury to life, liberty, and property."[158] It follows that justice is the absence of injury to one's life, liberty, or property. Smith states that justice is most times "a negative virtue, and only hinders us from hurting our neighbor."[159] While he believes that beneficence and justice are both virtues, coercion is appropriate for matters concerning justice but not beneficence.[160] Government should have no part in forcing individuals to be beneficent or charitable. Thus, it is easy to see that as a matter of social policy, Smith thinks that it is not the proper function of government to provide welfare assistance to the poor. It may be a virtue to help the poor, but one should not be forced or obliged to do so. This is because charity, kindness, philanthropy, and humanitarianism, according to Smith, do not come under the rubric of justice and thus are not part of the proper functions of a just state. Unlike Rousseau, Smith has a determinate view of justice, which allows him to state clearly what justice demands from the state for the poor. Later in the chapter, I will revisit Smith's views about justice but for now, this brief overview provides the necessary context for understanding his treatment of poverty.

Agreeing with Plato, Aristotle, and Rousseau, Smith says that once the state institutionalizes private ownership, poverty will become a problem. He spends little time analyzing the causes of poverty. Instead, he explains why poverty is a relative concept in a state with a free market economy. Smith views poverty in capitalist societies as a matter of material inequality. Thus, it is far less severe or detrimental to people than the absolute poverty found in other societies. Relative deprivation is much different from absolute deprivation since one has the minimum necessities for his or her subsistence in the former whereas in the latter, one may face starvation on a regular basis. He rejects Locke's negative views about the poor because like Rousseau, he believes that in market economies people want to work to accumulate wealth. Indeed, Smith is sympathetic to the plight of the poor and has many positive things to say about their character and work ethic. The irony is that unlike Aristotle, Rousseau, and Locke, he does not support public aid for the poor and completely rejects the English Poor Laws.[161] Smith does support higher wages for the working class, progressive taxation, lower taxes on necessities, and limited public education.

In line with his Stoicism, Smith stresses that self-denial and self-command bring honor and dignity to human beings.[162] He agrees with Locke about individual responsibility and that one of government's chief function is to protect private property. Infringements upon private property are punishable, including crimes committed because of extreme poverty.[163] It is his contention that justice demands that individuals have enough self-control to endure personal suffering from hunger instead of harming the innocent property owner by stealing. While this may sound harsh, it reflects Smith's allegiance to the Stoic tradition, which emphasizes self-control.

Smith does not share Locke's belief that poverty results entirely from lack of discipline or corruption of manners. He says, "Wherever there is great property, there is great inequality. For one very rich man, there must be at least five hundred poor, and the affluence of the few supposes the indigence of the many."[164] The advent of private property leads to the need for civil government.

> The affluence of the rich excites the indignation of the poor, who are often both driven by want, and prompted by envy to invade his possessions. It is only under the shelter of the civil magistrate that the owner of that valuable property, which is acquired by the labour of many years, or perhaps by many successive generations, can sleep a single night in security. . . . Where there is no property, or at least none that exceeds the value of two or three days labour, civil government is not so necessary.[165]

The conflicts about property between the wealthy and poor, according to Smith, make government necessary. "Civil Government, so far as it is instituted for the security of property, is in reality instituted for the defence of the rich against the poor, or of those who have some property against those who have none at all."[166] Notice that contrary to Hobbes, he does not emphasize self-preservation as the main motivation behind human beings' creation of civil government. Indeed, echoing Locke, he believes protection of private property is the fundamental force behind the need for government.

Smith agrees with Plato and Aristotle that it is not desirable for the bulk of society to be poor. "No society can surely be flourishing and happy, of which the far greater part of the members are poor and miserable."[167] Moreover, he believes that social stability is a prerequisite for a country to flourish economically. "The peace and order of society is of more importance than even the relief of the miserable."[168] People are naturally concerned with self-preservation and the continuation of the species. As a result, human beings are also endowed with a natural desire for the welfare and preservation of society.[169]

Smith's observations lead him to believe that people naturally want to be the center of attention because they are vain and thrive on being noticed by others.[170] The best way to be noticed is to be wealthy. Smith explains that it is not surprising that human beings have natural ambitions to pursue wealth. He explains why this is true:

> It is because mankind are disposed to sympathize[171] more entirely with our joy than with our sorrow, that we make parade of our riches, and conceal our poverty. . . . Nay, it is chiefly from this regard to the sentiments of mankind, that we pursue riches and avoid poverty. For to what purpose is all the toil and bustle of this world? What is the end of avarice and ambition, of the pursuit of wealth, power and pre-eminence? [172]

This is similar to Rousseau's claim when he said that no matter how high the tax rate was on luxuries, the wealthy would not do without these goods since they desire them to separate themselves from the poor.[173] Smith says that the poor man is not only ashamed of his poverty, but he is also overlooked. When he is noticed, he is met with disapproval. He observes how the rich and poor are treated differently:

> The poor man goes out and comes in unheeded, and when in the midst of a crowd is in the same obscurity as if shut up in his own hovel. Those humble cares and painful attentions, which occupy those in his situation, afford no amusement to the dissipated and the gay. They turn away their eyes from him, or if the extremity of his distress forces them to look at him, it is only to spurn so disagreeable object from among them. . . . The man of rank and distinction, on the contrary, is observed by all the world.[174]

Not only do people notice the rich, but they also sympathize with their misfortune and suffering more than that of the poor.[175] The poor are judged as more blameworthy for their mistakes and even when the rich and poor are of equal merit, the former garner more respect.[176] Smith argues that while this type of treatment may be unfair, it does have positive implications for society. Ambition causes men to work harder to gain material wealth.[177] The approval of the rich and powerful forms the basis for the distinction of ranks and the order of society.[178]

Smith asserts that men are imaginative, and most are frugal. Men's imaginations compel them to regard wealth and greatness as something grand, beautiful, and noble.[179] Most men are frugal because they have a desire to better their material conditions and thus, saving and accumulating some part of what they acquire comes naturally. Smith says:

However, the principle of expense [spending], therefore, prevails in almost all men upon some occasions, and in some men upon almost all occasions, yet in the greater part of men, taking the whole course of their life at an average, the principle of frugality seems not only to predominate, but to predominate very greatly.[180]

To sum up, Smith regards human beings as being naturally sympathetic, self-interested, social, ambitious, imaginative, and frugal. These combined characteristics fuel the capitalist economy and limit the problem of poverty. It is prudent to stop here and reflect on a significant difference between Smith and Rousseau's beliefs about human nature. While the former believes human beings are naturally social, one might remember that Rousseau did not think this was so since in his state of nature primitive man was also a solitary man.[181] It is true that the drive for self-perfection was one of the primary factors that caused primitive man to become civilized man; it is safe to say that Smith's idea of ambition is not what Rousseau had in mind. This type of ambition, according to Rousseau, only came about after human beings started living closer together.

Smith clearly believes that individuals' environments profoundly affect them since he says that human beings are born with few differences in their natural talents. The differences between the most dissimilar characters, for example, between a philosopher and a common street porter, seem to arise not so much from nature, he says, as from habit, custom, and education.[182] Once again, Rousseau would be in full agreement with him since individuals' environments as well as their governments, are crucial in shaping their characters.

Relative Poverty

To understand correctly the idea of poverty in an industrialized nation, Smith thinks that one must compare it with the poverty found in agrarian or pre-industrial nations. What Smith is describing is relative and absolute poverty. Absolute poverty means one is deprived of an adequate amount of food, housing, clothing, medical care, and other items necessary for a decent life. Relative poverty means there are inequalities in the distribution of income and material goods.[183] Therefore, if one thinks that she is relatively deprived compared to most of her neighbors, it does not follow that she has an insufficient amount of necessary goods to live a decent life. It does mean, however, that she may still feel a sense of relative deprivation in an affluent society when she compares her situation to that of others. In the opening paragraphs of the *Wealth of Nations*, Smith explains that the division of labor in industry increases productivity and allows even the frugal peasant to live comfortably:

> [A]nd yet it may be true, perhaps, that the accommodation of an European prince does not always so much exceed that of an industrious and frugal peasant, as the accommodation of the latter exceeds that of many an African king, the absolute master of the lives and liberties of ten thousand naked savages.[184]

Not only do the poor in England enjoy better accommodations than the wealthy in pre-industrial societies, but they are also happier and more comfortable. Smith says that the conditions of the working poor in a progressive state where society is advancing are the happiest and most comfortable in the world.[185] The upshot of this is that the conditions of the poor in an industrialized, capitalist country must be viewed in comparison to the poor in other places. What may look like poverty to some in a capitalist society is misleading because the poor are better off than the rich in other countries.[186] As Jerry Muller says, Smith's comparison of absolute and relative poverty has a moral component to it.

The ability of commercial society to provide greater wealth was also an important moral argument in its behalf. Smith advanced this argument implicitly, with his many references to the morally demeaning nature of life in a poor society. On the very first page of the *Wealth of Nations* he contrasts commercial nations with primitive nations that lack commerce and the division of labor and that "are so miserably poor, that, from mere want, they are frequently reduced, or, at least, think themselves reduced, to the necessity sometimes of directly destroying, and abandoning their infants, their old people, and those afflicted with lingering diseases, to perish with hunger, or to be devoured by wild beasts." Elsewhere, Smith cites the legitimization of infanticide as evidence of the moral degradation caused by the lack of material means. While wealth may corrupt, Smith implied, absolute poverty corrupts absolutely.[187] This is Smith's moral vindication of capitalism. He strongly believes that the poverty found in capitalist states is much less physically and morally devastating than the poverty in other economic and social systems.

In addition, E. G. West says that Smith thinks, "inequality is often illusory or superficial."[188] Once again, one may remember that Rousseau stresses this same point throughout his writings. Both agree there are few physical needs for many of the things that individuals want in society. Thus, Smith says, "avarice over-rates the difference between poverty and riches."[189] Men spend their time working not to procure the necessities of life such as food, clothing, and housing, but instead to have conveniences to please their tastes.[190]

These views explain why he spends little time focusing on the *causes* of poverty or *solutions* for it. Smith's beliefs, which he treats as empirical facts, satisfy any moral qualms that one may have about the poor in capitalist countries.

Self interest motivates people toward productivity. Through their endeavors, individuals promote the common good for all of society. D. O. Raphael states that the theme of mutual dependence runs throughout Smith's work. The benefits that come from the division of labor stem from individual self-interest in the practice of exchange.[191] If unnecessary regulations on trade and business are removed, the economy in a country improves. Natural balance occurs when the capitalist economy adopts *laissez-faire* policies so that productivity and consumption complement each other. In short, minimal government intervention allows the natural balance in economics to work properly.

Smith's argument against interventionist famine policies to regulate the internal corn trade during times of scarcity reflects his commitment to *laissez-faire* policies.[192] He believes that one must look at the economy in the long-term. Short-term fixes only serve to interrupt the natural balance of the market. What Smith fails to discuss is the human suffering during the interim between the crisis and the long-term fix. To be sure, he does not reject all government intervention. For example, he believes it is necessary for governments to construct roads and bridges to facilitate commerce.[193] He also advocates limited public education. "For a very small expense the public can facilitate, can encourage, and can even impose upon almost the whole body of the people, the necessity of acquiring those most essential parts of education."[194] The public should establish schools, but the families who have children attending them should pay small amounts to the schoolmaster privately for his salary. If paid by public funds, Smith thinks that the schoolmaster will neglect his duties.[195] He never changes his belief that public funds should back only things, which cannot be privately financed and are necessary to promote commerce.

Since he thinks that the poor are not that bad off and it would be morally wrong to take money from the wealthy to provide for them, he rejects the idea of public funded poor relief. One of his main criticisms of England's Poor Laws is that they do not permit the poor to travel freely. In the previous chapter, one may remember that the Poor Laws restricted the poor to their parish of residence with the threat of harsh punishment for violations. In contrast to Locke, who was preoccupied with limiting the poor's mobility, Smith strongly objects to these laws because they disrupt principles of *laissez-faire* doctrine by limiting the mobility and the freedom of the poor to find work.[196]

Without a doubt, Smith was not blind to the economic differences that existed in capitalist societies. He believes that tax rates should be based on individuals' wealth and their ability to pay them. Thus, he advocates progressive taxation. Unlike Rousseau, however, Smith wants all adults, no matter how poor they may be, to pay taxes.[197] He also observes that the constancy of employment fluctuates, and this may cause hardships for some workers. Inclement weather may limit the bricklayer's work, and thus Smith thinks that his daily wages should be higher than someone in manufacturing, for example, because it will help tide him over during times when he cannot work.[198] Moreover, he believes that higher wages for the working class are good not only for them but also for the rest of society. Healthier, happier workers are more productive, and they are able to buy more goods, which fuels the capitalist economy and benefits society.[199] While poverty does not prevent the poor from bearing children, it is not favorable to rearing them. He points to the high mortality rate among the children of the poor who cannot afford to raise them with the same care as those who have more wealth.[200] "The liberal reward of labor" enables the poor to provide better for their children. More wages would help to reduce infant mortality ensuring there will be sufficient workers to meet future demands.[201] Smith also observes that English merchants complain about the high wages and extravagant gains of British labor when compared to foreign labor costs. These same men, Smith says, never say anything about British stockholders' high profits and their tendencies toward extravagance. He concludes that these high profits contribute to the rising cost of manufacturing as much, or in many cases, more, than the high wages of British labor.[202]

Alienation?

The paradox in Smith's *Wealth of Nations* is that on the one hand, he extols the virtues that the division of labor brings to society, such as increased productivity, and high standards of living. On the other hand, Smith acknowledges that this productivity comes with a price. Since most laborers are confined to a few simple, repetitive operations, these men have no occasion to use their minds creatively to invent new things or to critically analyze and solve problems. As time passes, workers lose their abilities to carry on rational conversations and even more disturbing, they become incapable of exercising good judgment in their private lives. Indeed, Smith says they become "stupid and ignorant as it is possible for a human creature to become."[203] They are also unfit to serve as soldiers in war because the work has not only corrupted their minds, but also their bodies. Smith says,

> [The laborer's] dexterity at his own particular trade seems, in this manner, to be acquired at the expense of his intellectual, social, and martial virtues. But in every improved and civilized society this is the state into which these laboring

poor, that is, the great body of people, must necessarily fall, unless government takes some pains to prevent it.[204]

In spite of Smith's claims about the progress of humankind and the relative prosperity of the poor, this chilling statement exposes a pessimistic side to his thought. Moreover, one cannot help but to think about the alienation that Rousseau wrote about in the Second *Discourse* and the central role that it will play in Marx's work sixty years later.[205] To be sure, Rousseau's notion of alienation is different since he laments human beings' loss of autonomy, self-sufficiency, and most of all, freedom. Civilized man, according to him, is unhealthy, dependent, and in chains.[206] As West points out, Rousseau and Smith have opposite notions of the non-alienated world.[207] Indeed, West argues that the root of alienation for Marx comes from Rousseau and not from Smith. Moreover, Smith's 1756 "Letter to the Edinburgh Review" provides evidence that he did not agree with Rousseau's characterizations of society, especially the state of nature.[208] It is ironic that both point to the fact that civilization may have negative effects on human beings. Much has been written about this and it is important to note that Smith never uses the word alienation in his descriptions about the negative effects that the division of labor and increased productivity have on the workers. West says that alienation implies powerlessness, isolation, and self-estrangement, and one cannot claim that Smith's description encompasses the first two, that is, powerlessness and isolation.[209] Robert Lamb disagrees because he believes that Smith is indeed describing the concept of alienation. He points out that Smith's discussion of this effect was not limited to the *Wealth of Nations*, since he refers to the negative effects from the division of labor in his 1763 Glasgow lectures.[210] David Reisman thinks that Smith's pessimism was in line with the intellectual outlook of writers during the Scottish Enlightenment.[211] He names others, such as Lord Kames and Adam Ferguson, who shared Smith's bleak outlook about the future. Moreover, he claims that Smith looked to public education to remedy the situation he describes.[212] Patricia Werhane disagrees with Reisman because she says that the limited public education that Smith advocates would do little to change the life of the poor laborer.[213] She is correct and there are two additional reasons that support her claim. First, Smith says that parents must contribute to the teachers' salaries and this seems counterproductive if one is trying to motivate disadvantaged parents to send their children to school. Second, poor children are often forced to work to help support their families. It is not convincing that Smith's call for such limited public education could remedy the debilitating mental and physical effects from repetitive labor. Werhane also points to the obvious influence that Smith had on Marx's theory of the alienation of labor. She is quick to caution, however, that one may read too much into it because the two ideas are different.[214] Whatever the case, one will see the profound effect that both Smith and Rousseau had on Marx's political theory.

Smith's gloomy prediction potentially undermines his argument that material inequalities in market economies will not result in inadequate provisions for the poor. As the working poor become more incapacitated, they lose some of the very characteristics, such as good judgment in their private lives and imagination, which would allow them to maintain their place in society. That is to say, that some of the very qualities that Smith praises would no longer be applicable to the poor, and thus their situation in society would deteriorate. Of course, material equality in the state was never a goal for Smith. What one does find in Smith is a faith, albeit a qualified one, in human beings' abilities to produce great wealth. While poverty will always exist, one must look at just how well the poor fare in market economies compared to the poor in other places. Finally, while Smith like Mandeville admired the productivity of commercial society, the former wanted to show that self-interest and vanity could have positive effects and did not preclude one distinguishing between moral and immoral behavior. On the contrary, individuals could be virtuous, honest, successful, and moral in commercial society.

Earlier in the chapter, I explained Smith's definition of justice as an absence of harm or injury. It was a narrow definition that included threats to one's life, liberty, or property. I also mentioned that Smith's preoccupation with self-control was symptomatic of the Stoic influence on his work. One can also see that the great Stoic, Cicero, had what Nussbaum calls a narrow view of justice. Specifically, she persuasively argues that the idea of providing material aid to other countries is not included in Cicero's account of justice. She says,

> "Cicero's general account of the duties of justice (*justitia*) has two parts. Justice requires not doing any harm to anyone, unless provoked by a wrongful act. This is how Cicero thinks fundamentally about justice and injustice. Second, justice requires 'using common things as common, private possessions as one's own.' Cicero holds that it is a fundamental violation of justice to take property that is owned by someone else. He says that taking property 'violates the law of human fellowship.'"[215]

She thinks that one can trace contemporary beliefs about the duties of justice and material aid back to these ideas. Thus, while nations may object to rape, murder, and genocide on the grounds of justice, these same nations are silent when human beings lack food, shelter, and medical care because they do not view them as coming under the rubric of justice. While Nussbaum is concerned with justice among nations, one can apply her logic to a limited notion of justice in an individual state. If malnutrition, lack of medical care, and substandard housing cause harm to individuals and thus resentment, are these conditions not also matters of justice? While one must take seriously Smith's ideas about relative poverty, one should also recognize that poverty has negative and damaging consequences for human beings. It can cause great harm. Thus, the sympathetic spectator may feel the resentment that the poor experience.

One explanation for Smith's minimal view of justice is that he thinks it necessary to promote equality and fairness in the state. Indeed, Campbell argues that Smith's distrust of government policy stems from his dedication to justice and impartiality.[216] He correctly points to the following passage in Wealth of Nations to support his claim:

> All systems either of preference or of restraint, therefore, being thus completely taken away, the obvious and simple system of natural liberty establishes itself of its own accord. Every man, as long as he does not violate the laws of justice, is left perfectly free to pursue his own interest in his own way, and to bring both his industry and capital into competition with those of any other man, or order of men.[217]

Campbell focuses on the significance of this passage because it explains Smith's economic policies regarding monopolies and industry in general. It is also relevant to understand his minimal view of justice. Deciding who qualifies for government aid is not an easy matter. As was evident in the previous chapter, separating the deserving from the undeserving poor is not an exact science. What are the qualifications for aid? Should it be based on the number of children in a given family? How long should the government support last? These are judgments that Smith thinks are better left to private individuals who ought to help their fellow human beings in times of need. Instead of promoting impartiality and equality, the complexities and ambiguities inherent in public aid would do the opposite. Smith's minimal view of justice allows his political theory to keep government's primary functions specific. This, in turn, provides clarity and thus, impartiality and fairness. Moreover, as I have shown he did not support redistribution because it infringes on private property and it is not necessary since the poor are doing relatively well compared to others in nonindustrialized nations.

CONCLUSION

The tone of Rousseau and Smith's treatments of poverty stands in sharp contrast to Locke's since neither philosopher believes that the poor are lazy nor are they always to blame for their poverty. In fact, they argue that the poor work hard and often suffer indignities through no faults of their own. They both indict the wealthy for their extravagance and conspicuous consumption. In spite of all these agreements, there are some fundamental differences in their beliefs about human beings, society, poverty, and what justice demands for the poor. Rousseau laments human beings' forfeiture of freedom, autonomy, and self-sufficiency as they transitioned from primitive to civilized society. He views individuals in the state of nature as solitary, content beings who had few desires. Once civilized, they have become slaves to the material goods they believe are necessary for life when in fact, the loss of these goods causes them more grief than any pleasure they ever gain from their use. Most importantly, with the advent of private property came inequality, alienation, and poverty. Rousseau yearned for a simpler time when human beings were free from economic pressures. Since there was no turning back, however, he wanted to create the most just society possible. As I have shown, his ideas about the social contract and the general will aim toward building a state that is more just for all citizens, especially the poor. To create a more just state, he advocates eliminating taxes for the destitute, and providing public aid through the collection of revenue from the wealthier citizens. In Rousseau's ideal state, no one would do without the necessities.

In contrast, Smith rejects Rousseau's characterization of primitive man. He believes that human beings are social animals and thus find fulfillment in society. Moreover, any poverty found in a capitalist society pales in comparison to the absolute poverty found in primitive societies. In the latter, human beings die from starvation and disease and those who are fortunate enough to live barely survive with the most minimal of necessities. Far from making individuals less free, capitalist economies allow the poor to have a higher standard of living than anyone could have ever imagined. While Smith lauds the progress of humankind and the division of labor, one also sees a pessimistic turn in his thinking about the poor and their future in industrialized societies. Since truly free market economies provide the most just economic foundation for a society, justice and prudence demands *laissez-faire* policies, which exclude public aid. While the poor may not always be treated fairly in a free market economy, they have it better than in other pre-industrialized countries. The opportunities are so great that there is never any need to provide public aid and doing so would be unjust since it violates the sanctity of private property and Smith's negative notion of justice, which limits government's role to protecting from injury to life, liberty, or property.

Rousseau and Smith's treatment of poverty elevates the impoverished to a new status since both to some degree portray the poor as morally superior in many ways to the wealthy. Yet, in spite of their agreements about poor's character, their beliefs about what justice demands for them are quite different. In the next chapter, I explore how forty years later J. S. Mill and Alexis de Tocqueville's beliefs about the problem of poverty challenge many of Rousseau and Smith's assumptions. Like Smith and Rousseau, however, they share many similar beliefs about poverty but they will also reach different conclusions about the demands of justice for the poor.

NOTES

1. Bernard de Mandeville, *The Fable of the Bees and Other Writings*, Abridged and ed. E. J. Hundert (Indianapolis: Hackett Publishing Company, Inc., 1997), 19–182. This work was originally published in 1714 and it was expanded and republished in 1723. For a detailed discussion of this work by Adam Smith, see *Theory of Moral Sentiments* (New York: Prometheus Books, 200), Part VII, Section II, Chapter IV "Of Licentious Systems."

2. Sumptuary taxes are taxes that aim to regulate personal expenditures. The explanation for sumptuary taxes is often moral or religious and the aim is to discourage individuals from buying or consuming certain goods. An example of this is a tax on cigarettes to discourage smokers.

3. Jean-Jacques Rousseau, *The Reveries of the Solitary Walker*, trans. Charles Butterworth (Indianapolis: Hackett, 1992), 25, n.16 (hereafter cited as *Reveries*).

4. *Reveries*, 131.

5. Eli Friedlander discusses the autobiographical and imaginative qualities of Rousseau's writings in "Chambery, 12, June 1754: Rousseau's Writing on Inequality," in *Political Theory* 28, no.2 (April 2000): 254–72.

6. For examples see, John-Jacques Rousseau, *Confessions*, trans. Angela Scholar, ed. and intro. Patrick Coleman (New York: Oxford University Press, 2000), 30–31, 37, 41, 44, 52, 58, and 69–71.

7. *Confessions*, 5–7.

8. Ibid., 11–12.

9. Ibid., 29.

10. Ibid., 41.

11. *Reveries*, 28–30 and 80.

12. Ibid., 110–11.

13. Ibid., 127, 129.

14. Patrick Coleman says, "self-taught, Rousseau would always remain an outsider: a Protestant in Catholic France; a republican in a monarchy; a man who, earning his day-to-day living copying music, foregrounded his status as a paid worker in a culture where even hack writers sought to draw a veil of discretion over their involvement in the trade." Coleman's Introduction to Rousseau's, *Confessions*, xxii

15. *Confessions*, 244–46.

16. Ibid., 347–49.

17. Leo Damrosch, *Jean Jacques Rousseau: Restless Genius* (New York: Houghton Mifflin Company, 2005), 192.

18. Maurice Cranston, *The Early Life and Work of Jean-Jacques Rousseau 1712–1754* (New York: W.W. Norton and Company, 1982), 245.

19. *Confessions*, 347–49

20. Ibid., 349.

21. *Reveries*, 124.

22. *Confessions*, Book XIII, 347, 348.

23. See for example his discussion *in Confessions*, Book IX, 459 and 460.

24. Fleischacker, *Short History*, 59.

25. Ibid., 61.

26. Ibid., 59 and 60.

27. Ibid., 59.

28. Ibid., 58.

29. The process of interpretation, which I am referring to here is taken from Al Martinich in "The Interpretation of Covenants" in Leviathan *after 350 Years*, eds. Tom Sorrell and Luc Foisneau (Oxford: Clarendon Press, 2004), 216–40.

30. Robert Wokler, *Rousseau: A Very Short Introduction* (Oxford: Oxford University Press, 2001), 17; George Kateb, "Aspects of Rousseau's Political Thought," *Political Science Quarterly* 76, no. 4 (December 1961): 520, and John Rawls, *Lectures on the History of Political Philosophy*, ed. Samuel Freeman (Cambridge: The Belknap Press of Harvard University Press, 2007), 232.

31. Kateb, "Aspects of Rousseau's Political Thought," 520. Rousseau says that the general will produces justice in *On the Social Contract* in *Jean-Jacques Rousseau: The Basic Political Writings*, trans. Donald A. Cress (Indianapolis: Hackett Publishing Company, 1987), 157. All references to this work are from this edition and hereafter cited as *OSC*.

32. David Wooten, "Rousseau, the Enlightenment, and the Age of Reason," in *Modern Political Thought: Readings from Machiavelli to Nietzsche*, ed. David Wooten (Indianapolis: Hackett Publishing Company, 1996), 400.

33. Wooten, "Rousseau, the Enlightenment, and the Age of Reason," 400.

34. *OSC,* 170.

35. Ibid., 170.

36. Ibid., 170.

37. Ibid., 158.

38. Ibid., 180.

39. This interpretation has not been accepted by some notable scholars including Leo Strauss, *Natural Right and History* (Chicago: University of Chicago Press, 1953), Roger Masters, *The Political Philosophy of Rousseau* (Princeton: Princeton University Press, 1968), and Arthur M. Melzer, *The Natural Goodness of Man* (University of Chicago Press, 1990).

40. David Williams, "Justice and the General Will: Affirming Rousseau's Ancient Orientation." *Journal of the History of Ideas* 6, no.3 (July 2005): 383–411.

41. Shklar, "Jean-Jacques Rousseau and Equality," in *Rousseau's Political Writings*, Norton Critical Edition, eds. Alan Ritter and Julia Bondanella (New York: W. W. Norton, 1988), 274.

42. Rousseau, "Discourse on Political Economy" in *Rousseau's Political Writings,* trans. Julia Bondanella, eds. Allen Ritter and Julia Bondanella, 58.

43. Jean-Jacques Rousseau, "Discourse on the Sciences and the Arts," in *Jean-Jacques Rousseau: The Basic Political Writings,* trans. Donald A. Cress (Indianapolis: Hackett Publishing Company, 1987), 1–21. All references to this work are from this edition and hereafter cited as First *Discourse.*

44. Ibid., 17.

45. First *Discourse*, 17.

46. Ibid., 17.

47. Ibid., 4.

48. Ibid., 13.

49. Jean-Jacques Rousseau, "Discourse on the Origin and Foundations of Inequality Among Men," in *Jean-Jacques Rousseau, The Basic Political Writings*, trans. Donald A. Cress (Indianapolis: Hackett Publishing Company, 1987), 33, 36. All references to this work are from this edition and hereafter will be referred to as the Second *Discourse.*

50. Second *Discourse*, 33.

51. All references to Thomas Hobbes are from *Leviathan* with the page, chapter, and paragraph number. They are from *Leviathan*, ed. A. Martinich (Toronto: Broadview Press, Ltd., 2002), 95, 13.8.

52. Hobbes, *Leviathan*, 97, 13.13.

53. Ibid., 96, 13.9.

54. Ibid., 97, 13.14.

55. John Locke, *Second Treatise.* For example, compare Locke's description of the state of nature in Book II, 2.4–7, 269–70 with his later descriptions in Book II, 7.87, 318.

56. Ibid., Book II, 8.95–98, 332–33.

57. Second *Discourse*, 38.

58. Ibid., 37–38.

59. Ibid., 38.

60. Ibid., 41. He also rejects the idea that man is a timid, frightened creature in the state of nature as portrayed by Montesquieu, Cumberland, and Pufendorf.

61. Second Discourse, 45, 89, n.9.

62. Ibid., 35.

63. Ibid., 35.

64. Ibid., 39.

65. Ibid., 37–38.

66. Ibid., 39.

67. Ibid., 40, 52.

68. Ibid., 42–43.

69. Ibid., 43.

70. Ibid., 98, n.10.

71. Ibid., 44.

72. Leo Strauss and Roger Masters deny that Rousseau meant to give an argument for free will. See Leo Strauss, *Natural Right and History* (Chicago: Chicago University Press, 1953), 265–66, and Roger Masters, *The Political Philosophy of Rousseau*

(Princeton: Princeton University Press, 1976), 69–71. I endorse the interpretation provided by David Williams that Rousseau did mean to provide an argument for free will
in *Rousseau's Platonic Enlightenment* (University Park Pennsylvania State University Press, 2007). Williams' interpretation is in line with those of Wokler, 2001 and
Rawls, 2007.

73. Second *Discourse*, 45.

74. Ibid., 52–53.

75. Ibid., 57.

76. Ibid., 58–59.

77. Ibid., 53.

78. Ibid., 54–55.

79. Ibid., 55.

80. Maurice Cranston, *Jean-Jacques: The Early Life and Work of Jean-Jacques
Rousseau 1712–1754* (New York: W.W. Norton and Company, 1983, First American
Edition), 256–57; Jean Jacques Rousseau, *On Wealth and Fragments on Taste*, in *The
Collected Writings of Rousseau,* vol. 11, trans. Christopher Kelly and Judith Bush, ed.
Christopher Kelly (Hanover: Dartmouth College Press, 2005). 6–18.

81. *Second Discourse*, 60.

82. Ibid., 61.

83. Ibid., 63.

84. Ibid., 64.

85. Ibid., 70–71.

86. Ibid., 70.

87. Ibid., 99, n.10.

88. Ibid., 99 and 100, n.10.

89. Fleischacker, *Short History,* 59.

90. Bertril Fridén, *Rousseau's Economic Philosophy* (Dordrecht, The Netherlands: Kluwer Academic Publishers, 1998), 1. He argues that scholars, much to their
detriment have failed to take this work as a serious one in political economy.

91. Jean-Jacques Rousseau, *Discourse on Political Economy*, in *Jean-Jacques
Rousseau: The Basic Political Writings*, trans. Donald A. Cress (Indianapolis:
Hackett Publishing Company, 1987) 116. All references to this work are from this
edition and hereafter cited as *DPE*.

92. Ibid., 116.

93. Ibid., 116.

94. Ibid., 116 and 127.

95. Ibid., 132.

96. Ibid., 116.

97. Ibid., 124, 125, 136, and 137.

98. Ibid., 137.

99. Ibid., 119.

100. Ibid., 117.

101. Ibid., 122.

102. Ibid., 122, 123, 125, and 126.

103. Ibid., 125.

104. Ibid., 124.

105. Ibid., 124.

106. Ibid., 126.

107. Ibid., 131.

108. Ibid., 126 and 127.

109. Ibid., 127.

110. Ibid., 129.

111. Ibid., 119, 132, 133, and 136–138.

112. Ibid., 132–133.

113. Ibid., 132,133, and 136.

114. Ibid., 134–135.

115. Ibid., 133.

116. Ibid., 136.

117. Ibid., 137.

118. Ibid., 134.

119. For example, in the United States, farmers receive about 22 cents of every dollar in agricultural products sold. (United States Department of Agriculture, Statistics Services).

120. *DPE*, 135–136

121. Fleischacker, *Short History,* 62.

122. Jean-Jacques Rousseau, *Constitutional Project for Corsica* (drafted 1765; published 1772), in *Jean Jacques Rousseau Political Writings*, trans. and ed. Frederick Watkins with foreword by Patrick Riley (Madison: University of Wisconsin Press, 1986) 270–330. Jean Jacques Rousseau, *The Government of Poland*, trans. Wilmoore Kendall, Indianapolis: (Hackett Publishing Company, Inc., 1985). All citations are from these editions and hereafter cited as *CPC* and *GP* respectiely.

123. *GP,* 284.

124. *CPC,* 283

125. Ibid., 289 and 293.

126. Ibid., 291.

127. Ibid., 297, 298, 302, and 303.

128. Ibid., 304.

129. *GP,* 73.

130. *CPC,* 306 and 314.

131. Ibid., 308.

132. Ibid., 324.

133. Ibid., 325.

134. Ibid., 328 and 329.

135. *GP,* 20 and 21.

136. Ibid., 29–30.

137. Ibid., 74.

138. Ibid., 73 and 75.

139. Judith Shklar, "Jean-Jacques Rousseau and Equality,"in *Rousseau's Political Writings*, Norton Critical Edition, ed. Alan Ritter and Julia Bondanella, (New York: W.W. Norton & Company, Inc., 1988) 274.

140. For examples see T. Sowell, *Classical Economics Reconsidered*, (Princeton: Princeton University Press, 1974); M. Blaug, *Economic Theory in Retrospect*, (Cambridge, Oxford University Press, 1978); G. Himmelfarb, *The Idea of Poverty: England in the Early Industrial Age*, (New York: Alfred A. Knopf, 1984); I. Hont and M. Ignatieff, eds, *Wealth and Virtue: The Shaping of Political Economy in the Scottish* Enlightenment, (Cambridge: Cambridge University Press, 1983); E. Roll, *A History of Economic Thought*, (England: Farber and Farber, 1992); A. Sen, *On Ethics and Economics,*(Gateshead, Blackwell Publishers, 1997); E. Rothschild, *Economic Sentiments: Adam Smith, Condorcet, and the Enlightenment*, (Cambridge: Harvard University Press, 1991); A. Fitzgibbons, *Adam Smith's System of Liberty, Wealth, and Virtue*, (Oxford: Clarendon Press, 1995; paperback 1998), C. Griswold, Jr., *Adam Smith and the Virtues of Enlightenment* (Cambridge: Cambridge University Press, 1994); J. Muller, *Adam Smith in His Time and Ours: Designing the Decent Society* (New York: The Free Press, 1993; paperback rpt. Princeton: Princeton University Press, 1995); S., Darwall, "Sympathetic Liberalism: Recent Work on Adam Smith," Philosophy and Public Affairs, vol. 28, No. 2 (Spring 1999), 139–164; S. Fleischacker, *A Short History of Distributive Justice*, (Cambridge: Harvard University Press, 2005); and D. Rauhut, "Adam Smith— Champion for the Poor!" in *Economists and Poverty: From Adam Smith to Amartya Sen*, New Delhi: Vedams Books, 2005).

141. Alan Krueger, "The many faces of Adam Smith: "Rediscovering *The Wealth of Nations*," *New York Times,* Market Scene, section C, August 16, 2001.

142. Ibid., Section C.

143. Rothschild, *Economic Sentiments*, 2.

144. Fleischacker, *Short History*, 62.

145. Ibid., 59.

146. Rauhut, "Adam Smith—Champion for the Poor!," 30

147. Adam Smith, *The Theory of Moral Sentiments,* eds. D.D. Raphael and A. L. Macfie (Indianapolis: Liberty Fund, Inc. 1982), 78, (hereafter cited as *TMS*).

148. Ibid., 78.

149. Ibid., 16.

150. William F.Campbell, "Adam Smith's Theory of Justice, Prudence, and Beneficence," *The American Economic* Review, Vol. 57, No. 2, Papers and Proceedings of the Seventy-ninth Annual Meeting of the American Economic Association, (May, 1967), 572.

151. Smith, *TMS*, 25–26.

152. Ibid., 114.

153. Ibid., 1114–115.

154. Ibid., 79

155. Ibid., 78

156. Donald J. Levine, "Adam Smith and the Problem of Justice in Capitalist Society." *The Journal of Legal Studies* Vol. 6, No. 2 (June 1977), 405.

157. Smith, *WN*, 688, and Levine, "Adam Smith and the Problem of Justice," 405.

158. Levine, "Adam Smith and the Problem of Justice," 405.

159. Smith, *TMS*, 82.

160. Ibid., 78.

161. Ibid., 57.

162. Ibid., 23–24.

163. Ibid., 138. See also, John Salter, "Sympathy with the Poor: Theories of Punishment in Hugo Grotius and Adam Smith," *History of Political Thought* 20, no.2, (Summer 1999): 205–24.

164. Adam Smith, *WN*, 709–10.

165. *WN*, 710.

166. Ibid., 715.

167. Ibid., 96.

168. *TMS*, 226

169. Ibid., 160.

170. Ibid., 50–51.

171. Smith's use of the word sympathy connotes not only fellow feeling but also approval or disapproval of the feeling expressed under the circumstances. For example, if P falls down and skins her knee, Q will feel sympathy for P if P's response to her minor injury is appropriate. If P screams and cries for hours about a small scratch on her leg, Q will feel little sympathy for her.

172. *TMS*, 51.

173. *DPE*, 136–37.

174. *TMS*, 50. Notice how similar this is to Rousseau's observations in *Discourse on Political Economy*, 134.

175. *TMS*, 51–52.

176. Ibid., 61–62.

177. Smith makes this point about ambition more than once in both *TMS* and *WN*. For example, he argues that ambition forces the poor man's son to labor harder once he is filled with ambition to attain wealth, *TMS* 181.

178. *TMS*, 52.

179. Ibid., 183.

180. *WN*, 342.

181. For discussion about this point, see for example West, "Adam Smith and Rousseau's Discourse on Inequality: Inspiration or Provocation?" *Journal of Economic Issues* 5 (1971): 56–70.

182. *WN*, 28–29. See also John Danford, "Adam Smith and Equality," *American Journal of Political Science* 24, no.4, (November 1980): 674–95.

183. DiNitto, *Social Welfare: Politics and Policy*, 67 and 76.

184. *WN*, 23–24.

185. Ibid., 99.

186. Mandeville makes this same point in *The Fable of the Bees*, 28.

187. Muller, *Adam Smith In His Time And Ours*, 72.

188. E. G. West, "Adam Smith's Philosophy of Riches," *Philosophy*, 44, no.168 (April 1969): 109.

189. Ibid., 111.

190. Adam Smith, *Lectures on Justice, Policy, Revenue and Arms*, ed. Edwin Cannan 1896, 158, quoted in West, 114.

191. D. O. Raphael, *Adam Smith* (Oxford: Oxford University Press, 1985), 49.

192. Salim Rashid, "The Politics of *Laissez-Faire* during Scarcities" in *The Economic Journal* 90, no.359 (September 1980): 493–503.

193. *WN*, 723–24. The central government in England did control foreign trade but local authorities administered other policies. Local magistrates oversaw the regulation of markets in labor and land, internal trade, justice, police, county road maintenance, and poor relief. Thus, other than foreign trade, the *laissez-faire* policies that Smith advocates are in place, and some historians believe that it was not because of any libertarian principles, but because it was in the "pure self-interest of people who already had wealth and who were making more." *The Economics of the Industrial Revolution*, ed., Joel Mokyr (London: George Allen and Irwin, 1985), 13.

194. *WN*, 785.

195. Ibid., 785.

196. Ibid., 152–57, 470.

197. Ibid., 825.

198. Ibid., 120–21; Albert Rees, "Compensating Wage Differentials," *Essays on Adam Smith*, eds. Andrew Skinner and Thomas Wilson (Oxford: Oxford University Press, 1976), 342.

199. *WN*, 99.

200. Ibid., 97–98.

201. Ibid., 98.

202. Ibid., 599.

203. Ibid., 303.

204. Ibid., 303.

205. See especially Karl Marx's *Economic and Philosophic Manuscripts of 1844*.

206. See for example, Rousseau, *First Discourse*, 4 and *Second Discourse*, 42–43.

207. For example, West, "Adam Smith and Alienation: A Rejoinder," *Oxford Economic Papers* 27, no.2, (July 1975): 296

208. Adam Smith, "Letter to the Edinburgh Review" in *Essays on Philosophical Subjects*, ed. W. D. Wightman, first published 1756 (Indianapolis: Liberty Fund, Inc., 1982) 250–56.

209. For example, West, "The Political Economy of Alienation, Karl Marx and Adam Smith," *Oxford Economic Papers* 21, no.1 (March 1969): 1–23, hereafter cited as "Alienation."

210. Robert Lamb, "Adam Smith's Concept of Alienation," *Oxford Economic Papers* 25, no.2 (July 1973): 276.

211. David Reisman, *Adam Smith's Sociological Economics* (London: Croom Helm, Ltd. (1976), 153.

212. Ibid, 157.

213. Patricia Werhane, *Adam Smith and His Legacy for Modern Capitalism* (Oxford: Oxford University Press, 1991), 146.

214. Ibid., 144–47.

215. Martha Nussbaum, "Duties of Justice, Duties of Material Aid: Cicero's Problematic Legacy," *Bulletin of the American Academy of Arts and Sciences* 54, no.3. (Spring 2001): 42.

216. Campbell, "Adam Smith's Theory of Justice," 571–77.

217. *WN*, 576.

Chapter Five

Empirical Influences and the Complexities of Poverty: Alexis de Tocqueville and John Stuart Mill

Two of the most significant intellectuals of the nineteenth century, John Stuart Mill and Alexis de Tocqueville, spent a great deal of time thinking and writing about poverty. Both men show remarkable perceptiveness and bring a new depth of understanding about the complexity of the problem. Certainly, they were also concerned with justice and thus the problem of poverty necessarily engaged them because they witnessed increased poverty in England's urban centers as well as in Ireland. While the Industrial Revolution created tremendous wealth for some and improved living conditions for many, it also gave rise to urban centers with workers who were completely dependent on the will of their employers. Moreover, unlike rural workers, they had no way to produce their own subsistence. The excesses of capitalism renewed debates about state intervention and government aid. Tensions between capital and labor intensified and questions arose about the fairness of Smith's *laissez-faire* doctrine. This context created a fertile environment for discussions about what justice demanded from government as well as individual and societal responsibilities.

As we saw in chapter 3, the matter of public aid was a contentious issue in England. The controversy and debates continued and in 1832, a Royal Commission on the Poor Laws investigated their administration and practical application. This resulted in a New Poor Law, which Parliament passed in 1834. This was the most important piece of poverty legislation since the passage two centuries earlier of the original Poor Laws.[1] One of the aims of the new law was to make sure that the able-bodied poor would work by allowing them to receive relief only in workhouses. These offices would be located in every parish of considerable size while smaller parishes would share one. In addition to giving up one's freedom when entering the workhouse, the conditions inside were intended to discourage individuals from seeking help. The idea was that by limiting outside aid, officials would be able to separate paupers from the poor and thus, classify those who went to the workhouses as paupers. This distinction between the poor and indigent meant that only paupers could legally receive public aid.[2]

The heated debates about how to identify the deserving poor, why they were poor, and what legal or moral standing they had, only intensified during the nineteenth century because it was also the age of Malthusianism. First published in 1798, Thomas R. Malthus's influential work, *An Essay on the Principle of Population*, with its thesis that population growth can and will exceed the food supply, remained a much discussed and controversial topic that engaged theorists like Mill and Marx.[3] In much the same way that Mandeville's *Fable of the Bees* had dominated political discourse during the eighteenth century, Malthus's work sparked discussions about poverty and loomed over the arguments throughout the nineteenth century. Notice that his proposition stands in stark contrast to Adam Smith's belief that productivity and human beings' propensity to better themselves would be more than enough to sustain not only a healthy economy but also a working class that would continually better their situation. While some classify Mill as a committed Malthusian, this is incorrect since he does not entirely share Malthus's pessimistic outlook.[4] Mill does not think that population growth is inevitable.[5] With increased universal education and advances in women's rights, he believes that population growth can be controlled.[6] It is true that Mill advocates population control as being not only fundamental to addressing the problem of poverty but also to advancing women's rights.

While the Industrial Revolution brought public railroads, telegraphs, and industry to England, agrarian Ireland remained untouched. If the increasing numbers of paupers in urban areas such as Manchester and London were appalling, the abject poverty throughout Ireland was horrifying. Traveling in Ireland during the summer of 1835, Tocqueville writes about the devastating impoverishment because he not only witnesses the humiliation of the poor, but he also sees individuals who were literally starving to death. Moreover, this was before the Potato Famine, which dates from 1845 and did not end until 1851. More than one million Irish died from starvation and disease during that famine. In one decade, the Irish population went from eight million to six million. In spite of this debasing impoverishment, profitable exports from Ireland of grain and cattle continued during this time and the British property owners collected taxes and rents. Tocqueville's diary notes convey astonishment, disillusionment, and a strong sense of injustice about the Irish situation. On the anniversary of the famine 150 years later, Prime Minister Tony Blair expressed regret for British conduct during the catastrophe.[7] After all, as

Prime Minister Blair said, Ireland "was then part of the richest and most powerful nation in the world."[8]

Mill agrees with Tocqueville about the horrible conditions and injustices in Ireland. While he never travels to Ireland, he spends significant amounts of time and energy speaking and writing about the unfairness and offering ideas to help alleviate the problem. Mill's involvement in the issue spanned four decades and he used diverse means to address the situation including writing in periodicals, newspapers, a pamphlet, parliamentary speeches, and chapters in the *Principles of Political Economy*.[9] In his *Autobiography*, he says he had urged the reclamation of wastelands for the formation of peasant proprietaries during the famine.[10] He thought it was an opportune time to focus attention on the deplorable state of affairs, and perhaps improve the social and economic conditions of the Irish.[11] He condemns the rental arrangements where payments are determined by competition. This meant, according to Mill, that no matter how industrious and productive the tenants were, they could never get ahead since they were forced to pay more rent than they could afford.[12] Moreover, before the 1845 repeal of the British Corn Laws, English farmers were guaranteed a minimum price for their grain. As a result, the Irish could not afford to replace potatoes with the expensive grain. During the winter of 1867, Mill authors a pamphlet titled "England and Ireland" in which he proposes that existing tenants should be given permanent tenure at a fixed rate.[13]

On this point and many others, Tocqueville and Mill agree. Neither man approves of government aid since it removes the incentive to work. Instead of helping the poor, public aid creates new problems and does not address the real causes of poverty. Alan Kahan has called their type of European liberal thought, "Aristocratic Liberalism."[14] He says, "Their common distaste for the masses and the middle classes, their fear and contempt for mediocrity, the primacy of individuality and diversity among their values persuaded me that this was the proper label."[15] Certainly, the two men knew each other and they shared some similar ideas about the causes of poverty and possible preventive or corrective policies. Kahan's description, however, is difficult to reconcile with Mill's advocacy for the working class, the Irish, and his ideas about land redistribution. Moreover, I argue two of the most significant points of convergence in their social and political thought are their antipathy toward government aid and insistence that rich and poor alike needed to practice internal self-restraint. This might not seem to be a terribly ambitious argument since the emphasis on self-discipline runs throughout liberal thought. It is often overlooked. As we saw in chapters 3 and 4, it plays a critical role in Locke and Smith's works as well. I will go on to show that Mill and to some degree, Tocqueville, believe that the absence of self-control is a significant cause of poverty. It follows then if the poor exercise self-restraint, the number living in destitution declines dramatically. It is not just the poor, however, who lack this virtue. Both men see the wealthy as being culprits since they are greedy and lack self-control, which helps to create poverty. They agree that promoting property ownership is fundamental to alleviating poverty. While both theorists view public aid negatively because it creates dependency, they have different but provocative views about the proper role of private charity.

Most importantly, I will show that at the heart of their treatments of poverty, both reject intuition as a basis for making policy decisions because it leads to sentimentality and ineffective policies. Instead, Tocqueville and Mill rely on empirical evidence and reason. Tocqueville is not as straightforward about this because of his projection of certain natural traits onto the poor, such as laziness and lack of planning. Because of his nuanced and thoughtful treatment as well as his willingness to entertain a variety of solutions, it is clear that he joins Mill in believing that empirical evidence and rational analysis are the keys to understanding poverty and working to reduce it. In this chapter, we will see how the crisis in Ireland and the ongoing problem of poverty in England affect, and to some degree modify their beliefs about the poor and the problem of poverty. Once we explore each theorist's views, we will be able to answer the central question in this study; what are Tocqueville and Mill's judgments about the relationship between justice and poverty in the state? To that end, we will explore Tocqueville's treatment of poverty and then turn to Mill's analysis.

ALEXIS DE TOCQUEVILLE'S *MEMOIRS ON PAUPERISM*

Tocqueville, as political scientist, historian, and sociologist never states a theory of justice per se. In spite of this, one could also add moralist to the list above since he makes ethical judgments throughout his work. This is especially true in his treatment of poverty. Tocqueville's beliefs are similar to Locke's since he is a classical liberal who believes in the sanctity of private property, limited government, rule of law, avoidance of arbitrary and discretionary power, and that each individual is responsible for his or her own fate in society. In *Democracy in America* and *The Old Regime and the French Revolution*, he writes about the decline of distinctions of social status and the principle of equality. The problem for modern society, as Tocqueville sees it, is how to reconcile liberty with equality. With the erosion of aristocracy came more centralized power. This in turn reduced regional and local attachments and concentrated power in the central government. Tocqueville is concerned about this consolidation of power and his treatment of poverty reflects it. He has a keen sense of fairness and thus, it is proper to use the word just and un-just regarding his moral judgments. Given his preoccupation with the prob-lem of poverty, it is clear that to a large degree he engages the problem to find the root causes, effects, and possible solutions not only because of political concerns but also because it is a matter of justice. This explains, in part, why he provides a nuanced and sophisticated analysis. Without a doubt, he be-lieves individual responsibility is paramount to solving the problem. Like Mill, however, his criticisms apply to the wealthy as much as to the poor. He also recognizes that governments have a role to play in alleviating poverty and this is especially true in the case of Ireland. Before visiting Ireland, how-ever, it was his visit to England that inspired his *Memoir on Pauperism*.[16]

During an 1833 trip to England, Tocqueville was appalled by the numbers of people living in poverty. Inspired by that journey, he wrote the first of a two-part work on poverty. He completed his first *Memoir on Pauperism* in 1835 and delivered it before the Royal Academic Society of Cherbourg in France that same year.[17] In this piece, he searches for possible explanations for increased poverty in industrialized nations as well as ways to alleviate, or at a minimum, moderate the problem. He delivers a harsh critique of public aid and explains why private charity is better for everyone in society. He be-gins to explore other causes and solutions with a sincere desire to try to un-derstand the reasons for so much poverty in such a wealthy nation. In this concise work, Tocqueville covers a lot of territory and provides some provocative suggestions not only about the causes of poverty, but also possi-ble solutions. As a result, it is well worth systematically exploring it.

Tocqueville begins by asking why the poorest countries in Europe have the fewest number of poor people. He claims that in England, "the Eden of mod-ern civilization," one-sixth of the population depends on public charity.[18] He thinks it is possible to explain the state of affairs in Europe, but to do that he must first examine the beginning of human societies.[19]

The Tocquvillean state of nature is composed of savages who associate only for survival and do the minimum required to obtain subsistence because they are naturally lazy. Their lives are analogous to that of non-human ani-mals because they exert the least amount of effort necessary to satisfy their basic needs. There is no inequality because no one person or family holds a superior position in this pre-political state.[20] These savages, according to Toc-queville, learn about agriculture and are able to produce enough food to feed themselves and their families. Private property is created and society "enters the most active element of progress."[21] Once individuals settle permanently and their food sources become less precarious, they begin thinking and look-ing beyond their subsistence needs to discover other sources of pleasure. Ig-norant about how to protect their property, men turn to any kind of tyranny.

This is the origin of aristocracy where property and power are concentrated in the hands of a few.[22] Violence threatens the property of every citizen and "inequality reaches its extreme limits."[23] Tocqueville says:

> If one looks clearly at what has happened to the world since the beginning of societies, it is easy to see that equality is prevalent only at the historical poles of civilization. Savages are equal because they are equally weak and ignorant. Very civilized men can all become equal because they all have at their disposal similar means of attaining comfort and happiness. Between these two extremes is found inequality of conditions, wealth, knowledge—the power of the few, the poverty, ignorance, and weakness of all the rest.[24]

He proceeds to the twelfth century to investigate feudal societies. Only two groups made up the entire population—those who worked the land but did not own it and those who owned the land but did not work it. Workers were provided with food and shelter. They had few desires or worries because they did not have any decisions or choices to make about their lives, or as Tocqueville says, "they enjoyed a kind of vegetative happiness."[25] It is curious that he associates having no control over one's life with happiness. One may remember from the last chapter that Rousseau's description of savage man, who was not a slave to anyone, enjoyed freedom and happiness, and not the man who had become a slave in society. Tocqueville says the opposite was true for the landowners because their lives were "brilliant, ostentatious, but not comfortable."[26] Discomfort for them came from the lack of cooperation among all members of the class to make life easier and from the absence of things like adequate heating for their homes and proper clothing. Like Smith and Rousseau, Tocqueville calls attention to the relative nature of poverty:

> I am convinced that there is not a provincial town today whose more fortunate inhabitants do not have more true comforts of life in their homes and do not find it easier to satisfy the thousand needs created by civilization than the proudest medieval baron.[27]

During this period, he believes that individuals had few needs, but slowly they began to desire better housing, clothing, and more of life's comforts and pleasures. They left the land to find work to make money to satisfy these new needs. While the majority still worked in agriculture, a new class arose who made their living by working at a trade.[28] In the following passage, Tocqueville implies that it is the Creator's will that society changes.[29]

> Each century, as it emerges from the hand of the Creator, extends the range of thought, increases the desires and the power of man. The poor and the rich,

each in his sphere, conceive of new enjoyments, which were unknown to the ancestors.[30]

"Immutable laws" govern the growth of organized societies. And only the Creator knows the limits to this growth or to human perfectibility.[31] Again, Tocqueville's ideas are similar to Rousseau's proposition that human beings have the faculty of self-perfection, which ultimately leads them down a road to creating their own misery.[32]

As civilization progressed, he says that a prodigious number of new goods became available and people's lives became not only more comfortable, but also happier. During the middle ages, when everyone survived through agriculture, there was always enough food to prevent starvation. By 1835, however, the majority of people in England would be on the verge of starvation if not for government aid.[33] Tocqueville observes that this is how the free market system works. When the market takes a downturn, unemployment rises, and workers are left without the means to survive. God has given these workers the "special and dangerous mission" of supplying goods for others while they must also take all the risks and dangers associated with their work. In the following passage, he states some of the problems associated with economic growth.

Each year needs multiply and diversify, and with them grows the number of individuals who hope to achieve greater comfort by working to satisfy those new needs rather than by remaining occupied in agriculture. Contemporary statesmen would do well to consider this fact.[34]

Education and habit compel men to want more than mere subsistence because nonessential items are no longer thought of as luxuries. Once again, he echoes Rousseau's observation in the Second *Discourse* that deprivation of these luxuries causes more suffering than any enjoyment that one may derive from having them.[35] Tocqueville puts forth Native Americans as an example because they have become beggars for tobacco, which is now something they need. This cause of beggary is new, and civilized man is far more vulnerable to it than savages ever were because they relied on fortune to meet their basic needs. He contrasts civilized and savage men by saying that "Among very civilized peoples, the lack of a multitude of things causes poverty; in the savage state, poverty consists only in not finding something to eat."[36] This is one of the main causes of pauperism in England.[37]

Tocqueville provides four primary causes for poverty: human beings' propensity toward laziness, private property ownership, unstable labor markets, and the proliferation of needs in civilized society. Additionally, he mentions that industrialization rapidly displaced people who left the land to move into industry before the latter could meet their needs. He shares Rousseau and

Smith's views about private property and the growth of people's needs in modern societies. Again, like his two predecessors, these observations lead him to compare absolute and relative poverty. He is much less optimistic about human nature than either Rousseau or Smith. Although Tocqueville does not think that laziness or lack of virtue can account for explaining the entire problem, he does believe that people are basically lazy and that religion is an important mitigating factor in staving off poverty. He rejects Smith's idea that people are motivated to work to get ahead or that they are naturally frugal. Moreover, he is a harsh critic of public aid, which he also calls public charity. He recognizes, however, that structural forces, such as mass urban migration and market fluctuations, contribute to increasing poverty. He sympathizes with the working poor who produce goods because he says that their jobs, and thus their survival are precarious in market societies. The inexactness of the relationship between the production and consumption of manufactured goods, that is, supply and demand in a free market economy, contributes to the problem and this "inexactness" greatly concerns him.[38] That being said, in spite of all these factors listed, he believes that public aid is the principle cause of greater poverty in industrialized nations.

Why has England created this unmanageable situation? Tocqueville offers a psychological explanation that hinges on the effects of wealthy and poor living near each other because he believes that society feels compelled to relieve the needs of the poor. In a backward country, no one would think of giving clean clothes, healthy food, and comfortable shelter to the poor. In contrast, since English citizens have such high standards of living, individuals believe that they must provide for the poor and it is this compulsion that exacerbates pauperism. While the relative nature of poverty partially explains the English situation, Tocqueville takes it a step further by describing the psychological inclination because of guilt to provide for the poor. The result is that in prosperous nations, large numbers of people live off government aid. The most vulnerable people in society multiply while their needs grow and change along with their exposures for failing to meet them. The continued growth of public charity, he says, is an "inevitable evil" that foreshadows the future of modern society and the best that one can hope to do is to moderate its effects.[39]

Tocqueville explores two ways that poor relief may be provided. First, it can be administered by individuals according to their means. This approach has been around since the beginning of time. Christianity made it a private virtue and called it charity. Protestantism created the second type, that is, public charity, and it led society to attempt to deal with the problem systematically. Since public charity was created and regulated by society, it is no longer a private virtue.[40] The notion of public charity is psychologically seductive because society reflects on its problems, then tries to fix them, all the while assuring that the rich enjoy their wealth, and the poor are relieved from excessive suffering. This logic is fallacious, Tocqueville says, because it created legalized public charity, which led to the rapid growth of pauperism.[41] Public aid is a disastrous policy because it removes incentives for individuals to work for their living. The need to live, and the desire to improve the conditions of one's life are the two principal incentives for one to work. Experience, Tocqueville believes, has shown that the first is the only reason why the majority of human beings work. Public aid removes that motivation and most individuals are not moved by the second one. Therefore, he outright rejects Smith's claim that individuals work hard because they want to improve their material conditions. Again, refuting Smith's assessment of the poor as being frugal, Tocqueville says that when poor people do work, they have no interest in saving money. The poor do the least amount of work possible to get by and then foolishly spend whatever they earn. Echoing Locke's assessment, he says that by removing the only incentive to work, hardworking and generous people are forced to pay for the poor's idleness.[42] In short, with guaranteed public aid, why would anyone want to work?

Tocqueville turns to what he believes is some of the insurmountable difficulties when trying to decide who is truly worthy of charity and getting able-bodied people to work. He says that it is nearly impossible to decide who merits assistance because of all the nuances and myriad circumstances surrounding individuals. No one possesses sufficient knowledge, foresight, conscience, time, and talent to decide who deserves aid. More importantly, he asks, "Who would dare to let a poor man die of hunger because it's his own fault that he is dying?"[43] He says that the English have tried to find a person who can determine merit for assistance by putting an overseer of the poor in each Parish. The result has been disastrous because it is easier for the overseer to give public aid than to deny it. He succinctly sums up the problem in the following passage:

> Since public aid is only indirectly harmful to society, while the refusal of aid instantly hurts the poor and the overseer himself, the overseer's choice cannot be in doubt. The laws may declare that only innocent poverty will be relieved; practice will alleviate all poverty.[44]

Putting the poor to work is also fraught with difficulties. Public work is not always available or may be necessary only in specific locations, which in turn creates logistical problems in getting the poor to the geographical area where their labor may be truly necessary. Even if there is public work that needs to be done, Tocqueville says it will be difficult to prioritize the work, to supervise the laborers, and to determine their salaries. He doubts that anyone possesses the knowledge or courage to "force the most inactive and vicious part of the population into sustained and productive effort."[45] In this last passage, one can see that his negative views toward the poor, which are almost identical to Locke's in his Report, lead to Tocqueville's doubts about the poor's motivation to work even if jobs were provided by the government. One may remember in chapter 3 that Locke begins his report to the Board of Trade with the same indictment against the poor and the same conclusion about their laziness.

Another reason that England's Poor Laws have failed, according to Tocqueville, is that they were utopian. He says that, "Laws must be made for men and not in terms of a perfect world, which cannot be sustained by human nature, or of models, which it offers only very occasionally."[46] He believes that in the process of implementing their utopian ideas, the English have created an intractable problem. Tocqueville says that, "Any measure that establishes legal charity on a permanent basis and gives it an administrative form thereby creates an idle and lazy class, living at the expense of the industrial and working class."[47] While America has escaped this problem so far, he predicts that if preemptive measures are not taken, the same thing that is happening in England, "will devour the well-being of generations [in America] to come."[48]

Tocqueville compares public aid to a monastic system that lacks morality and religion. He believes that the moral dimension of public aid is just as important as the economic one because it "depraves men even more than it impoverishes them."[49] Once the poor had a legal right to aid, the act of asking for help was removed and the recipient was on the same level as the provider. Public aid also removes any privacy by requiring indigents to be listed as such on the parish poor rolls. The poor may demand relief, but they must publicly admit to their misery, weakness, and misconduct. As a result, the poor's inferiority is proclaimed publicly.[50] Legal aid also destroys any hope of establishing important moral ties between the rich and poor. In fact, he believes that public charity drives a deeper chasm between them because they form two rival nations where the rich view the poor with fear and contempt, and the poor feel despair and envy toward the wealthy. The poor's future has been destroyed because they have lost their fellow citizens' respect. While they may live without fear of starvation, they also live without hope. He compares their outlook to that of non-human animals because of their present-orientedness. They live only to satisfy their needs for the present and they have no idea about their future.[51] One may remember that this is his description of prepolitical man so one may conclude that he thinks that the poor have returned to the savage state. Moreover, public aid has led to increased laziness, criminal activity, and illegitimate births, and it has become difficult for the poor to live virtuous lives. As if those evils were not enough, Tocqueville ticks off a list of the other negative effects that result from public aid:

- The rich are reduced to tenant farmers of the poor.
- The source of savings disappears.
- The accumulation of capital stops.
- Trade development is retarded.
- Human industry and activity slow down.
- A violent revolution will be the final result because those who receive public aid outnumber those who give it and the poor will steal property to satisfy their needs.[52]

Finally, he says that public charity is not a virtue because it is a weak and unreflecting inclination and not a reasoned act. The aim of charity, according to Tocqueville, should be to do what is most useful for the poor and not merely please the giver. The welfare of the majority of the population should be considered instead of rescuing a few.[53]

He praises private charity because in contrast to public aid, it is privately given by reason of a recognized inferiority of the recipient. It forces givers to be concerned about the lives of the needy. Recipients feel gratitude because they know they had no right to ask for help and these feelings are healthy and inspirational for them. Tocqueville says:

> A moral tie is established between those two classes whose interests and passions so often conspire to separate them from each other, and although divided by circumstance they are willingly reconciled. This is not the case with legal charity. The latter allows the alms to persist but removes its morality. . . . Public alms guarantee life but do not make it happier or more comfortable than individual alms giving; legal charity does not thereby eliminate wealth or poverty in society.[54]

Thus, one of the most important qualities of private charity is the forging of a moral link between rich and poor in society. Moreover, it is a virtue and it provides what is most useful for the poor.[55] So far, one can see that Tocqueville has a negative opinion about the poor's character and government aid. One may be led to think that he believes that justice does not necessitate government aid for the poor. As we shall see, it is not that simple because future experiences will continue to shape and change his views about what is practical as well as just when confronting the problem of poverty. Moreover, Tocqueville's beliefs reflect the English debate about public aid and charity during this time. Some thought that charity demonstrated the virtue of mercy that would guarantee eternal life for the provider. Greater mercy meant that providers should only give to those who were "deserving." Deserving meant that recipients should demonstrate correct social behaviors and be of sound character. Organizations such as the Proclamation Society, the Society for the Suppression of Vice, and the Society for the Support and Encouragement of Sunday Schools called for a "moral regeneration" of society.[56] Others saw the opportunity for charity to remake people by converting them to their organizations' religious views or to the individuals' beliefs who were supplying relief. The idea was that since the poor were often wicked, charity should be provided to them ". . . in a way which would produce a moral transformation."[57] Moreover, these groups shared Tocqueville's beliefs because their ambition was not only to moralize the poor, but also to reform the English Poor Laws. These reformers thought that the Poor Laws had removed work incentives. If public aid were not available, individuals would be motivated to be more self-sufficient instead of depending on society to provide for them.

In spite of his praise for private relief, Tocqueville recognizes that the demand for relief is too great for private charity. He entertains the idea that by "regulating" relief, private charity organizations could bring more power and activity to individual philanthropy.[58] It is not clear what he means by "regulating" relief. One possibility is that he thinks that private organizations could join forces to oversee the administration of poor relief, resulting in greater coordination and a more concentrated effort than individual philanthropists could provide. He does acknowledge public aid's utility and necessity for those who are least able to care for themselves such as infants, old people, the sick, and insane. Temporary public aid may also be necessary in "times of public calamities which God sometimes allows to slip from his hand, proclaiming his anger to the nation."[59]

Tocqueville concludes the *Memoir* with questions about what ought to be done about poverty. He returns to the inherent problem of calculating production and consumption in capitalist economies so that workers do not lose their jobs when the former exceeds the latter. He mentions two new ideas as possible solutions. First, he wonders if there is a way to discourage urban migration to industrial areas; and second, he asks whether one could devise a way to help the working class accumulate savings as a safety net for times of unemployment or misfortune.[60] These questions show that while Tocqueville shared some of Locke's negative views about the nature of the poor, he is acutely aware of the complexity surrounding poverty and thus one could argue that he provides a more sophisticated analysis of it. He ends the work with the promise of a second one that will deal with the problem of poverty and perhaps, answer some of the questions that he poses at the end of this one.[61]

In 1837, he composed the *Second Work on Pauperism*, which consists of only sixteen numbered pages.[62] Like his previous piece, it begins with an historical overview of the problem. He returns to his belief that capitalist industrialization exacerbates the problem of poverty because the working class has no property while the capitalist class has great wealth. Property ownership instills moral and social values that help to prevent poverty. Tocqueville wonders if there is some way to provide the industrial worker with "the spirit and the habits of property."[63] He provides several ideas as possible solutions, but then almost in the same breath he rejects or finds fault with each of them. He first wonders if perhaps laborers could be provided with an interest in the factories where they work. He rejects this because the capitalist owners will never agree to this idea. He then asks if workers' cooperatives could be established. This would probably not work, he says because of the internal conflicts and inefficiencies. An "association of workers" might succeed in the future. Finally, he has an idea of creating state-run savings banks, which would motivate workers to save money by giving them higher interest rates or savings banks merged with local pawnshops, which would allow the poor to borrow money at lower rates than normal. Tocqueville says that both of these ideas have the significant disadvantage of giving and promoting state control and centralization.[64] The manuscript ends abruptly but one can see that Tocqueville thought that the industrial laboring class needed a stake in property in order to avoid pauperism. Moreover, one could also conclude that he sees that the poor are not entirely responsible for their situation. Thus to be fair and just, he considers some structural and institutional changes that may level the playing field a bit and give the poor more opportunities to be full participants in free market economies.

Like Locke, Tocqueville describes what contemporary social scientists call a culture of poverty. This notion involves much more than a lack of material wealth. They believe that poor people share certain attitudes like indifference, present-orientedness, the need for immediate gratification, and a lack of motivation to work or to save money.[65] Both theorists share contempt for the poor because they believe that "able-bodied" people are taking advantage of government aid. While policy debates in England centered on the idea that relief was being provided for the able-bodied poor, empirical studies show that in practice, this was not a problem.[66] That is to say that the bulk of relief in the late seventeenth and eighteenth centuries went to the impotent poor and not to the able-bodied.[67] So while Tocqueville probably more than any other theorist based many of his views on observations and experiences, his negative beliefs about the poor to some degree clouded his empirical findings. That is until his trip to Ireland. His journey to Ireland provided him with empirical evidence that forced him to rethink some of his moral judgments about the poor as well as the role of private charity and government aid.

Poverty in Ireland

In July and August of 1835, Tocqueville spent six weeks in Ireland with his friend Gustave de Beaumont, who had accompanied him to America and Canada in 1831. The latter trip resulted in Tocqueville's remarkable work, *Democracy in America*. While this short piece on Ireland consists of his notes, comments, descriptions, interviews, conversations, and essays that he wrote during the trip, his analysis is nonetheless brilliant.[68] Emmet Larkin says that while Tocqueville's notes are based on his experiences, a close reading reveals that he was preoccupied with three issues; (1) the devastating poverty of the Irish people; (2) their complete hatred of the Irish aristocracy, and (3) their devotion and loyalty to the Catholic Church.[69] Indeed, his preoccupation with the problem of poverty intertwines with the other two topics throughout his notes. Tocqueville's descriptions and thoughts about the destitute Irish people are provocative not only for his rich detailed descriptions, but also because he foresees the future violence and civil unrest that will plague that country for many years after his visit.

What Tocqueville witnessed in Ireland was abject poverty, which was different and more shocking than anything he had ever seen in England or anywhere else for that matter. He saw people living in disgusting conditions with no hope of ever bettering their lot in life. His notes are replete with vivid descriptions of how miserable life is for the vast majority of the Irish people. In brief, the situation was one where a few wealthy property owners, who were overwhelmingly British, owned the incredibly fertile and productive land.[70] Through time, the property owners evicted nearly all of the small farmers and converted their land to large farms.[71] Most of the wealthy landowners lived in England and spent their money there also. Therefore, while they reaped significant financial benefits from the fertile Irish land and cheap peasant labor, they invested nothing back into Ireland.[72] One cannot overlook the religious component to this because Catholics could not own land before 1782.[73] In addition, while they could own land by the time Tocqueville is writing, Protestants still owned the majority of Irish land. In 1835 then, what one finds is a small minority of wealthy Protestants and a large oppressed Catholic population who live in absolute poverty. As Tocqueville noted, "There is an upper class and a lower class. The middle class evidently does not exist; or at least it is confined to towns as in the middle ages."[74]

Tocqueville was shocked by the number of people who were literally starving to death. Unlike England, Ireland had no public aid so one inferior potato harvest could result in widespread famine. On the verge of starvation, the poor were so desperate for food that they would dig up the new harvest when the potatoes were not as large as nuts. This effort did nothing to curb their hunger because it only had the effect of making them terribly ill.[75] In one of his most descriptive passages, Tocqueville writes about his visit to the Poorhouse in Dublin where 1,800 to 2,000 paupers gathered daily. He said that the sight inside was "the most hideous and disgusting aspect of destitution."[76] In the following passage, he describes how the poor gather food.

> On leaving there [the Poorhouse] we came upon a small covered wheelbarrow pushed by two paupers. This wheelbarrow goes to the doors of the houses of the rich; into it is thrown the remains of the meals, and this debris is brought to the poorhouse to make the soup.[77]

While in the first *Memoir*, Tocqueville favored private charity and provided a harsh critique of public aid, it was immediately clear to him that the immensity of the problem in Ireland could not be solved by private charity. Besides, where was the charity to come from when the vast majority of the wealthy refused to have any dealings whatsoever with the poor? The poor hated and distrusted the aristocracy and in return, the wealthy felt no compassion for them.[78] Only a few days into his trip, Tocqueville observed there was no moral tie between the rich and poor in Ireland.[79] In one of his conversations, the priest tells him "It is the poor who support the poor."[80]

Regarding the poor there are several provocative aspects of this piece in light of his other writings about poverty. The first is Tocqueville's preoccupation with land distribution. In a conversation with William Murphy, a wealthy Catholic merchant in Dublin, they discuss where land might be found to help the poor have a better life. Tocqueville first asks if there is uncultivated land available and if so, would the poor be willing to relocate. Murphy responds that such land exists, but it is owned by the wealthy. He adds that the poor would relocate if it became available because of their desperation. Tocqueville says that this is "the most complete proof that one could give of the wretchedness of the population."[81] He then wonders whether or not a larger number of people could live in greater comfort in the same space if the large landed estates were divided.[82] Murphy responds that the division of land is unlikely since the poor do not have any money to buy it. Owners would only get a good price if they sold the entire parcel.[83] Tocqueville makes a note, which states, "It is the opposite in France. A difference that ought to be well considered."[84] In another meeting, he returns to the issue of landed property and he asks Thomas Kelly, who is a Protestant, "Is it true that the Irish landlords squeeze the agricultural population to the extent of almost depriving them of their means of living?"[85] Kelly says yes and since there are few, if any, alternatives for individuals to make a living, the poor must rely on agriculture.[86] Finally, in a conversation with Bishop Edward Nolan, Tocqueville returns to the subject of landed property and thinking about the division of landed property in France, he makes a note in his journal that reads, "Clear advantage here of the laws that divide up landed estates."[87]

A second intriguing aspect of this work is Tocqueville's moral assessment of the Irish poor and wealthy. Throughout the trip, he asks about the poor's morality.[88] In spite of the ubiquitous poverty in Ireland, theft is rare and the poor only steal food when they are desperate.[89] Moreover, there are extremely few illegitimate births along with a low incidence of adultery.[90] Drunkenness can be a problem among the poor since it is sometimes accompanied by violence, and he is concerned about their lack of respect for the law.[91] He notes that the poor man "seeks in violence a support that he cannot find in the law."[92] Thus, he acknowledges the lack of justice and fairness in the legal system. Critics of the poor point to their lack of foresight and planning.[93] Tocqueville comments on how his reaction to idleness in Ireland cannot be one of indignation because he knows that it is lack of employment and not laziness.[94] Moreover, he notes that good morals and modesty do not always go together. He observes how the Irish are not nearly as conscientious about covering their bodies as the English, yet they have purer morals and much lower illegitimate birth rates.[95] Indeed, Tocqueville directs his moral indignation toward the wealthy. The Irish aristocracy imitates the English, according to him, but they do not have the same attitude and spirit toward freedom for the lower classes.[96] During several of his interviews and conversations, it becomes clear to him that the rich care little about the poor, or for that matter, Ireland. As a direct result of his visit, he realizes that it is not always the case that the poor are to be blamed for their poverty. In fact, just the opposite is true in Ireland, because it is the wealthy, not the poor, who Tocqueville holds responsible for the widespread poverty.

His journal entry ends with a discussion about the chilling prospect of civil war since there is no separation between politics and religion. Tocqueville knew that the tyranny of the few not only politically, but also economically, could not sustain itself in Ireland. This latter fact combined with the omnipotent influence of the Catholic clergy left him with great concern for Ireland's future. Thus, he was sensitive to the injustices and believed that the poor deserved much better. Because of the injustice, which permeated Ireland's legal, political, and economic structures, he predicted a future of civil strife for Ireland. In addition to the religious divisions, Ireland was a society divided between rich and poor with no middle class. Plato and Aristotle warned of the conflict that accompanies this state of affairs. In fact, Aristotle favors a large middle class because it is the mean and thus provides stability for the state. Adam Smith warned that no society could be happy or flourishing where the bulk of the citizenry are poor. Moreover, like Rousseau's critiques of the wealthy, Tocqueville puts the blame squarely on them for the destitution in Ireland.

One can also see that Tocqueville's work captures the inherent tensions in liberal theory. On the one hand, there is an uncompromising commitment to private property and minimal government intervention. On the other hand, there is a belief that it is unjust to allow human beings to die for want of food or shelter. When people lack subsistence or the ability to care for themselves, Tocqueville, like Locke, agrees that government must act to promote their welfare or else violate God's law to promote the preservation of humankind. One may remember, however, that Adam Smith never viewed poverty as being a serious threat to human life in capitalist societies since material inequality did not justify government intervention. It is ironic that Locke and Tocqueville, who share negative views of the poor's character, believe that public aid may be justified in some cases, while Smith, who views the poor as hard working and frugal, rejects public aid altogether.

As we shall see, John Stuart Mill, much like Tocqueville, looks at the paradox of poverty in the midst of the richest and most powerful nation in the world. As we turn to Mill, one will see how the historical context and thus empirical influences causes him to agree often with Tocqueville. This is especially true in his conclusions about the causes and possible approaches to reducing poverty. It is somewhat surprising that they strongly disagree about the role of private charity and public aid.

JOHN STUART MILL

Mill says in his *Autobiography* that he never accepted half solutions or abandoned difficult problems.[97] This is certainly true of his preoccupation with the problem of poverty. Throughout his writings, he repeatedly discusses the causes and possible solutions. Indeed, Mill's first argumentative essay was a piece that denied the wealthy's superiority in moral qualities when compared to those of the poor.[98] The story of his rigorous education under the tutelage of his father is well known. Mill writes about how his father, James Mill, emphasized logic and analysis, instead of feelings or emotions, to justify one's ethical conduct.[99] He wants to bring this logic and philosophical analysis to the subject of poverty since he laments that "sentimentality rather than common sense" dominates discussions about the poor.[100] Some people, he says, have characterized his views as "hard hearted" and "anti-population" because he wants evidence to analyze problems before he comes to conclusions.[101] To understand Mill's social and political philosophy, one must first know that he distinguishes between two schools of philosophy. He says that one relies on intuition, which treats feelings and ideas about human nature as intuitive truths that come from God, laws of nature, or some higher authority than reason. Those who follow intuition ignore empirical evidence. The second school relies on empirical evidence and uses reason to understand and solve social problems. The latter school knows that differences in circumstances produce different results. Mill believes that the way in which one approaches social problems has profound practical implications. These different orientations to understanding the world and human beings lay at the heart of all the greatest differences in opinion.[102] In fact, Mill says, this rejection of reason and empirical evidence is the principal impediment to the rational treatment of significant social questions. Thus, it is also the greatest obstacle to human improvement.

Mill's notion of justice is concerned with utility or the Greatest Happiness Principle.[103] An action is right provided it maximizes human welfare. While individuals always act to maximize their own pleasure, Mill believes that maximizing general human welfare can be among the pleasures they seek. Not all pleasures are equal because Mill thinks there are differences in the kind of pleasures one pursues. He divides pleasures by whether one uses her higher faculties, which are intellect, imagination, feeling, and the moral sentiments or the lower faculties, which deal with satisfying bodily needs. The aim is for human beings to order their faculties (that is, higher and lower) appropriately so that they may have a happy life.[104] It is not too strong to say that Mill believed that individuals *ought* to maximize human beings' welfare. He admired moralists such as Jesus and Socrates and believed that reading about them helped to improve one's own morality. Mill derives moral rules by applying this principle of utility to empirical information. As John Rawls states, "Justice is not an independent separate standard along side of and possibly having greater weight contrary to the principle of utility. Instead, it is a derivative from it."[105] In *Utilitarianism*, Mill says the following about justice:

> While I dispute the pretensions of any theory which sets up an imaginary standard of justice not grounded on utility, I account the justice which is grounded on utility to be the chief part, and incomparably the most sacred and binding part, of all morality. Justice is a name for certain classes of moral rules, which concern the essentials of human well-being more nearly and are therefore of more absolute obligation, than any other rules for the guidance of life; and the notion which we have found to be the essence of the idea of justice, that of a right residing in an individual, implies and testifies to this more binding obligation.[106]

Using empirical evidence and the principle of utility, Mill thinks there are solutions to end poverty. According to him, "Poverty, in any sense implying suffering, may be completely extinguished by the wisdom of society, combined with good sense and providence of individuals."[107]

Like Tocqueville, Mill says that understanding the paradox of poverty in a rich and industrious community is one of the most important and fundamental questions in political economy.[108] He believes that the populace is unwilling to confront, or even discuss, the real causes of poverty.[109] Since Mill was a liberal who as a utilitarian was interested in promoting the greatest happiness for the greatest number, it is not surprising that he put great emphasis on individual responsibility and self-control. Without moral and intellectual education, individuals, and thus society, would never be able to achieve its potential.

Daniel Rauhut argues that Mill believes there are four causes that explain poverty. He says:

> To sum up, Mill pointed at four causes of poverty; (1) the primitive instincts to reproduce in large numbers; (2) the inability of the poor to understand, due to lacking intelligence and a low moral cultivation, what is good for them at an aggregate level; (3) a too numerous labour force creates a hard competition for each vacancy, which, in turn, press down the wages; and (4) the poor relief system in itself contained mechanisms for keeping the poor in poverty.[110]

While Mill examines all of these issues, one could argue that he believes the root cause of poverty is the poor and wealthy's lack of self-control. For example, overpopulation, which results from lack of self-restraint, creates a large labor force. In turn, this creates a glut of workers among the laboring class thus driving down wages. Mill's criticisms of public aid are the same as his critique of communism. He worries that both create dependence on state support, causing individuals to lose their motivation to work or to practice self-restraint in marriage and having children.[111] Communism, however, may be more effective in promoting self-restraint since the power of public opinion against "selfish intemperance" may be decisive.[112] Again, one can see that his concern is self-control because the greatest problem that public aid causes is that it removes the motives for self-restraint.[113] In fact, when one reads Mill, one cannot help but think of Plato's theory of the tripartite soul. Like Plato, Mill advocates that reason should be in control of the appetites. This not only applies to the poor, but to all classes. Like Aristotle, Mill acknowledges how the accident of birth influences one's circumstances. In turn, those circumstances help to form one's character.[114] This is especially true for women, who are victims of an accident of gender.[115] That Mill would appeal to ideas of the Ancients is not surprising since he says that reading *Plutarch's*

Lives and Plato's writings about Socrates greatly influenced him.[116] In this section, I explore Mill's treatment of poverty focusing on his views about self-restraint, public aid, private charity, and finally, his policy recommendations for relieving indigence.

The Power of Self-Control

In Book Two chapter 8, of *Principles of Political Economy*, Mill says, "Poverty, like most social evils, exists because men follow their brute instincts without due consideration."[117] Indeed, he believes that many, if not most problems in society result from human beings' lack of self-control. That is to say, poor and rich alike allow their appetites to pursue things such as sex, money, material goods, and alcohol with no regard to the consequences of their behavior. Regarding the poor, this conduct leads to disastrous results not only for them, but also for the rest of society. In fact, he says that without self-control, it will be impossible to improve the lives of the poor.[118]

Mill's chief complaint about the poor's lack of self-restraint is that it leads to hasty and ill-advised marriages followed by high birth rates among men who cannot support themselves much less their wives and children. That he would focus on population control is not surprising since as was mentioned earlier, it was the age of Malthusianism. Himmelfarb says that Mill was a "strict Malthusian." One must be cautious, however, about equating him with all of Malthus's beliefs because Mill did not have the same grim and catastrophic view of society's future.[119] While he was not committed to communism nor strict *laissez-faire* policies, he is more optimistic in his outlook for humankind than Malthus, yet less so than Adam Smith. Himmelfarb explains that Malthus never approved of any "artificial or unnatural" type of birth control because he believed in moral restraint to control birth rates. By the 1860s, population control came to be called "Malthusianism" and later it was called "Neo-Malthusianism." The latter more accurately describes Mill's views.[120] Thus if one calls Mill a committed Malthusian, it should be understood in light of his advocacy of population and birth control in general.

One of the main reasons that he was so concerned about high birth rates was because of its depressing effect on the labor market. Fierce competition among a glut of laborers drives wages down and this in turn leads to poverty.[121] If the government were to guarantee employment with generous wages to everyone born, then any motivation for self-restraint would be removed and other methods of restraint would have to be enforced.[122] Perhaps the government, as a matter of survival, would have to legislate that births would not be allowed without its consent. Mill suggests that it may become necessary for the English to look to the Germans, who control marriage by restricting it among those who cannot support themselves. Individuals who have children but are unable to support them should face severe penalties.[123] The upshot of this discussion is that Mill adamantly believes that population control is fundamental to securing full employment at high wages for the working class.[124]

As mentioned earlier, Mill is an empiricist who believes that evidence and reason are paramount to solving social problems such as poverty. Therefore, it is no surprise that he indicts religion, along with morality, and leadership as culprits that have contributed to the population problem by encouraging early marriages, which in turn lead to pregnancies.[125] Like Tocqueville, Mill observes how much control the Catholic clergy has over the poor, and how their encouragement for the poor to marry to prevent premarital sex contributes to the problem. Blinded by religious prejudices, the poor and rich alike look upon children as being sent by God and thus both groups abdicate their responsibility to discuss the subject rationally.[126] In his *Autobiography*, Mill says that he never believed in religion.[127] Moreover, he argues that religion serves as a great hindrance to rationally addressing social issues and as a result, it impedes humankind's development. Finally, he says that if it is possible for the unmarried to abstain from sex, then it is also possible for married individuals to do the same. Instead, he says, they act as if they have no control and it is simply God's will that they have children.[128]

As a feminist, Mill believes that birth control would help contribute to the emancipation of women. Since women seldom have any choice about becoming pregnant, he says they would welcome the idea since it would not only relieve them from the physical suffering but also the "intolerable domestic drudgery" that results from having so many children.[129] While he held onto commonplace ideas about the traditional family and the separate spheres, that is, women rear children and keep house while men work outside the home to earn a living, he at least acknowledged the difficult physical and mental aspects of childbirth.[130] After all, one's social class corresponded to the type of care a woman received during childbirth. Poor women and their infants had much higher mortality rates than wealthy women. Whereas wealthy women had the luxury of bed rest for much of their pregnancies, poor women did not even have the comfort of sterile conditions when they gave birth. It was during this time that puerperal fever, which was an infection that was fatal to women and infants, was an epidemic throughout England and other parts of Europe.[131] Poor women risked their life with every pregnancy.

Mill's critical statements about individuals' lack of self-restraint in society are not limited to the poor. He is just as severe in evaluating the rich. In his *Autobiography*, Mill clearly states his views about the aristocracy:

> I thought the predominance of the aristocratic classes, the noble, and the rich, in the English Constitution, an evil worth any struggle to get rid of; not on account of taxes, or any such comparatively small inconvenience, but as the great demoralizing agency in the country.[132]

The wealthy are immoral because they put selfish interests above the common good. Hereditary or acquired riches are the "chief passport" to political power in England, and the rich abuse their powers to legislate for their advantages. Moreover, the wealthy commit their entire lives to pursuing wealth. They fail to see that it is in their interest to educate the poor since Mill says that the wealthy have much more to fear from them when uneducated, than when educated.[133]

In many ways, Mill is Lockean in his beliefs about property with one important exception. Mill believes that one should take into account the accident of birth. Thus, he wants to level the playing field to some degree by limiting the number of enormous fortunes.[134] The law of primogeniture, entitling the eldest son to the exclusive right of inheritance, violates the general principles of justice because it is based on the accident of birth. Besides, unearned wealth can damage one's character.[135] There are also economic considerations because Mill believes this law leads to imprudence among the large landowners who tend to be ostentatious and guilty of conspicuous consumption.[136] As a result, they end up mortgaging their properties to pay their expenses. This increases the land's value, which in turn creates a new class of property owners. Mill believes that a large middle class is advantageous to a healthy society. Instead of large concentrations of wealth held by the few, with the poor envying their riches, he thinks it is far better if no one is rich or poor. In that respect, he follows Plato, Aristotle, and Rousseau. These beliefs lead Mill to endorse the idea of a progressive inheritance tax levied on the recipient of the inheritance. One could avoid this tax by dispersing one's wealth among several instead of leaving it to the eldest son. It is important to note here that Mill did not favor a progressive income tax because it would be unfair and penalize those who work hard and save money.[137] This would be tantamount to penalizing individuals who showed self-restraint by saving instead of consuming.

This brings us to his idea of the stationary state, which is basically a no growth economy.[138] Mill says that contrary to Adam Smith's beliefs, this is an attractive state of affairs because,

I confess I am not charmed with the ideal of life held out by those who think that the normal state of human beings is that of struggling to get on; that the trampling, crushing, elbowing, and treading on each others' heels, which form the existing type of social life, are the most desirable lot of human kind, or anything but the disagreeable symptoms of one of the phases of industrial progress.[139]

He believes that the ideal state for human beings is when there are no poor but no one desires to be richer.[140] Thus, he does not find it wise for a country continually to increase its production so that those who are already richer than anyone needs to be consume more for the sole purpose of showing off their wealth.[141] Obviously, he is concerned about the negative effects that acquisitive ethos has on individuals and societies over time. The incessant desire and quest for more material possessions destroy individuals' characters and lessen their inclinations toward self-restraint. In addition, he says that it is saving, and not spending, that enriches a country.[142] It comes as no surprise that Mill supports sumptuary taxes. He believes that these taxes will never affect those who buy only the necessities. It is not that he begrudges those who have money to indulge themselves with luxuries. The problem is that individuals desire luxuries not for their personal enjoyment, but because they are vain and wish to impress others.[143]

Ireland illustrates the irresponsible selfishness of the rich. Mill says that one would think that the property owners in Ireland out of concern for justice or just from good sense would not take advantage of the competition for land. They are not unique; he says because, "it is never safe to expect that a class or body of men will act in opposition to their pecuniary interest."[144] Indeed, for the most part Mill blamed the aristocrats for the deplorable situation in Ireland. Not only did they exploit the peasants with their high rents, but they also denied the Irish justice because they controlled the legal systems.[145] Interestingly, Mill said, "It is not about the power of the Protestant over the Catholic, which has made Ireland what she is, it is about the power of the rich over the poor."[146]

Kinzer's work on Mill's involvement with the Irish question shows just how much antipathy he held toward the aristocracy. That he came to this position is no surprise since his father, James Mill, took every opportunity to reproach the rich for their selfishness and lack of public spiritedness. One can sense the younger Mill's pride when he writes about his father's public censuring of the nobility.[147] Writing in the *Morning Chronicle* in 1846, Mill berates Parliament for doing nothing for the poor while always doing something for the rich.[148] While he favored peasant proprietorship in Ireland as a matter of distributive justice, he was skeptical of legalized aid to the poor.

Public Aid and Private Charity

The claim one makes for help out of destitution is one of the strongest moral claims that can be made according to Mill. Desperate situations, such as when an individual is suffering from starvation, demand that society do whatever is necessary to relieve the destitution.[149] That being said, he had little good to say about legal aid or England's Poor Laws. Mill's chief fear is that individuals become dependent on public aid. In fact, he is so concerned about the loss of economic independence among the needy that he says the negative effects of aid may well outweigh any good that comes from it.[150] Much like Tocqueville, he wonders why an individual would be motivated to work if he could live as well as his neighbor without working. Additionally, he thinks public aid encourages the poor to continue to have large numbers of children since they can live well on public aid. This is especially true when parishes provide aid based on the number of children in the family.[151] Finally, the poor will never learn self-restraint or good judgment if the government does too much for them.[152] Interestingly, he thinks that the greater the need for subsistence, the more likely individuals will become dependent. As a result, Mill says the problem is "how to give the greatest amount of needful help, with the smallest encouragement to undue reliance on it."[153] Given Mill's views about public aid, it is curious that Fleischacker says, "John Stuart Mill was a prominent advocate of government programs to aid the poor."[154] Fleischacker's statement is misleading because as we shall see, Mill does think it is only fair to give aid to the poor since even criminals are supported by the government. He based his limited support for public aid on reason and logic. It is safe to say that he strongly opposed government-sponsored aid for the poor but given the situation, it was rational and just to provide some government aid.

If individuals are truly needy, Mill thinks it necessary to give them hope because if there is no hope, they may give up and become completely dependent forever. If public aid is to be provided, then the poor should continue to use their skills, to develop their prudence, and to work while getting this help. When public aid is distributed in this manner, it offers hope without creating dependency.[155] This is what Mill hoped would result from the Poor Law Reforms of 1834. The idea was to give enough aid to keep people from starving but not enough to make them comfortable. If the conditions of those receiving public aid are less desirable than those who work for their living, he thinks this will motivate those receiving aid to seek a better life. In addition, under the reform, outside aid was severely limited so that the vast majority who received aid would have to go to the workhouses to get it. Mill strongly supported this revision.

His beliefs about private charity are provocative. At first reading, one can match Mill and Tocqueville's critique of public aid and private charity point for point. One will remember that Tocqueville thought that private charity should be the primary source for poor relief. He emphasizes private charity because he thinks it creates a moral tie between the rich and poor, and it would not create the debilitating dependency that public aid engendered. Mill says that private charity is problematic for three reasons; first, charity almost always does too much or too little; second, since the government provides for the criminal poor, justice demands that it must do the same for those who are innocent; and third, if the poor are left to depend on charity, then a lot of deception will take place.[156] Mill views the role for private charity as one of supplementing public aid. That is to say, private charity should give more to those who really need or deserve it. Since the government must act according to general rules, it should not distinguish between the deserving and undeserving poor. Like Tocqueville, Mill thinks that the poor guardians and overseers are neither qualified nor motivated to discern between those who truly deserve aid and those who do not. To allow those administering aid to make judgments based on their views about the poor's morality is irrational. Private charity can make those judgments and thus Mill says this is their "peculiar role and appropriate province."[157] Most importantly, however, he does not think it is just to make the poor depend on the rich. This sharply contrasts with Tocqueville's belief that dependence on private charity creates moral ties between rich and poor. Perhaps, Mill's view is connected to his feminist beliefs since he finds it a "flagrant social injustice" that women must depend upon their husbands for their livelihood.[158] Since women are without legal standing and the rights of inheritance, they are completely dependent upon men for their welfare. This is the second time that his views about the subjection of women informed his convictions about how the poor ought to be treated. He also believed that reducing the number of births among the poor would greatly benefit women.

Mill's Proposals to Reduce Poverty

Mill's beliefs about the causes of poverty lead him to believe that universal education, population control, some redistribution of property, and colonization are the most effective means to reduce it. Most important of all is universal education because without it nothing will be successful. As an empiricist, Mill emphasizes the role of education because it helps to develop an enlightened populous, which will be more likely to exercise self-restraint to control unhealthy urges. The chief aims of universal education should be to develop individuals' common sense and judgment. Anything else that an individual gains from it is extra.[159] Once individuals become educated, they will act as a check on each other's behavior since the enlightened will have less tolerance for shortsighted and irresponsible conduct. For example, he believes that if public opinion turned against the working class having large families it could be extremely effective in controlling the population.[160]

Mill argues that it is impossible to educate individuals who are living in severe poverty. To remedy this, he makes the radical proposal that government must alleviate poverty for an entire generation.[161] The idea is that once individuals become accustomed to comfortable lives, they will not want to return to poverty. To this end, he proposes that the English government should provide public financing for colonization. Instead of using public money for aid to the poor, it makes more sense to help to establish them in a systematic program of colonization.[162] Second, he wants to use all English common land that had been brought into cultivation under the General Enclosure Act to establish small proprietors. Like Tocqueville, Mill thinks that property ownership is also fundamental to solving the problem. The idea is to provide five-acre plots to the poor along with the tools, manure, and in some cases, enough subsistence to get them by until their land becomes productive. The desire for this land would be so great that it would positively influence the poor to control their behavior.[163]

The nineteenth century saw rapid expansion of European colonialism with Great Britain being the dominant colonial power. That fact, combined with the economic success of the American colonies and his desire for opportunities for the poor, convinced Mill that creating new colonies would be one of the most effective measures to relieve poverty in England and Ireland. The reclamation of wastelands in Ireland and common land use in England were additional strategies to provide land and to create hope among the poor. He knew that both of these policies were not overnight solutions. In fact, Mill says that it would take at least a generation for them to relieve indigence.[164] One may remember that Aristotle had similar ideas to alleviate poverty. Since his aim was to create the environment where a large middle class would flourish, he advocated population control. He also believed in providing the poor with what they needed to be productive. As empiricists, they were acutely aware of the complexity of the problem so both Aristotle and Mill were pragmatists who wanted sensible solutions.

Early on, Mill found the idea of communism provocative but in *Principles of Political Economy*, he says that no one has enough information to know if it would be a viable system.[165] He believed that many criticisms of it were grossly exaggerated, often unfounded, and thus unfair.[166] His chief concern was its compatibility with freedom. He did not think that exchanging comforts for liberty was a rational choice.[167] Some types of socialism, such as "Fourierism" were more appealing to him and he believed that they should be tried on a limited basis because they may lead to a better society. For the meantime and into the near future, however, Mill says that one should accept that the system of private property would prevail.[168]

That being said, Mill is critical of capitalist states for creating barriers for some, while removing them unfairly for others. While the accident of birth meant that individuals had different starts in life, the system of private property "purposely fostered inequalities and prevented all from starting fair in the race."[169] He says the poor are forced to take the most offensive jobs yet they make the least amount of money. Salaries are unjust when compared to the amount and type of work individuals perform in capitalist societies.[170] One can reasonably say that it was probably a combination of his marriage to Harriett Taylor and his advancing years that caused him to say in his *Autobiography*, that he and his wife could be classified as socialists.[171] As Stephen Nathanson says, one should remember that while they may have approved of the idea in theory, the question about how to unite socialism with the greatest individual liberty remained.[172] In a memorable passage, Mill addresses his and Harriet Taylor's beliefs:

> While we repudiated with the greatest energy that tyranny of society over the individual which most Socialistic systems are supposed to involve, we yet look forward to a time when society will no longer be divided into the idle and the industrious; when the rule that they who do not work shall not eat, will be applied not to paupers only, but impartially to all; when the division of the produce of labour, instead of depending, as in so great a degree it now does, on the accident of birth, will be made by concert on an acknowledged principle of justice; and when it will no longer either be, or be thought to be, impossible for human beings to exert themselves strenuously in procuring benefits which are not to be exclusively their own, but to be shared with the society they belong to.[173]

While he articulates more forceful than ever, his and Harriett's penchant for socialism, it is not a new sentiment. Throughout his life, he believed that human beings were capable of caring for each other and the common good, and thereby demonstrating their ability for self-control for the public good.[174] As an empiricist, he believed that different economies and societal structures could be tried on an experimental bases since that is how progress is made.

The problem of poverty and what justice demands from individuals and government figure prominently in Tocqueville and Mill's respective works. With so many poor in the midst of such great wealth, both men recognize the perplexities and challenges that impoverishment presents to governments. It is also clear that what concerns them is absolute poverty and not relative poverty. This is why both theorists find the abject poverty in Ireland disturbing and unjust. Tocqueville and Mill indict the rich landowners in Ireland since they show no self-restraint in their greed and care nothing for the common good. Justice demands that the British government intervene and find land so that the Irish can at least raise food for their own survival. Mill supports reclamation of wastelands while Tocqueville believes that the government should follow the French and outlaw huge land holdings. Increased property ownership figures prominently as one of their proposals not only for the Irish, but also for the poor elsewhere.

Mill points to the injustice inherent in a system where the rich control the legal system and thus have enormous power over the poor. The power that the rich held over the poor was unjust, and while Mill did not like the idea of public aid because it created dependency, he realized that justice demanded intervention. This is so because there is a need to level the playing field so that the poor may have a fair start in a competitive and demanding economic system such as capitalism. Like Aristotle, he takes into account that through no fault of their own some individuals are either born into poverty or become poor because of myriad reasons that are truly beyond their control. Thus, Mill advocates for universal education, and the unique idea that the government invest to raise significantly the living standards of the poor for at least a generation. When they get used to the higher standard of living, the poor will become more industrious because they will fear returning to poverty. Again, like Aristotle he believes that the state must supply the poor with land, tools, and other necessities so that they can get out of poverty. If the cycle of poverty is not broken with positive programs to encourage self-sufficiency there is no chance of ever making progress toward solving the problem. This is not only just it is also the rational approach toward addressing the problem.

Excluding the Irish situation, Tocqueville places his hope for solutions in private charity while Mill places his greatest hope in universal education. That they agreed on so many points makes it all the more provocative that when it came to private charity they disagreed. Tocqueville lauded the dependence and subservience that the poor should show toward those who had the means to help them. He believed it created moral ties that would reduce the antagonism between rich and poor. In contrast, Mill did not think it just for the poor to have to depend on private means for their survival. He abhorred treating the poor as children. No doubt, his work on behalf of women's rights reinforced his belief that no human being should have to depend on others for charity, since there are no guarantees that the wealthy will feel either benevolence or compassion toward the poor. Private charity, Mill argued, should supplement government aid since justice demands that the government treat all equally and do away with categories of deserving and undeserving. While government cannot make these judgments, private individuals can and thus, they can provide more money to those who are deemed to need more help.

Tocqueville and Mill's logic and empirical approaches make for compelling arguments because what justice demands is that individuals and politicians avoid irresponsible sentimental approaches to this serious problem. Likewise, denouncing the poor and putting all the blame on them was no solution either since both held the rich responsible as well because both groups lacked self-restraint. Echoing an earlier empiricist, Aristotle, Mill and Tocqueville do not think government aid is the solution. Instead, they want to understand the root causes of poverty, which will lead to pragmatic policy proposals to alleviate it.

As we turn to Hegel and Marx, we will see two political theorists who like Tocqueville and Mill spend a lot of time thinking and writing about poverty. Hegel worries about poverty and struggles to understand and find solutions to alleviate it. Unlike Hegel, Marx believes that he has a clear grasp on the causes of poverty as well as the solutions. While both take into account the empirical circumstances, they offer distinct interpretations about the demands of justice and poverty.

NOTES

1. Gertrude Himmelfarb, *The Idea of Poverty* (New York: Albert A. Knopf, 1984), 153.

2. Ibid., 159.

3. Thomas R. Malthus, *An Essay on the Principle of Population*, with an Introduction by Geoffrey Gilbert (New York: Oxford University Press, Reissue Edition, 1999).

4. Himmelfarb, *Idea of Poverty*, 127. The issue of peasant proprietorships illustrates their differences. Bruce Kinzer says that while Mill was an advocate for peasant proprietorships, Malthus was against them. Bruce L. Kinzer, *England's Disgrace?: J .S. Mill and the Irish Question* (Toronto: University of Toronto Press, Incorporated, 2001), 53.

5. Stephen Nathanson, "Editor's Introduction" to John Stuart Mill, *Principles of Political Economy with Some of Their Applications to Social Philosophy*. Abridged (Indianapolis: Hackett Publishing Company, Inc., 2004), xxiv–xxv.

6. Ibid., xxv.

7. Sarah Lyall, "Past as Prologue: Blair Faults Britain in Irish Potato Blight," *New York Times*, page 3, June 3, 1997.

8. Ibid., 3

9. Kinzer, *England's Disgrace?: J. S. Mill and the Irish Question*, 3–4.

10. John Stuart Mill, *Autobiography of John Stuart Mill*, with preface by John Jacob Coss (New York: Colombia University Press, 1944), 163 and 165, hereafter cited as *Autobiography*.

11. Ibid., 163.

12. John Stuart Mill, *Principles of Political Economy*, in *Collected Works of John Stuart Mill, Principles of Political Economy*, vols 2, 3 ed. J. M. Robson (Indianapolis: The Liberty Fund, 2006), 314–315. Future references hereafter cited as *PPE* with the volume and page numbers.

13. *Autobiography*, 206.

14. Alan S. Kahan, *Aristocratic Liberalism* (New York: Oxford University Press, 1992), 3. Kahan's study includes Jacob Burkhart in addition to Mill and Tocqueville.

15. Ibid., 5.

16. Alexis deTocqueville, *Journeys to England and Ireland*, trans. George Lawrence and K. Mayer, ed. J. Mayer (London: 1958).

17. Alexis de Tocqueville, *Memoir on Pauperism*, trans. Seymour Drescher with an introduction by Gertrude Himmelfarb (Chicago: Ivan R. Dee, 1997). Referenced hereafter as *MP*.

18. Ibid., 37–39.

19. Ibid., 39.

20. Ibid., 40.

21. Ibid., 40.

22. Ibid., 41–42.

23. Ibid., 42.

24. Ibid., 42–43.

25. Ibid., 43–44.

26. Ibid., 44.

27. Ibid., 44.

28. Ibid., 45.

29. Unlike Locke, Tocqueville's religious beliefs are not clear. On this point, I follow McClendon's conclusion that Tocqueville was an admirer of religion but was probably an agnostic. Michael McClendon, "Tocqueville, Jansenism, and the Psychology of Freedom," *American Journal of Political Science* 50, no.3 (July 2006): 664–75.

30. *MP*, 45.

31. Ibid., 46. Rousseau and Smith share Tocqueville's idea of human perfectibility, which is typical of the Enlightenment period. Smith says, "Nature, however, when she implanted the seeds of this irregularity in the human breast, seems, as upon all other occasions, to have intended the happiness and perfection of the species," *TMS* II.iii.3: 152.

32. Second *Discourse,* 45.

33. *MP*, 45–46.

34. Ibid., 48.

35. Second *Discourse*, 63.

36. *MP*, 49.

37. Ibid., 50.

38. Ibid., 72.

39. Ibid., 50.

40. Ibid., 51.

41. Ibid., 51–53.

42. Ibid., 54–55.

43. Ibid., 56.

44. Ibid., 57.

45. Ibid., 58.

46. Ibid., 58.

47. Ibid., 58.

48. Ibid., 58.

49. Ibid., 58.

50. Ibid., 59.

51. Ibid., 60.

52. Ibid., 62, 70.

53. Ibid., 69.

54. Ibid., 69.

55. Ibid., 69.

56. Ibid., 470–71.

57. M. J. Daunton, *Progress and Poverty: An Economic and Social History of Britain, 1700–1850* (Oxford: Oxford University Press, 1995), 468.

58. *MP*, 69.

59. Ibid., 69–70.

60. Ibid., 71–72.

61. Ibid., 72.

62. Alexis de Tocqueville, *Second Mémoire Sur Le Paupérisme*, *Oeuvres Complètes, Tome XVI*, ed., J. Mayer (Paris, 1990), 140–57, hereafter referred to as *SM*.

63. *SM*, 146.

64. Ibid, 153–56.

65. DiNitto, *Social Welfare: Politics and Public Policy*, 80.

66. Daunton, *Progress and Poverty*, 449.

67. Ibid.

68. Alexis de Tocqueville, *Alexis de Tocqueville's Journey to Ireland*, ed., trans., and with introduction by Emmet Larkin (Washington, D.C.: Catholic University Press, 1990), 147.

69. Ibid., 7.

70. Ibid., 29.

71. Ibid., 40.

72. Ibid., 29.

73. Ibid., 53.

74. Ibid., 51.

75. Ibid., 131.

76. Ibid., 24–25.

77. Ibid., 7.

78. Ibid., 134.

79. Ibid., 29, 40.

80. Ibid., 78–79, 134.

81. Ibid., 23.

82. Ibid., 22–23.

83. Ibid., 24.

84. Ibid., 24.

85. Ibid., 29.

86. Ibid., 29.

87. Ibid., 40.

88. Ibid., 20, 23, 41, 53, 62, 64, 69, 72, 73, 98, 99.

89. Ibid., 20, 41, 99.

90. Ibid., 99 and 137.

91. Ibid., 41, 72, 82, 98.

92. Ibid., 82.

93. Ibid., 20, 23, 62, 64.

94. Ibid., 112–13.

95. Ibid., 137.

96. Ibid., 89.

97. *Autobiography*, 86.

98. Ibid., 50.

99. Ibid., 77.

100. *PPE*, vol. 2, 351–352.

101. *Autobiography*, 77.

102. Ibid., 191–92.

103. Mill defines it as follows: "The creed which accepts as the foundation of morals, Utility, or the Greatest Happiness Principle, holds that actions are right in proportion as they tend to promote happiness, wrong as they tend to produce the reverse of happiness. By happiness is intended pleasure, and the absence of pain; by unhappiness, pain, and the privation of pleasure." John Stuart Mill, *Utilitarianism*, in *Collected Works of John Stuart Mill, Essays on Ethics, Religion, and Society*, vol. 10, ed. J. M. Robson (Indianapolis: The Liberty Fund, 2006), 210.

104. *Utilitarianism*, 211.

105. Rawls, *Lectures on the History of Political Philosophy*, 272.

106. *Utilitarianism*, 225.

107. Ibid., 216.

108. *PPE*, vol. 2, 173.

109. *Autobiography*, 346.

110. Rauhut, *Economists and Poverty*, 63 and 74.

111. *PPE*, vol. 2, 206.

112. Ibid., vol. 2, 206–207.

113. Ibid., vol 2, 206.

114. *Autobiography*, 119, 162; *PPE*, vol. 2, 207.

115. *PPE*, vol. 3, 765–766.

116. *Autobiography*, 79.

117. *PPE*, vol. 2, 367.

118. Ibid., vol. 2, 354.

119. Himmelfarb, *The Idea of Poverty*, 127.

120. Ibid., 115.

121. *PPE*, vol. 2, 341–344.

122. Ibid., vol. 2, 358–359.

123. Ibid., vol. 2, 347.

124. *Autobiography*, 74.

125. *PPE*, vol. 2, 367–368.

126. Ibid., vol. 2, 369–370.

127. *Autobiography*, 27–34.

128. *PPE*, vol. 2, 369.

129. Ibid., vol. 2, 372.

130. Okin, *Women in Western Political Thought*, 230.

131. Liza Picard, *Dr. Johnson's London* (New York: St. Martin's Griffin, 2000), 96.

132. *Autobiography*, 120.

133. Ibid., 120–21.

134. *PPE*, vol. 3, 754–755.

135. Ibid., vol. 3, 889.

136. Ibid., vol. 3, 890.

137. Ibid., vol. 3, 806–808.

138. Ibid., vol. 3, 738.

139. Ibid., vol. 3, 753–754.

140. Ibid., vol. 3, 754.

141. Ibid., vol. 3, 754–755.

142. Ibid., vol.. 2, 68.

143. Ibid., vol. 2, 869.

144. Ibid., vol. 2, 315.

145. Kinzer, *England's Disgrace?: J. S. Mill and the Irish Question*, 18.

146. John Stuart Mill, *Essays on England, Ireland, and the Empire*, ed., John M. Robson with introduction by Joseph Hamburger (Toronto: University of Toronto Press, 1982), 67.

147. *Autobiography*, 65–66.

148. Kinzer, *England's disgrace?: J. S. Mill and the Irish question*, 51.

149. *PPE*, vol. 3, 960.

150. Ibid., vol. 3, 960.

151. Ibid., vol. 2, 346.

152. Ibid., vol. 3, 943.

153. Ibid., vol. 3, 960–961.

154. Fleischacker, *Short History*, 103.

155. *PPE*, vol. 3, 960–961.

156. Ibid., vol. 3, 962.

157. Ibid., vol. 3, 962.

158. Ibid., vol. 3, 765.

159. Ibid., vol. 2, 375.

160. Ibid., vol. 2, 370–372, 374, 375.

161. Ibid., vol. 2, 375.

162. Ibid., vol. 2, 376.

163. Ibid., vol. 2, 376–377.

164. Ibid., vol. 2, 374–375.
165. Ibid., vol. 2, 213–214.
166. Ibid., vol. 2, 213–214.
167. Ibid., vol. 2, 208–209.
168. Ibid.,vol. 2, 214.
169. Ibid., vol. 2, 207.
170. Ibid., vol. 2, 382–383.
171. *Autobiography*, 162.
172. Nathanson, "Editor's Introduction," xxix–xxx.
173. *Autobiography*, 162.
174. *PPE*, vol. 2, 205.

Chapter Six

Poverty as a Challenge to Capitalism: G. W. F. Hegel and Karl Marx

G. W. F. Hegel and Karl Marx's political theories reflect the great influence that Adam Smith had upon them. Smith wrote *The Wealth of Nations* in 1776 at an early stage of the Industrial Revolution while Hegel's *Philosophy of Right* was published forty-five years later in 1821. Marx wrote during the nineteenth-century heights of it from 1839, when he completed his doctoral dissertation, to his death in 1883. Both philosophers witnessed the expansion of the Industrial Revolution, the free market economy, and European colonialism as well as increased productivity and poverty. Hegel and Marx reject the idea that *laissez-faire* capitalism is capable of reconciling property inequalities with adequate provisions for the excluded. Their grounds for rejecting this theory, however, are quite different.

Hegel accepts many of Smith's views about civil society. He agrees with Smith's portrayal and subsequent effect of self-interested behavior benefitting society. Contrary to Smith, however, he rejects *laissez-faire* because he thought that poverty was an inevitable by-product of a free market economy. Echoing Rousseau and foreshadowing Marx, Hegel says that social forces shape individuals' beliefs about objectivity. This means that that the society one lives in has a tremendous role in conditioning one's perceptions about needs and desires, and thus relative poverty matters. Moreover, poverty in the midst of prosperity creates resentment among the poor who in turn have a negative influence upon the state.

Hegel's idea of justice rests upon his aim to promote individual freedom, which one achieves by being a part of a society based on reason. The historical progression toward freedom begins with individuals having private property. It then advances to the moral realm, which is where individuals recognize the importance of moral norms, and finally, one enters the realm of ethical life when one interacts with others through the institutions of the family, civil society, and the state. The aim is to bring together the individual will and the universal will so that one may be free. Hegel wants to reconcile the separation of civil society from the political state because he believes it causes basic social divisions, which in turn hinders historical progress. Institutions that stand above and outside civil society are necessary to resolve the contradiction between civil society as the sphere of selfish interests and the state as the sphere of public interests. These are the institutions of the estates, the bureaucracy, and hereditary monarchy. Thus, while Hegel agrees with much of Smith's positive portrayal of civil society, he thinks political control is necessary to ensure the rationality of the state and individual freedom. As Peter Singer says, "Hegel finds the unity of individual satisfaction and freedom in the conformity to a social ethos of an organic community."[1]

Arguably, it is reasonable to think that with Hegel's rejection of *laissez-faire* and penchant for state control he would incorporate policies to provide assistance to those who become destitute. Most importantly, one must ask, if his project is to join together individual self-interest and concern for the common good to promote freedom, would it not be reasonable to assume that he should provide some ideas for civil society to alleviate the problem of poverty? While he analyzes the problem of poverty and writes about it with great concern, in the end his treatment of poverty is sorely lacking. Throughout this study, I argue that the demands of justice necessarily entail that the political theorists engage with the problem of poverty with the goal being to suggest some reasonable steps to address it in the context of their political theories. On one hand, Hegel does engage the problem since he spends time explicating the causes with thoughtful analysis. On the other hand, he does not put forth any ideas within the state to deal with the problem. Instead, one finds that the Hegelian state is rather callous to the plight of the poor and thus, fails to answer his demands of justice as a society based on promoting individual freedom.

Karl Marx wants to make radical changes to society by eliminating some of the very institutions that Hegel advocates. He rejects Hegel's conclusions about private property, the family, civil society, and the state's political role. He believes that capitalist economies inevitably lead to class divisions, recurring crises, and the eventual breakdown of the free market itself. He argues that capitalism is based on irreconcilable contradictions. Indeed, the only resolution is through revolution and the establishment of a communist society. Thus for him, views about human nature, the effect of the invisible hand, and the concepts of relative and absolute poverty, are myths that political philosophers use to justify private property ownership and the exploitation of the poor. According to Marx, the idea that human beings have some innate characteristics is absurd. Like Hegel, he believes societies shape individual characters including their ideas about needs and desires. Building upon Rousseau's ideas in the *Second Discourse*, he argues that one must look to civil society to understand human beings. Unlike Rousseau, however, he never claims that human beings are naturally good, since he says that he does not believe in the idea of human nature. Since one cannot create a political theory, however, without some ideas about what one thinks human beings are like and what it means to be human, Marx's political theory leads one to believe that he has a positive view of human nature. The corrupting forces of capitalist society have contributed to the decline of the species. Thus, one may safely say that on the nature/nurture question, he clearly favors the nurture side.

Like Rousseau, Marx writes with great sensitivity and understanding about the poor, but he combines those qualities with both passion and indignation. He, along with Freidrich Engels, not only documents the human suffering that accompanies poverty, but also indicts the entire capitalist system. In this chapter, I show how Marx's polemic skills and command of empirical facts have a potently seductive quality. The problem lies in the fact that after the seduction one is left with sorrow for the poor and a utopian dream. It is the same utopian dream that the Athenian Stranger laments is fit only "for gods or children of gods" in Plato's *Laws*.[2] After exposing the excesses of the capitalist system, Marx offers what appears to be a somewhat alluring alternative to liberalism. While one theorist accused Rousseau of disingenuously seducing his readers with his prose about the suffering of the poor, one could argue that it is Marx's provocative writings that appeal to not only his readers' intellects, but also to their compassion for the less fortunate.[3] Indeed, his writings can inspire and enrage one about the injustices he describes and thus, he forcefully shows the power of philosophy and ideas. He lived by his own admonition to philosophers that they should not aim to interpret the world but to change it.[4]

That being said, one can reasonably ask; was Marx concerned with justice. To be sure, he never describes his project as one of establishing a just state or a just society. On the contrary, he would scoff at the liberal bourgeoisie idea of justice. Yet, surely, he is making the argument that the lower economic classes are treated unfairly. Indeed, he believes that the capitalists exploit the poor and are unjust. Marx argues that not only are the individual capitalists unjust but also the entire free market enterprise including the institutions, processes, and even the basic components of society, such as the family. Admittedly, he never uses the word "justice" but his moral outrage spills forth on page after page and thus, it is clear that he thinks capitalism is unjust and that the poor are on the receiving end of the abuse and exploitation that accompanies the injustices of capitalist societies. As I shall show, Marx's idea of justice is when communism has reached the state where societal arrangements rest upon the following declaration, "From each according to his ability, to each according to his needs!"[5]

In this chapter, I explore Hegel's work and in turn that of Marx. As in earlier chapters, I investigate how they define poverty and what they think are the primary causes for it. This is done in the context of their entire political theories. With that work complete, I turn to their individual prescriptions for alleviating poverty and the central question of this study, which explores the problem of poverty and the demands of justice.

HEGEL

To understand Hegel's treatment of poverty, one must be acquainted with some critical elements of his political theory put forth in his *Elements of the Philosophy of Right*. In the preface to this work, he writes that it is an attempt to "comprehend and portray the state as an inherently rational entity" and not as a project to construct the state, as it ought to be but to show how the state as an ethical universe should be recognized.[6] I argue that Hegel fails to deliver on this promise. He bases his political theory on the belief that reason is the fundamental principle that explains all reality. He says, "What is rational is actual; and what is actual is rational."[7] Poverty is a particularly challenging problem for his political theory. He says, "The important question of how poverty can be remedied is one which agitates and torments modern societies especially."[8] The poor are deprived of all societal advantages and thus, do not have opportunities or abilities to acquire skills and education. He says they are denied justice, health care, and the comfort of religion.[9] In fact, he describes the perennial poor as "rabble," (*Pöbel*), which connotes more than just poverty. Hegel describes the poor in the following way:

> Poverty in itself does not reduce people to a rabble; a rabble is created only by the disposition associated with poverty, by inward rebellion against the rich, against society, the government, etc. It also follows that those who are dependent on contingency become frivolous and lazy like the *lassaroni* of Naples, for example. This gives rise to the evil that the rabble do not have sufficient honor to gain their livelihood through their own work, yet claim that they have a right to receive their livelihood.[10]

Hegel's use of the term, rabble, implies that the poor are not only outside of the mainstream of society but that they also have negative affects upon the state.[11] If he is interpreting the world as reason, as one scholar has noted,

"Poverty either finds its place in that interpretation or the interpretation itself is revealed to have at least one gaping hole."[12]

Freedom, according to Hegel, is not simply doing what one wants to do.[13] Human beings may experience freedom only when they live in a rational society, such as the one in the *Philosophy of Right*. Individuals obtain freedom, according to Hegel, when they have overcome their "particularity" and act "universally" according to the concept of the universal will."[14] By particularity, he means that people must look beyond their own subjective ideas, needs, and desires. When one consciously acts in an objective way, or for the good of the whole, then one is acting universally. A community can only be a rational community if it has rational social institutions, that is, those institutions that facilitate joining universal interests with the objective good of the individual. Therefore, for Hegel, the citizen may say that he is free only when he identifies himself with the institutions of his community. Citizens must feel that they are part of the institutions and that the institutions are part of them. The family, civil society, the police, corporations, and the state are entities, which have specific meanings as well as distinct functions that according to Hegel, advance individual freedom.

The family is the first phase of ethical life and it is where individuals find love and unity, and subsequent to being a part of a family, they experience individuality.[15] He says, "Marriage, and essentially monogamy, is one of the absolute principles on which the ethical life of a community is based."[16] Hegel believes that the family has its external reality in *property* because it provides them with personality.[17] Moreover, the family needs resources to survive, and the acquisition and care of property provide a communal purpose, which also has an ethical quality.[18] As heads of households, husbands should provide and care for their families' needs as well as control and administer their resources.[19] Sharing resources, Hegel cautions, is only an external action that lacks objectivity. Marriage becomes a spiritual unity only when couples have children because it allows husbands and wives to see the whole of their union.[20]

Hegel says that children have a *right* to be reared and supported at the expense of the family.[21] Rearing a child properly is important because children do not instinctively arrive at their life's destiny. He compares children who are not properly reared to people who live under paternalistic governments and those who are dependent on their state for subsistence.[22] These individuals can never become self-sufficient because that can only be learned through one's own efforts. Children should feel subordinate to their parents because he believes it instills in them a desire to mature.[23]

Since most families do not produce their own subsistence in the modern state, they must interact with the economic and civil life of society. In fact,

Hegel says that the "individual becomes a *son of civil society*" because it "tears the individual away from family ties."[24] As a result, the entire family becomes dependent on civil society and it intervenes between the family and state.[25] Hegel presupposes the structure of a state because it must exist before civil society can fully develop. His definition of civil society includes the economic and legal structures, the public authority, and social arrangements. Because families have interdependent needs, they are driven to come together. The circumstances may vary; they may share natural origins, be under a dominant power; or be a voluntary union. What do not vary are their interdependent needs. The reciprocity generated by the satisfaction of those needs help to compose civil society.[26] Unlike the love and trust found in the family, self-interest governs civil society. Hegel describes "three moments" in civil society. The first he calls the system of needs and it is "the mediation of *need* and the satisfaction of the *individual* through his work and through the work and satisfaction of the needs of *all the others*." Second, he says is the protection of property through the administration of justice, which is the actuality of the universal of *freedom*. Finally, he says that "provisions against contingency, which remains present in the above systems, and care for the particular interest as a *common* interest, by means of the *police* and the *corporation*."[27]

Individuals may achieve their ends, according to Hegel, only when they act in a way that makes them "*links* in the chain of this continuum."[28] While individuals may think, they are acting only to attain their ends, in reality they are acting for others' ends also. There is a unity present because social and economic interdependence necessitate it. Thus, individuals gain personal satisfaction while simultaneously providing for others' welfare.[29]

One can see Adam Smith's influences in Hegel's political theory. The latter's views about individuals' collective market behavior in civil society read like pages from *The Wealth of Nations*.[30] He also describes the same invisible hand effect that Smith so aptly explained in his work. Contrary to Smith, however, he rebuffs *laissez-faire* policies. Therefore, while Hegel accepts Smith's description of civil society, he rejects his argument for limiting government intervention. In the Hegelian state, the government is omnipresent, and (as will be shown later) the authority of public power reaches into many aspects of civil life.

Civil society leads to the division of labor and the three estates. The estates of agriculture, trade and industry, and civil servants help to connect individual selfishness with the universal, that is, the state.[31] The agricultural estate, which Hegel also calls the substantial estate, normally has the resources to provide subsistence for its members. He describes it as a patriarchal system whose members are not concerned with acquiring wealth because human industry is subordinate to nature.[32] In contrast, people in the estate of trade and industry must rely on themselves and their labor to meet their needs. The estates of craftsmanship, manufacturers, and commerce all fall under this category.[33] The universal estate, which Hegel also calls the estate of civil servants, has the universal interests of society as its main concern.[34] Because civil servants do not work for their individual interests, they must have private resources or be compensated by the state. They receive personal satisfaction by working for the state's common good.[35] All members of their respective estates have status, a right of recognition, and a professional ethic. In fact, Hegel says that, "A human being with no estate is merely a private person and does not possess actual universality."[36] Thus, he believes that human beings experience individual freedom in civil society through their memberships in one of these estates.

Laws are codified and promulgated to promote the administration of justice and to protect individuals from arbitrary decisions. Hegel says that justice is an important factor in civil society because good laws help a state to flourish. Since free ownership is fundamental to the state's success, laws are necessary to protect private property.[37]

While laws protect certain legal rights, it is the role of the police and corporations to protect and promote citizens' welfare.[38] When Hegel uses the term "police," he is referring to the idea of police power in the sense that governments are given the public power and authority to protect citizens' health, morals, and safety (*öffentliche Macht*).[39] This authority includes law enforcement, but it also denotes many other functions such as regulating the prices of necessities, public health, public works, and moderation of economic fluctuations (including unemployment), poor relief, and the authorization and regulation of corporations.[40] Hegel says, "The aim of oversight and provisions on the part of the police is to mediate between the individual and the universal possibility which is available for the attainment of individual ends."[41] He never provides any specifics about poor relief measures but he does say that one of the main functions of the public authority is to prevent the formation of a rabble.[42]

Corporations are the associations that bring people together because of common professions and trades, and according to Hegel, they are civil society's second ethical root. The corporations mitigate the competitive individualism of the system of needs, educate their members for life in the state, and assume the role of a second family.[43] Since corporations have resources, Hegel looks to them to help their members during times of unemployment and economic downturns.[44]

Kenneth Westphal believes that the idea of the corporation is crucial to Hegel's political theory because it mediates the divisive tendencies of individual self-seeking in commerce.[45] Most importantly, he says, corporations bring people together who would otherwise form two antagonistic groups: an underclass of rabble and a class of elite corporate leaders.[46] Clearly, Hegel intends for the corporations to play a mediating role and to offer some security to their members during times of crisis. What is not clear, however, is how the corporations could prevent the formation of rabble. First, members of corporations are members of an estate. As noted earlier, membership in the estate provides its members with status, a right of recognition and a professional ethic.[47] In addition, corporation membership is limited to the urban male middle class, which would exclude wage laborers.[48]

The rabble, as described by Hegel, does not have a sense of self-respect or a sense of right and wrong in their own lives.[49] Since one must be a member of an estate before becoming a member of a corporation, it is not clear what role, if any, the corporation plays in preventing the formation of a poor, disenfranchised rabble. Perhaps Hegel thinks that corporations can prevent the unemployed from falling into poverty. The problem with this is that Hegel would have to change his definition of who the poor are because he says that they "are more or less deprived of all advantages of society" and belonging to a corporation is a definite advantage in the Hegelian society.[50] The upshot of this is that it is hard to understand how corporations can mitigate poverty and prevent the formation of a rabble.

The state, according to Hegel, is distinct from civil society because it is not concerned with satisfying individual needs or wishes. Instead, the state brings unity to society. Hegel believes that all rational human beings are destined to live within a state because that is where the law of reason merges with the law of subjective freedom.[51] As a result, each person's end becomes identical with the universal objective. Like Aristotle, he thinks that citizens' happiness is the chief end of the state. If society's welfare is not protected, there is no happiness, and the state itself rests on shaky ground.[52] Hegel rejects the sharp conflict between the state and individuals because the state fosters citizenship.[53] Most important for Hegel is that, "The state is the actuality of concrete freedom."[54] He believes this is so because individuals pursue their particular interests in the family and civil society while they knowingly look out for the interests of the state and accept the universal interest as their own "and *actively pursue* it as their *ultimate end*."[55] Echoing Kant, he says that duties and rights are united in citizenship because as individuals fulfill their duties as citizens, they gain protection for their lives and property and have membership as part of the whole.[56]

After providing an overview of the state, Hegel discusses five possible causes for poverty. First, human beings do not have equal resources or skills, which lead some to poverty.[57] Second, there are numerous circumstances and contingencies, such as natural ones like the weather and soil infertility, which may contribute to it.[58] Third, some people are lazy and simply do not want to work.[59] Finally, he says that poverty is a natural by-product of a free-market society. Even in the best of times, there will never be enough consumers to purchase all the products being produced. There is too much capital, and more is being produced all the time. This leads to the fifth and main cause of poverty, which Hegel says is unemployment.[60]

He follows the list of causes with a discussion of some of the approaches that have been used to alleviate poverty. First, wealthier citizens could assume the burden of support for the poor by establishing hospitals, foundations, or monasteries to maintain some decent standard of living for them. Hegel dismisses this approach because it violates a fundamental principle of civil society, which requires that individuals should work to meet their needs. Moreover, it is only through work that human beings achieve feelings of honor and self-sufficiency.[61] Second, money in the form of taxes could be collected from wealthier citizens and redistributed to the poor. Hegel thinks that this solution aggravates the problem of poverty because the poor lose their self-respect and independence. Taxing the wealthy to provide for the poor will also be an interruption to the market and the rich will suffer because they will have less money to spend on their own needs.[62] Just as important is the fact that wealthy citizens would have less money to buy things, which only exacerbates overproduction. The third possibility is that the state could provide employment for the poor. Hegel thinks this is a bad idea because like taxing citizens, it leads to over overproduction, which is one of the chief causes of poverty. Finding no solution to remedy the problem within civil society or the state, Hegel suggests colonization.[63] The problem of poverty can be attacked on two fronts through imperialism. Poor people can gain property from the process of colonization and goods produced in the homeland could be sold in the new colonial markets.[64]

Hegel's preference is that these new colonies should retain strong links with their home countries.[65] He advocates a systematic approach to colonization, which should be initiated and regulated by the state. Using the ancient Greeks as an example, Hegel sees colonization as a relief to overpopulation and a practical way to deal with poverty. Even if the colonies are liberated later, they are a great advantage to the mother state. He cites the example of the American colonies, which continued to buy English goods after their independence.[66]

The question then becomes an empirical one, which is; where can one find land for colonies? Hegel thinks it should be overseas because, "The sea is primarily the natural element of industry, towards which civil society must strive in its development."[67] That Hegel would look to colonialism to address the problem makes sense when one reads his work in its historical context. As mentioned, earlier, the nineteenth century was the age of intense European expansionism throughout the world. The upshot of this discussion is that colonialism is the only possible solution that he offers for dealing with the problem of poverty. Shlomo Avineri views Hegel's state as the "protector of the weaker classes in society."[68] The question is how would Hegel protect these weaker individuals in society? While he says that the state should mediate between the individual and civil society to regulate the pricing of necessities and public health, this can hardly qualify the Hegelian state as a protector of the poor.[69] Instead, Hegel provides a dismal account of a society in which the poor not only remain marginalized, but also have little hope for happiness, freedom, or an escape from poverty. In fact, Hegel seems to suggest that the poor ought to be left to their own fate by begging from public.[70] The one exception is the possibility that the state establish new colonies to alleviate the problem. If, as Hegel states, the chief end of society is to promote citizens' welfare, happiness, and freedom, it appears that with no internal solutions to alleviate poverty, the state fails the poor. Thus, Hegel's notion of a just state is one that offers little hope for the poor. This is surprising since he seems preoccupied with the problem and provides a thoughtful examination of its causes. That being said, the demands of justice seem to exclude the poor in the Hegelian state. This provides fertile ground for Marx who challenges the core tenants of liberalism.

MARX

Marx rejects Hegel's thesis that his version of civil society represents a rational entity. The Hegelian state is merely a fantasy. It is not surprising that Hegel has no ideas to alleviate the problem of poverty because according to Marx, it is an intractable problem. The capitalist system promotes profit making as a goal rather than meeting human needs. In the free market society, the growth of poverty is inevitable because it is a necessary condition for capitalism to flourish.[71] Marx also rejects Hegel's portrayal of the separation of civil society and the state because he believes that civil society and the mode of production shape human beings.[72] History, according to Marx, is divided into epochs that are defined by the mode of production.[73] In turn, the mode of production dictates the social relations in society. Economic roles assigning control over the means, processes, and fruits of production to one group in society while excluding other groups define these societal roles.[74] This is Marx's definition of historical materialism and these groups form the basis of class differences in society.

The bourgeoisie, the petty bourgeoisie, the proletariat, and the *lumpen-proletariat* are the different classes. The bourgeoisie are the capitalists who own the means of production and employ wage laborers. The petty bourgeoisie control some means of production but for the most part, they use their own labor for production. They may buy some labor power to supplement their needs, such as a small business owner who needs to employ others during peak times of business. Marx defines the proletariat as "a class of laborers, who live only so long as they find work, and who find work only so long as their labor increases capital."[75] The *lumpenproletariat*, which literally means "ragged proletariat," is described by Marx as the criminals and prostitutes who form a group distinct from industrial workers who compose the bulk of the proletariat.[76] Marx describes capitalism as a system of exploitation arising from private ownership of the means of production. The wealth generated by the proletariat is used against them as they are used as means to an end. That end is great wealth for the capitalist owners and poverty for the workers.[77] Class antagonism arises between the proletariat and the bourgeoisie because of the inherent conflicts between the sellers and buyers of labor power.[78]

Exploitation under capitalism occurs when the proletariat produces a surplus whose use is controlled by the capitalists. The proletariat sells their labor power to subsist. Capitalist production generates a surplus because capitalists buy workers' labor power at a wage equal to its value but extract labor greater than the equivalent of that wage. Marx is not saying that exploitation arises from the unequal exchange of labor for wages. Labor power is what workers sell to capitalists for a money wage. Labor is the actual exercise of human productive powers to alter the use value of, and add value to, commodities. The amount capitalists pay for labor power is smaller than the value they pay for the labor that adds the value to it. This is Marx's labor theory of value that is linked to surplus value. He believes that the distinction between labor and labor power is that the latter is sold at its value while the former creates the surplus. In capitalist societies, value must be measured by labor since everyone's continued existence depends on surplus value. The illusion of free and equal exchange masks the actual exploitation in the capitalist mode of production. Even if wages rise, workers will always provide a certain amount of unpaid labor, which means they will always be exploited.[79] Economists criticize Marx's labor theory of value for a variety of reasons. One common criticism is that value cannot be linked to the labor time that a worker spends on producing a given product. For example, if a worker P, who is inept, takes sixteen hours to produce a lamp that is of poor quality and another worker Q, who

has superior talent to P, takes ten hours to produce a lamp that is of superior quality to P's lamp, how can one assign value to the two lamps based on the amount
of labor that it took to produce them?[80] This and other criticisms raise questions
about Marx's labor theory of value that go beyond the scope of this chapter. In
spite of the criticisms, his critical investigation into labor, wages, and exploitation has influenced not only twentieth-century economics but also the fields of
social science, political philosophy, and history.[81] While economists may reject
his labor theory of value and thus, his theory of exploitation, no one can deny
the influence his ideas have had upon the world.[82]

Unemployed or part-time workers compose the reserve army of labor or
the industrial reserve army, as Marx sometimes calls it. These people are ripe
for exploitation because they desperately need wages for subsistence. Industry expands from increased demand, new technology, and better means of
transporting products like the expansion of the railroads. A surplus of workers must exist, according to Marx, so that industry can put them to work without negatively affecting other areas of production.[83] He describes the cycles
in the capitalist economy as periods of average activity, high production, crisis production, and stagnation. This cyclical feature of industry depends on
the "constant transformation of a part of the working population into unemployed or semi-employed hands."[84]

On the one hand, the growth of capital may mean a demand for more labor.
On the other hand, surplus capital may be used to purchase new machinery
that may reduce the demand for labor. Moreover, if there is a lengthy period
of high employment, it may shrink the reserve army and force wage increases. Wage increases, however, slow the accumulation of capital and future employment opportunities, leading to increased emphasis on mechaniza-
tion by the capitalists, followed by layoffs, which in turn replenish the reserve
army of labor.

Another way capitalists assure a pool of potential employees is by over-
working those who are already employed. Driven by competition from those
waiting to take their jobs, wage laborers submit to long hours of work while
those who are unemployed willingly work part-time to receive some wages.
This is a means of "enriching the capitalists" because it is in their interest to
"extort a given quantity of labor out of a smaller rather than greater number
of workers, if the cost is about the same."[85] Marx provides an example of an
1863 English cotton-spinning operation where workers were forced to work
twelve to thirteen hours a day while hundreds of unemployed would have
willingly worked part-time.[86] This practice not only accelerates production
and enriches the capitalists, but it also ensures a dependable supply of potential laborers.[87] Capitalists, according to Marx, may also use a greater mass of
labor for less money by progressively replacing skilled workers with less

skilled ones. For example, female workers replace male workers or children replace adults.[88] Finally, labor may be imported from areas with high unemployment and low wages to reestablish a larger pool of workers.

Marx describes three forms of exploited workers who always exist in the reserve army of labor.[89] The floating form consists of a large number of male workers who are dismissed from their jobs by the time they reach the age of maturity. These unemployed men may emigrate to other areas following capital and look for employment, but capital demands youthful workers and fewer adults.[90] The second form is the latent one that describes a worker who has "completely lived himself out when he is only halfway through his life."[91] As a result, this individual falls into the ranks of the surplus labor force or he must take a lower paying job. Marx points to empirical data to show that the working class has much shorter life expectancies than the middle or upper classes. This contributes to rapid displacement of one generation of workers by another among the proletariat. Another consequence of this latent form of labor is that it leads to the exploitation of the workers' children who are used to replace their parents.[92] The third form is the stagnant one, which happens when the capitalists take possession of agriculture. As the demand for a rural working population falls, some workers move to urban areas and become part of the manufacturing proletariat. In the countryside, a constant latent surplus population remains who receive minimum wages. This worker, according to Marx, "always stands with one foot already in the swamp of pauperism."[93] The final groups, who are not an active part of the industrial reserve army, are those who "dwell in the sphere of pauperism."[94]

Distinct from the *lumpenproletariats*, Marx describes three categories of paupers. The first group includes those who are able to work. The second group is comprised of orphans and pauper children, who are prime candidates for the industrial reserve army during times of great prosperity. The final group is demoralized, physically ravaged, and unable to work. They have succumbed to their inabilities to adapt to the harsh conditions of the division of labor. They are the victims of industry. These individuals labor in dangerous conditions, like mines and chemical plants, and they are the sick, the mutilated, and the widowed that are unemployed.[95] Marx's remarks about this last group merits quoting.

Pauperism is the hospital of the industrial reserve army. Its production is included in that of the relative surplus population, its necessity is implied by their necessity; along with the surplus population, pauperism forms a condition of capitalist production, and of the capitalist development of wealth. It forms part of the *faux frais** of capitalist production: but capital usually knows how to

---

*incidental expenses

transfer these from its own shoulders to those of the working class and the petty bourgeoisie.[96]

Marx says that the hard work by the proletariat, which results in increased productivity, only serves to make their situations more capricious. Capitalism is responsible for the brutalization and moral degradation of the proletariat. By making hunger a permanent condition among the working class, the capitalists control them and force them to work harder and longer. In chilling language, Marx describes the relationship between the bourgeoisie and the proletariat as one of absolute control, "He [the worker] can work only with their [the capitalists'] permission, hence live only with their permission."[97] All the while, the bourgeoisie continue to accumulate more wealth.[98] The capitalists not only control wealth, but they also control the ideas and the intellectual forces of society.[99] Marx says, "The ruling ideas are nothing more than the ideal expression of the dominant material relationships."[100] There is no freedom for the proletariat because the ruling class controls their physical and mental lives.

"Alienation" is a term used throughout Marx's writings. He speaks about the alienation of labor and more generally about the alienation of human beings from themselves. The capitalist system erodes the connection that individuals feel to themselves and to others as human beings in the world who are conscious of their own life-activities. Labor is external to workers because it is not an expression of their creativity, nor does it affirm them as human beings. Workers are not free to develop physically or mentally. In fact, the labor they undertake ruins their bodies and minds.[101] The worker feels himself as a human being only when he is not working. Marx says, "It [work] is not a satisfaction of a need; it is merely a *means* to satisfy needs external to it."[102] In the same way that religion alienates people by asking them to give up themselves and put everything into God, people are alienated by giving themselves over to work while retaining none of themselves.[103] Marx defines the alienation of labor in the following passage:

> The *alienation* of the worker in his product means not only that his labor becomes an object, an *external* existence, but that it exists *outside him*, independently, as something alien to him, and that it becomes a power of its own confronting him; it means that the life he has conferred on the object confronts him as something hostile and alien.[104]

The proletariat exists in the world as workers and subjects, and Marx concludes, "life itself appears only as *a means to life*."[105]

Marx directly addresses Adam Smith's claim that poverty is not a serious problem in capitalist societies. One may remember that Smith's argument rested on his comparison of absolute and relative poverty. He concluded that what might look like poverty to some in a capitalist society is misleading because the poor are better off than the rich in other countries are.[106] Marx examines this conclusion by granting the most favorable conditions for the workers in capitalist societies. Capital is growing and there is low unemployment with higher wages for the proletariat. Even under these favorable conditions, Marx rejects Smith's conclusion about relative poverty in the following passage:

> A house may be large or small; as long as the surrounding houses are equally small it satisfies all social demands for a dwelling. But let a palace arise beside the little house and it shrinks from a little house to a hut. The little house shows now that its owner has only very slight or no demands to make; and however high it may shoot up in the course of civilization, if the neighboring palace grows to an equal or even greater extent, the occupant of the relatively small house will feel more uncomfortable, dissatisfied and cramped within its four walls.[107]

Because an individual's pleasures and desires spring from society, according to Marx, human beings measure their satisfaction by society's standards and not by the mere objects that satisfy them. Since one's needs and desires are of a social nature, they are of a relative nature.[108] When wages increase for the proletariat, the capitalists' profits increase even more. Marx says that the relative share of wages is reduced under these circumstances because of the increased cost of goods. Items such as cereal, meat, butter, and cheese cost more and this fact diminishes any real increase in wages.[109] While the workers may receive higher wages, the gulf between the proletariat and bourgeoisie is greater than ever and the workers feel little satisfaction in the gains they may have made.[110] Thus, while Smith claims that inequality in society is often illusory or superficial with no overwhelming physical needs for many of the things that individuals want, Marx says that relative poverty is directly connected to individuals' feelings of satisfaction in society and that the inequality is neither illusory nor superficial.[111] It is an *actual* economic fact that the worker becomes poorer the more wealth he produces and he adds, "With the *increasing value* of the world of things proceeds in direct proportion the *devaluation* of the world of men."[112]

Marx paints a picture of exploitation at every turn and for every step forward the worker takes, he takes three steps backward. Surely, one can reasonably conclude that he thinks capitalist societies are unjust. The poor live at the mercy of the capitalists and even under the best circumstances, the lower classes are still being exploited and economic destitution looms heavily over their entire lives.

Marx believes that a revolution will occur in advanced capitalist societies and result in the establishment of a communist society. The communist society will remedy, for the most part, the problem of poverty. As the proletariat becomes aware of its own spiritual and physical poverty, its members will recognize their own dehumanization. This theoretical consciousness will turn into indignation against the inhumanity of the capitalist system and the proletariat will be driven to liberate itself.[113] Philosophy plays an important role in bringing forth the revolution because according to Marx, the proletariat finds its intellectual weapons in philosophy, just as philosophy finds its material weapons in the proletariat.[114] In one of his most famous passages, Marx tells us what the role of philosophy ought to be when he says that "The philosophers have only *interpreted* the world, in various ways; the point, however, is to *change* it."[115] Ultimately, the revolution will occur because of historical progress. The conflict between the bourgeoisie and the proletariat represents the ongoing conflict between individual interests and the common good. Capitalism exacerbates this conflict and ultimately destroys itself because of it.[116]

After the revolution has taken place, there will have to be an interim structure, which Marx calls the dictatorship of the proletariat. Since this new society is starting from the foundation of capitalism, changes will occur gradually. Marx says:

> What we have to deal with here is a communist society, not as it has *developed* on its own foundations, but, on the contrary, just as it *emerges* from capitalist society; which is thus in every respect, economically, morally and intellectually, still stamped with the birth marks of the old society from whose womb it emerges.[117]

Marx provides some details about how society ought to be structured to limit the incidence of poverty and care for those who are unable to work. Communism demands the conversion of land and all instruments of production into common property. Economic necessity requires certain deductions from the proceeds of labor to cover the replacement cost of the means of production, to fund future expansion, and to establish a reserve or insurance fund for accidents and dislocations caused by natural disasters, etc. The general costs of administration not belonging to production must be deducted as well as funds to support health care, schools, and other services to meet the common satisfaction of needs and to provide for those who are unable to work. Marx says that these deductions will grow considerably when compared to present-day society because it will increase in proportion as the new society develops.[118]

After these deductions, the individual will receive back from society exactly what he or she has contributed to it. Marx recognizes that some people who are physically or mentally superior will supply more labor in the same time or may choose to work longer hours. Communism recognizes labor as a measure defined by intensity or duration. There will be no class differences but unequal individual endowments will be recognized and thus one's productive capacity will be viewed as a natural privilege.[119] Marx admits that all types of different economic situations arise in society, such as one man who is married while another is single, or one man may have five children while another has only one. It is also true, Marx says, that one man will in fact receive more than another will and one will be richer than another. These defects are inevitable in the first phase of communism, which is just emerging from capitalism. After time has passed and the problems associated with the division of labor have subsided, labor will not only be a means to life but "life's prime want" and productivity will increase because individuals will have become better developed in all facets of their lives. It is then, Marx says, that society may say, "From each according to his ability, to each according to his needs!"[120] This is Marx's picture of a just society.

Criticisms of Marx's theory are many. His idea of historical progression did not take place. Capitalism's productivity continued to surpass his expectations and wages increased so that many, though certainly not all, individuals were able to purchase more than mere subsistence. Proletariat revolutions did not occur in the most advanced capitalist societies. As Peter Singer says, perhaps the flaw in his reasoning that looms the largest is his absolute belief that common interests will take precedence over individual interests, thus dissolving individual motivations for power and control. Through the abolition of private property and the transformation of the economic and social conditions of society, Marx believed that people would change.[121] Self-interest would be replaced with a concern for the common good, and the state as a political entity would cease to exist. Rejecting claims that his theory was utopian, Marx believed that he had discovered a scientific basis for his claims. The laws of history would necessarily entail the dissolution of capitalism and the creation of the communist state. It is clear from Marx's writings that he failed to consider the possibility that his theory could be used to establish authoritarian regimes that would not promote the well-being of all people. Critics like Mikhail Bakunin believed that power would reside in a few and result in tyranny.[122] In an exchange with Bakunin in 1874, Marx fails to answer his concerns about tyranny after revolution. At one point in the exchange,

Bakunin says that anyone who believes that some of the former proletari-
ats will not want power and control over the people simply does not understand human nature.[123]

Scholars debate whether Marx is concerned with justice as his primary goal
or whether freedom for all human beings is his first concern.[124] Regardless of
those academic arguments, it is safe to say that Marx is deeply concerned
with the mental and physical well being of human beings. He is concerned
about poverty, whether it is absolute or relative physical deprivation, or the
mental poverty that results from lack of education and the drudgery of working long shifts in factories. Poverty prevents human beings not only from
reaching their potential as a species, but also from enjoying their lives. Since
Marx rejects religion and believes that an individual has one life to live, he
does not accept that it has to be a life full of pain and suffering resulting from
deprivation and poverty. While Marx concentrates on individuals achieving
happiness and self-fulfillment, his belief is that individuals can only be happy
when they work for the good of the whole. The seemingly inherent conflict
between self-interest and the common good is eliminated once the social and
economic forces have been changed to communism because these forces
shape human beings.

Hegel describes a culture of poverty because he says that the rabble have
internalized attitudes, which contribute to their alienation from society. While
he thinks that laziness may account for some poverty, unlike Locke, he believes that unemployment is the chief cause of it. As such, the problem of
poverty is an inevitable by-product of a free market economy. Unfortunately,
Hegel provides few answers that would help the rabble or the other poor people. Void of solutions within the Hegelian state, poverty becomes an intractable problem unless new colonies are established outside the homeland.
Like Mill, who also lived during the era of European colonial expansion, he
thinks that new colonies would not only take pressure off the homeland, but
also contribute to its economic growth. Unlike Mill, however, this is the only
suggestion that he has to relieve poverty. The Hegelian state fails to meet the
demands of justice for the poor.

In contrast, Marx wants to solve the problem of poverty through the careful study of philosophy, history, economics, and of course, by taking actions
resulting in revolutions. He offers an alternative view of poverty as a product
of factors and processes, which other philosophers, including Hegel for all his
attention to the organic links within the whole of society, simply did not see.
Hegel's solution to the problem of poverty at home is to export it somewhere
else. In short, he is really moving poverty around like a shell game. No doubt,
this is one reason why Marx insists that the solution must be an international
one.[125] Not only does Marx foresee the international aspects of poverty, he

also writes about poverty as structure because of the institutional and structural elements of society that contribute to and cultivate its continuation and expansion.

One cannot easily dismiss Marx's response to Adam Smith's claims about relative poverty. Relative poverty does matter because many human needs and desires are of a social nature. As a result, individuals often measure their personal satisfaction by society's standards rather than abstract ones. Finally, Marx, along with Engels, provides a sobering account of the physical and mental deprivation of women, men, and children who were victims of a system that not only ignored their needs, but also profited from their misery. His writings are powerful because of their polemical force that exposes and examines human suffering and the plight of poor people. In the end, however, the inherent problems with his political theory are too great to be overlooked. As mentioned at the beginning of the chapter, Marx's rhetoric has a seductive quality to it and one ignores the vagueness of his writings about the post revolutionary state at his or her own peril. Singer is correct when he says that Marx's greatest flaw was his belief that individuals would change and that concern for the common good would supplant self-interest.

Hegel and Marx undoubtedly aim to promote a just state. Both engage the problem of poverty. As I said earlier, however, mere concern is not enough to meet the demands of justice. For all of Hegel's anxiety about the problem he does little to alleviate it. As we have seen, Marx demands fairness for the poor and exploited and while he never mentions justice, I have shown that he indeed thinks that capitalism is unjust and that he has a better political theory to ensure that no one in society does without the necessities nor lives by the whims of others. No doubt that Marx, like Rousseau, is concerned with individual freedom, but that does not preclude his preoccupation with the relationship between poverty and justice. In fact, one could say that an individual's freedom from exploitation has everything to do with justice. Since neither Hegel nor Marx directly address the demands of a just state, one has to deconstruct their political theories to some degree to tease out their treatments of poverty and explore how they relate to a just society. As we turn to two contemporary political theorists in the next chapter, we will see their unmistakable preoccupation with justice, which necessitates an overt confrontation with the problem of poverty.

.

NOTES

1. Peter Singer, *Hegel: A Very Short Introduction* (New York: Oxford University Press, 2001), 45.

2. *Laws*, 739c–e.

3. Fleischacker, *Short History*, 59–60.

4. Karl Marx, "Theses on Feuerbach," in *The Marx-Engels Reader*, 2nd ed., ed. Robert Tucker (New York: W.W. Norton and Company, Inc., 1978), 145.

5. Karl Marx "Critique of the Gotha Program," in *The Marx Engels Reader*, 2nd ed., ed. Robert Tucker (New York: W.W. Norton and Company, Inc., 1978), 531. Hereafter cited as *CGP*.

6. Hegel, G. W. F. *Elements of the Philosophy of Right*, ed. Allen Wood, trans. H. B. Nisbet (Cambridge: Cambridge University Press, 1991), 21. All references to this work are from this edition and hereafter cited as *PR*, the page number indicated for the preface and notes and the paragraph symbol (¶) along with the number of the paragraph indicated for the rest of the work.

7. *PR*, 20.

8. Ibid., ¶244A.

9. Ibid., ¶241.

10. Ibid., ¶244.

11. Some writers, especially in the United States use the term "underclass" in a similar way. The underclass describes poor, black, urban communities where people experience long-term unemployment and long-term welfare dependency accompanied by high levels of street crime and overall social disorganization (DiNitto, 84). Like Hegel's description of the rabble, this group is outside the mainstream of the economic, social, and political structures that are part of the lives of most citizens.

12. Richard Teichgraeber, "Hegel on Property and Poverty," *Journal of the History of Ideas* 38, no. 1, (January–March, 1977): 59.

13. *PR*, ¶15.

14. Ibid., ¶23.

15. Ibid., ¶158–81.

16. Ibid., ¶167.

17. Ibid., ¶169. Hegel believes that ownership of private property is an individual's central right. Property ownership does not satisfy physical needs but helps people to develop or fulfill their individual personhood. Hegel says that everyone ought to have property (*PR*, ¶49 Addition). Equality in property is a moral *wish* because one cannot speak of an *injustice* in nature (*PR*, ¶49). Only the state, and this is in exceptional cases, may cancel private ownership (*PR*, ¶46 Addition).

18. Ibid., ¶170.

19. Ibid., ¶71.

20. Ibid., ¶173.

21. Ibid., ¶174.

22. Ibid., ¶174, Addition.

23. Ibid., ¶174, Addition.

24. Ibid., ¶238.

25. Ibid., ¶238.

26. Ibid., ¶181.

27. Ibid., ¶188.

28. Ibid., ¶187.

29. Ibid., ¶182.

30. Smith, *WN*, I.iv.ii: 477–78.

31. *PR*, ¶201.

32. Ibid., ¶204.

33. Ibid., ¶204.

34. Ibid., ¶205.

35. Ibid.

36. Ibid., ¶207.

37. Ibid., ¶229.

38. Ibid., ¶229–30.

39. Inwood, Michael, *A Hegel Dictionary* (Oxford: Blackwell Publishers, Ltd., 1998), 55.

40. *PR*, ¶236, ¶240, ¶241, ¶242, ¶244, ¶252.

41. Ibid., ¶236 Addition.

42. Ibid., ¶240.

43. Ibid., ¶252.

44. Ibid., ¶2534.

45. Westphal, Kenneth, "The Basic Context and Structure of Hegel's *Philosophy of Right*," in *The Cambridge Companion to Hegel*, ed., Frederick C. Beiser (Cambridge: Cambridge University Press, 1993), 259.

46. Westphal, "Basic Context and Structure," 259.

47. *PR*, ¶206, ¶207.

48. Ibid., ¶250.

49. Ibid., ¶240, ¶241, ¶244.

50. Ibid., ¶241.

51. Ibid., ¶75.

52. Ibid., ¶265.

53. Inwood, *A Hegel Dictionary*, 55.

54. *PR*, ¶260.

55. Ibid., ¶260.

56. Ibid., ¶261.

57. Ibid., ¶200.

58. Ibid., ¶189, ¶241.

59. Ibid., ¶189.

60. Ibid., ¶245 and Hegel, *Philosophie des Rechts: die Vorlesung von 1819/20 in eigner Nachschrift*, ed. Dieter Henrich (Frankfurt am Man: Suhrkamp, 1983) Trans. Shlomo Avineri, "The Discovery of Hegel's Early Lectures on the Philosophy of Right," *The Owl of Minerva* 16, no. 2 (Spring 1985): 205–8. This translation appears as the appendix to Avineri's article and all references to this work are from this translation and hereafter cited as *Lectures*.

61. *PR*, ¶145.

62. *Lectures*, 207.

63. *PR*, ¶248; *Lectures*, 208.

64. *Lectures*, 208.

65. *PR*, ¶248.

66. *Lectures*, 208.

67. Ibid.

68. Shlomo Avineri, *Hegel's Theory of the Modern State* (Cambridge: Cambridge University Press, 1972), 101.

69. *PR*, ¶236A.

70. Ibid., ¶245.

71. Karl Marx, *Capital*, vol. 1, ch. 25, trans. Ben Fowkes (New York: Vintage Books, 1977), 798–99. All references to *Capital* are from this volume and edition and hereafter cited as *Capital* with the volume, chapter, and page number.

72. "In short, it is not history but old Hegelian junk, it is not profane history— a history of man—but sacred history—a history of ideas." Karl Marx, letter to V. Annekov, 28 December 1846, *The Marx-Engels Reader*, 2nd ed., ed. Robert Tucker (New York: W.W. Norton and Company, Inc., 1978), 137–8. All references to *The Marx-Engels Reader* are from this edition. Marx discusses civil society's differences from Hegel's conception in "The German Ideology" in *The Marx-Engels Reader*, 163.

73. Karl Marx, "Society and Economy in History," in *The Marx-Engels Reader*, 138; "German Ideology," 161.

74. Karl Marx, "The German Ideology," in *The Marx-Engels Reader*, 150, 157.

75. Karl Marx, "The Communist Manifesto," in *The Marx-Engels Reader*, 473.

76. *Capital*, I.25: 797. See also Richard W. Miller, "Social and Political Theory: Class, State, Revolution," in *The Cambridge Companion to Marx* (Cambridge: Cambridge University Press, 1991), 63.

77. *Capital*, I.25: 798–99.

78. Miller, "Social and Political Theory," 37.

79. *Capital*, I.25: 769–71.

80. See for example, Cohen, G. A. "The Labor Theory of Value and the Concept of Exploitation," *Philosophy and Public Affairs* 8, no.4 (Summer, 1979): 339–60.

81. Thomas, Paul, "Critical Reception: Marx Then and Now" in *The Cambridge Companion to Marx*, ed. Terrell Carver (Cambridge: Cambridge University Press, 1991) 25.

82. For example see, Allen Buchanan, *Marx and Justice* (Totawa, NJ: Rowman and Littlefield, 1982) and Ziyad Husami "Marx on Distributive Justice," *Philosophy and Public Affairs* 8, no.1 (Autumn 1978): 27–64.

83. *Capital*, I.25: 785.

84. Ibid., 784–86.

85. Ibid., 788–89.

86. Ibid., 789.

87. Ibid., 789–90.

88. Ibid., 788.

89. Ibid., 794.

90. Ibid., 794–95.

91. Ibid., 794.

92. Ibid., 795.

93. Ibid., 795–96.

94. Ibid., 797.

95. Ibid., 797.

96. *Capital*, I.25, 797.

97. *CGP*, 526.

98. *Capital*, I.25, 799–800.

99. "German Ideology," 172.

100. Ibid., 172–173.

101. *Economic and Philosophic Manuscripts of 1844* in *The Marx-Engels Reader*, 75–76. All references to this work are from this translation and hereafter cited as *Manuscripts 1844*.

102. *Manuscripts 1844*, 74.

103. Ibid., 72.

104. Ibid., 72.

105. Ibid., 75–76.

106. Adam Smith, *WN* I.i.1, 16 and I.i.8, 90–91. See also Adam Smith's *Lectures on Justice, Policy, Revenue and Arms*, ed. Edwin Cannan 1896, 158, quoted in E. G. West's "Adam Smith's Philosophy of Riches," *Philosophy* 44, no.168 (April 1969): 114.

107. Marx, "Wages, Labour and Capital," in *Karl Marx and Frederick Engels Selected Works, Volume I* (Moscow: Foreign Languages Publishing House, 1958), 93–94. All future references to this work are from this edition and hereafter cited as *WLC*.

108. *WLC*, 94.

109. Ibid., 94–95.

110. Smith, *Lectures on Justice, Policy, Revenue and Arms*, ed. Edwin Cannan 1896, 158, quoted in West "Adam Smith's Philosophy of Riches," *Philosophy* 44 no. 168 (April 1969): 109.

111. Peter Singer *Marx: A Very Short Introduction* (Oxford: Oxford University Press, 2000), 62.

112. *Manuscripts 1844*, 71.

113. Marx, "Alienation and Social Classes," in *The Marx-Engels Reader*, 134.

114. Marx, "Contribution to the Critique of Hegel's *Philosophy of Right:* Introduction," in *The Marx-Engels Reader*, 65.

115. Marx, "Theses on Feuerbach," 145.

116. Singer, *A Very Short Introduction*, 80–81.

117. *CGP*, 529.

118. Ibid., 528–29.

119. Ibid., 530.

120. Ibid., 531.

121. Singer, *A Very Short Introduction*, 94.

122. Mikhail Bakunin was a Russian revolutionary who published a book in 1873, *Statehood and Anarchy*. He was a harsh critic of Marx and he was active in workers' movements. Marx read Bakunin's book and wrote a rebuttal in 1874 in *The Marx-Engels Reader*, 542.

123. Marx, "After the Revolution: Marx Debates Bakunin," in *The Marx-Engels Reader*, 546.

124. For example, Allen Buchanan claims that Marx holds that justice is the first virtue of society and that respect for individuals as right-holders is the first virtue of individuals (*Marx and Justice*, xiv). Ziyad Husami maintains that justice in the moral, not legal sense, is to be found in Marx and his critique of capitalism rests on a moral critique of injustice ("Marx on Distributive Justice," 63). Peter Singer says that "Marx was devoted to the cause of human freedom" and that was his central concern (*A Very Short Introduction*, 89–93).

125. Credit goes to David Williams for this point.

Chapter Seven

Poverty and Justice: John Rawls and Robert Nozick

In chapters 3 and 5, we saw how the problem of poverty exposed tensions in Locke and Tocqueville's work, and liberalism in general. Both theorists held firm commitments to liberal values including private property and limited government, while at the same time they believed that human beings were morally equal. When individuals lack subsistence or the ability to care for themselves, Locke believed that government had a moral obligation to act because of God's law to promote the preservation of humankind. This was his moral justification for public aid for the poor. While other liberals, like Tocqueville and Smith resisted public aid, modern liberals are not only supportive of it, but they also do not appeal to any theological or metaphysical justifications for it. Another tenant of classical liberalism is the idea that individuals are responsible for their own fate in society. Certainly, Locke, and other theorists that we have explored agreed with this view. Naturally, this value is reflected in American political culture, and until the 1930s, there was little discussion about the value of individual responsibility. The watershed event of the Great Depression caused a seismic shift in the way Americans viewed public aid. In recent decades, attention has focused on government programs and welfare policies that critics say not only fail to help the poor, but also hurt them by creating a cycle of dependency. That is to say, some argue that what started out to be a helping hand for a short period turned into entitlement programs that did not help individuals to get out of poverty but instead created a permanent underclass.[1] At the same time, extensive developments in worldwide patterns of economic relations and interconnectivity among nations, has raised questions of fairness and justice among them. This phenomena, which is commonly called globalization, points to the worldwide integration of human beings. Globalization is not without its critics because some view it as an expansion of economic exploitation by the wealthy countries, which aggravates and even creates more inequality among nations. All of this is to say that whether we are looking at poverty and the idea of justice in the United States or globally, the question of this study remains as relevant today as it was in Plato's time. What does justice demand for the poor not only in the United States but also for the poor throughout the world?

Two contemporary political philosophers, John Rawls and Robert Nozick provide accounts of justice that appeal to John Locke and Immanuel Kant's political theories. Both invoke Kant's imperative to treat individuals as ends in themselves and not merely as means. Rawls appeals to Locke's idea of social contract theory as a justification for his theory of justice. Nozick uses Locke's ideas about self-ownership and just acquisition in constructing his ideal state. While both seek principles of justice that embody Kantian and Lockean principles, they arrive at quite different answers as to what constitutes just distribution in the state. As Michael Sandel notes, they present the clearest alternatives on the subject of distributive justice that the American political agenda has to offer.[2]

Rawls represents one branch of modern liberalism that focuses on individual personal freedom with a plan for significantly reducing the problem of poverty in the democratic capitalist state. He rejects Marxist ideas for the abolition of private property ownership because he believes that it is essential for individual self-expression. He also rejects utilitarianism because he wants to protect individual rights. Like Rawls, Nozick is committed to promoting individual freedom and protecting private property. He proposes a libertarian variety of liberalism. Compulsory taxation for helping the poor, according to Nozick, violates personal freedom. Thus, it is morally wrong for governments to force individuals to pay for welfare programs to help the needy. Rawls and Nozick's commitments to Kantian and Lockean principles present contrasting visions for a just society. Since the central goal for both authors is to create a just state, we will look for their answers to the fundamental question this study asks; what is the relationship between poverty and justice in the state?

JOHN RAWLS

John Rawls's *A Theory of Justice* is one of the most influential works in contemporary political theory.[3] The number of journal articles and books in response to it attests to this fact.[4] *Justice as Fairness* provides a response to Rawls's critics and allows him to develop his original theory.[5] He provides a political conception of justice that creates the framework for a liberal egalitarian society. Rawls tries to answer the normative question: how should society structure political and social institutions so that they promote political and economic justice for all citizens, especially the least-advantaged members of society? Just as important to him is the question: what morally justified procedure could be used to find the just conditions that would form a basis for commitment in civil society?

Rawls's answers are provocative but also ambiguous at times. On the one hand, as I shall show, there are ideas that would restructure society so that those who are least advantaged would have a fair chance to pursue their life plans with greater opportunities and security. On the other hand, he seems to shy away from dealing with the problems of people who are the most disadvantaged in society, like those with severe physical or mental disabilities.[6]

Rawls uses a Kantian version of social contract theory to establish moral obligation based on people being ends in themselves. As such, human beings are entitled to equal consideration in virtue of their individual moral worth. The contract in Rawls's account is neither tacit nor explicit but hypothetical. Free, equal, rational, and properly informed individuals make an agreement in the original position, a hypothetical situation, on the principles of political justice for society's basic structure, that is, its social and political institutions. Included in the basic structure are the ideas of a political constitution, an independent judiciary, legally recognized forms of property ownership, the structure of the economy, and the family.[7] The society is democratic and the economic system is capitalist. Rawls makes it clear, however, that he does not want merely to re-create welfare state capitalism.[8] He refers to the society as a property-owning democracy. The basic structure makes cooperation possible, according to Rawls, by securing background justice for all citizens in society.

In addition, Rawls wants to make justice as fairness compatible with liberal pluralism. In *Political Liberalism*, he assumes that it is inevitable that different religious, moral, and philosophical views exist in liberal societies.[9] A public conception of justice, according to Rawls, can be a unifying feature of society.[10] He believes that an overlapping consensus of justice exists in spite of myriad individual differences. Most individuals share certain moral ideas, such as citizens being free and equal moral persons. As a result, human beings with different ethical, religious, and philosophical views can endorse a public conception of justice if only for their own individual reasons. Rawls's basic belief is that free and equal persons have a capacity for reason and a sense of justice.[11] This is what he calls the idea of "reasonable pluralism."[12]

To reach a fair agreement, he wants individuals to think about what kind of society they would design if their particular features or circumstances did not influence them. They must not have too much knowledge of the basic structure because that would distort their points of view. This hypothetical state, that is, the original position, and the "veil of ignorance" limits individuals' information about their particular social position, race, ethnicity, gender, or native endowments, such as intelligence and strength. Nor are individuals to know what their comprehensive doctrines are, that is, their conceptions of what they value in human life such as religious, moral, and political beliefs.[13] Since no one knows what position he or she will occupy in society, asking individuals what is best for them also calls upon them to decide impartially what is best for everyone. If one is to decide from behind a veil of ignorance what is best, then one must also imagine that through the accident of birth, he or she could be anyone in society. Individuals must ask what promotes their good. Self-interest joins with an awareness of benevolence because one must be able to identify sympathetically with others. To give others equal consideration, one should attempt to take an account of what would promote their good. Since no one should be advantaged or disadvantaged by natural fortune or social circumstances in the choice of principles, the original position and the veil of ignorance make it impossible to tailor principles to one's own circumstances.[14] If one takes seriously the idea of the moral equality of all human beings, then the original position combined with the veil of ignorance, according to Rawls, will be a useful device for determining the content of a political conception of justice.

The most fundamental idea of a political conception of justice is the idea of society as a fair system of social cooperation over time from one generation to the next.[15] To determine if an arrangement is just, Rawls asks what the outcome of a social contract would be under his stated conditions. He believes that justice, as fairness is the best political conception to obtain that idea.[16] The impartial agreement among free and equal citizens is made in view of what individuals regard as their reciprocal advantages or good.[17] Rawls wants to persuade us that individuals would agree to two intuitively attractive principles of justice in the original position. An arrangement is just if and only if, according to Rawls it fulfills the following two principles:

- Each person has the same indefeasible claim to a fully adequate scheme of equal basic liberties, which scheme is compatible with the same scheme of liberties for all; and
- Social and economic inequalities must satisfy two conditions: first, they attach to offices and positions open to all under conditions of fair equality of opportunity; and second, they are to be the greatest benefit of the least-advantaged members of society (the difference principle).[18]

Principle (a), according to Rawls, is a constitutional essential. It applies primarily to the basic structure of society by securing equality in the assignment of basic rights and duties.[19] This includes political liberties such as voting and running for political office, freedom of speech and assembly, liberty of conscience, freedom of thought, personal property ownership, freedom from arbitrary arrest and seizure, and the rule of law.[20] Each person is to have an equal right to the most extensive basic liberty compatible with a similar liberty for others. Rawls uses constitutional guarantees of rights and civil liberties in the first principle to make everyone alike and equal.[21] Principle (a) must be satisfied before principle (b). Thus, (a) has priority over (b). This means that any departure from principle (a) may not be justified or compensated for by greater social and economic advantages in principle (b).[22]

Principle (b) is more complicated because it really contains two components. First is the idea of fair equality of opportunity. I shall refer to this as the opportunity principle. Second is the idea that social and economic inequalities are to be to the greatest benefit of the least-advantaged members of society. This is the difference principle. The opportunity principle has priority over the difference principle. Thus, fair equality of opportunity must be fully satisfied, according to Rawls, before applying the difference principle.

Rawls admits that the meaning of fair equality of opportunity is unclear and difficult to explain. He says that it is necessary to try to correct the defect of the system of natural liberty.[23] A system that is formally open to all individuals based upon their talents and abilities is a system of natural liberty. Fair equality of opportunity means liberal equality for Rawls. Individuals, who have the same levels of talent and abilities with the same motivation and willingness to use them, should have similar prospects for success in pursuing their life plans regardless of what social class into which they are born. In addition, those who are similarly gifted and motivated should have roughly equal opportunities to influence government policies irrespective of their economic or social class.[24] Instead of a procedural statement of equal opportunity, Rawls wants to adjust the long-run trend of economic forces to preclude excessive concentrations of property and wealth among certain individuals in society. He aims to equalize the influence that individuals may exert on politicians and policies. Rawls also aims to broaden educational and career opportunities and choices for citizens. All individuals, according to Rawls, should have equal opportunities for education regardless of family income. This is one of the most important requirements to ensure that the opportunity principle effectively applies to a given society.[25]

The difference principle applies to the basic structure of society. Parties in the original position are forced to think about the worst outcomes. They must then answer the question about what individuals' fundamental interests would be in those situations.[26] Rawls says that no rational person would be willing to risk ending up as one of the least advantaged without having an agreement to ensure that he or she would be better off than in any other agreement.[27] The difference principle, he believes, fulfills that requirement because it calls for the maximization of the distributive shares for the least advantaged in society. He says that it provides for the best worst outcome or a "guaranteeable level."[28] It is also called the maximin rule because individuals in the original position would want to adopt the principle whose worst outcome is better than the worst outcomes of other alternatives. Rawls explains the difference principle in the following way:

> The difference principle requires that however great the inequalities in wealth and income may be, and however willing people are to work to earn their greater shares of output, existing inequalities must contribute effectively to the benefit of the least advantaged. Otherwise, the inequalities are not permissible. The general level of wealth in society, including the well being of the least advantaged, depends on people's decisions as to how to lead their lives. The priority of liberty means that we cannot be forced to engage in work that is highly productive in terms of material goods. What kind of work people do, and how hard they do it, is up to them to decide in light of the various incentives society offers. What the difference principle requires, then, is that however great the general level of wealth—whether high or low—the existing inequalities are to fulfill the condition of benefiting others as well as us. This condition brings out that even if it uses the idea of maximizing the expectation of the least advantaged; the difference principle is essentially a principle of reciprocity.[29]

Rawls explores the idea of a social minimum, which would be a constitutionally protected level of material well-being that no member of society should be allowed to fall below.[30] In *Theory of Justice*, he provides two reasons for his rejection of the idea of a social minimum.[31] First, there are too many variables and changing circumstances to determine what the social minimum should be. Seung aptly calls this the argument from indeterminacy.[32] The second argument is that the idea of an appropriate social minimum is so indeterminate that in actuality it would turn out to be the same as the solution that the difference principle provides.[33] Thus, he provides an argument from equivalence.[34] These two arguments are incompatible because if the idea of a social minimum is unachievable because it is indeterminate, then it cannot be equivalent to the difference principle.[35] In *Justice as Fairness*, Rawls still rejects the social minimum but for different reasons.[36] Since individuals make the original agreement in good faith, he wants to ensure that the strains of commitment are not so great as to weaken individuals' resolve to honor it. He asks, what is the lowest minimum necessary to assure that the strains of commitment are not too great? If the social minimum is inadequate, people may withdraw from political society and become cynical about any conception of justice. More threatening to society is when poor people become bitter and feel oppressed. The least advantaged will view society's conception of justice as a hollow statement and may take violent actions to protest against their situation. To avoid either of these scenarios, he thinks that the difference principal should meet the basic human needs essential for a decent life and presumably more.[37] He says:

> The idea is that in virtue of our humanity—our common human needs—everyone is owed at least that much; and this is not merely, on the grounds that it is politically prudent to eliminate the causes of unrest. It is claimed, though, that the argument from the strains of commitment requires no more than this.[38]

Rawls questions whether establishing a social minimum as a guarantee of a certain standard of living would be adequate to ensure that poor people will feel that they are a part of political society. He wants the idea of justice to have meaning for the least advantaged so that they will view political society as being significant to their lives. He concludes that a social minimum alone may indeed be adequate to prevent revolution. It is inadequate, according to Rawls, to prevent the poor from becoming cynical and withdrawing from political society. A social minimum may be adequate for a capitalist welfare state but not for a property-owning democracy in which the principles of justice as fairness could be realized.[39]

To answer the question, "who is the least advantaged in society?" Rawls introduces the idea of primary goods. These are the social conditions and the means necessary to allow citizens to develop as free and equal persons who pursue their conception of what constitutes a good life. He lists five items and circumstances as these primary goods. First, are the basic rights and liberties, for example, freedom of thought and liberty of conscience, that all should enjoy. These are necessary so that individuals may make judgments about the justice of basic institutions and social policies and so that they may have the necessary freedom to pursue their own good.[40] Second, for individuals to pursue a variety of ends and have opportunities to make, revise, and even change their decisions, they must have freedom of movement and free choice of occupation with diverse opportunities. The powers and prerogatives of offices and positions of authority and responsibility are the third category of primary goods. Fourth is income and wealth, which may be understood as all-purpose means (having an exchange value). This would encompass what individuals generally need to achieve a wide range of ends whatever they may be. Finally, Rawls says that it is necessary to establish a social basis of self-respect, which he believes may be understood as those aspects of basic institutions normally essential for human beings to have a lively sense of their worth as persons and to be able to advance their ends with self-confidence.[41] The two principles of justice will force a government to look at the basic structure to see how it regulates citizens' shares of primary goods. Since equal basic rights, liberties, and opportunities will be secured constitutionally, the least advantaged are those who belong to the income class with the lowest expectations.[42] Rather than identifying qualities or features, such as race, gender, or social class, Rawls chooses to identify the least advantaged solely by their income and wealth. The difference principle as a principle of distributive justice, according to Rawls, will not require continual economic growth over generations to maximize upward the income and wealth of the least advantaged. In economic downturns, the expectations of all citizens will be less.[43]

Rawls says that self-respect is the most important primary good, but one has to ask; what does he mean by self-respect?[44] First, according to him, it includes a person's sense of his or her own value. Second, it means that individuals must have the secure conviction that his or her conception of their own good and plans of life, are worth carrying out as far as it is within his or her power to fulfill their intentions. If individuals feel their life plans are of little or no value, then it is difficult for them to pursue or to take any satisfaction in accomplishing things contributing to them. Human beings, according to Rawls, desire recognition by others that their lives are worthwhile and that their deeds are appreciated.[45] He believes that a political society based on justice as fairness is good for citizens because it secures mutual self-respect among them. Equal basic rights, fair equality of opportunities, and the difference principle guarantee the essentials of an individual's public recognition as a free and equal citizen. It also means that political society has upheld the fundamental needs of citizens.[46]

Having defined what Rawls means by self-respect as a primary good, two questions must be answered; why is it government's role to secure self-respect among its citizens and how can government accomplish this goal? He provides two answers. First, mutual self-respect among citizens enhances cooperation in society. This is so because public recognition of these two principles of justice provides greater support to individual self-respect, which in turn increases the chances for social cooperation.[47] Since to some degree self-esteem depends on the respect of others, Rawls argues that self-respect is a reciprocal relationship that promotes societal interests. By arranging inequalities for reciprocal advantage and by avoiding the exploitation of the contingencies of nature and social circumstances, individuals are allowed to express their respect for each other in the constitution of their society. It is a rational process to ensure not only their individual self-esteem, but also that of their fellow citizens.[48]

Second, Rawls argues that lack of self-respect among citizens leads to envy, which can be destructive to society.[49] He assumes that the main psychological root of envy lies in a lack of self-confidence in one's own worth combined with a sense of inadequacy.[50] As a result, he says that the least favored in society tend to be more envious of the better situated when they lack self-respect. Rawls points to three conditions that promote envy. First, the psychological condition where one lacks self-respect and has a sense of hopelessness about improving his or her situation.[51] Second, the social structure and style of life in one's society reinforces number one, which results in painful and humiliating experiences for the least favored in society.[52] Third, he says that the least favored do not see any positive alternatives to opposing the favored circumstances of the more advantaged. The latter causes the least favored to desire to impose a loss on those better-situated individuals even if it comes at some cost to them. Of course, not all will want revenge and Rawls says that some individuals will merely accept their situation and become cynical and apathetic.[53]

Society should be organized in a way to reduce these conditions because envy leads to jealousy, resentment, and spite among all members of society. Rawls admits that envy is endemic to human beings since it is associated with rivalry. His goal is to reduce the amount of envy so that cooperation and political justice will flourish.[54] The way that a society is organized directly affects the opportunities for its citizens to have self-respect. Since self-respect promotes cooperation, reduces envy, and helps to ensure a more stable body politic, Rawls believes that governments should promote it as a good in society. This may be accomplished by applying his two principles of justice to society's basic structure. He thinks that individual needs for status will be satisfied by the public recognition of just institutions along with equal liberty. The basis of self-esteem cannot be equated with an equal distribution of goods or wealth. Instead, it relies on an equal distribution of fundamental rights and liberties that promote self-respect among citizens.[55]

It is worthwhile to think about Rawls's claims about rivalry and envy in light of some of the other theorists' beliefs we have explored. While Adam Smith did not provide a detailed account of human psychology, one may remember that he thinks that individuals desire attention and that being wealthy is an effective way to garner it. Conversely, he says that the poor are to some degree ashamed of their poverty, and Smith sees this as a positive impetus for all to work harder to become better off. Smith's positive remarks stand in stark contrast to Rawls's ideas since the latter would probably view this situation as problematic since one could infer that the poor may lack self-respect, which is a primary good that benefits all of society. Moreover, in the first two chapters we saw that Plato and Aristotle identified human greed as one of the root causes of poverty. This leads one to ask: do Plato and Aristotle's notion of greed stem from this rivalry, which Rawls says manifests itself in envy? If not, how are they different? When Rawls uses the word rivalry, one could infer that obtaining material goods and accumulating wealth could be symptomatic of rivalry among individuals. Individual P gets a new Lexus and this stirs the rivalry and in turn the envy of neighbor Q, who thinks she works harder than P and is thus more deserving of a new Lexus. On the other hand, is it that P and Q simply want to acquire as much stuff as possible so that the one who has the most and best stuff wins the rivalry? Alternatively, are individuals just naturally greedy? Significantly, one may remember that Aristotle believes that individuals are not just competitive or sensitive about the abundance or lack of material goods, but also about honors and privileges. That is to say, individuals resent those who receive honors and privileges when they deem the latter unworthy of receiving them. Human beings also take offense when they do not receive what they think they deserve. It is not too far a stretch to say that Rawls's moral psychology in this respect is similar to that of the Ancients. Certainly, at a minimum, rivalry and envy can be contributing factors to one becoming greedy.

The most problematic aspect of Rawls's account of self-respect is that it relies partially on the premise that human beings need the approval of others to obtain self-respect. Moreover, others must acknowledge and appreciate an individual's accomplishments or choice of work as being worthy. This aspect of his definition of self-respect is questionable since history is replete with individuals, who far from receiving approval or appreciation from others, suffered because of their moral integrity to go against the prevailing norms of their society. For example, abolitionists, women suffragists, or animal rights activists have all been ridiculed and marginalized in society. Often, those who were first to point out the immorality and injustice of a social practice or institution were labeled as lunatics. Did these individuals lose their self-respect? On the contrary, one may think that they had a strong sense of self-respect because they acted on their moral convictions. Thus, approval and appreciation of others is not a necessary condition for self-respect. In fact, it would appear that one's moral integrity is a source of self-respect. Seeking the approval and appreciation of others who are immoral, for example, Nazis who want to murder Jews, works against the notion of self-respect. Of course, Rawls is offering a political conception of self-respect, but as shown by the examples, the two are often intertwined. If approval and appreciation from others is a necessary condition for self-respect, then we can easily see why Rawls believes that self-respect will enhance social cooperation and lessen envy. That misses the point, however, because when Rawls lists the primary goods for citizens, he has chosen a moral point of view that is bound to a specific culture.[56] If he relies in part on the approval of others as one of the benchmarks for individuals to obtain self-respect, how can individuals who provide different moral viewpoints from their society's prevailing norms ever obtain self-respect? Since Rawls wants to ensure that society allows for personal autonomy and the objectivity of individuals' judgments of right and justice, it is puzzling that his explanation of self-respect is somewhat other-regarding and not a function of individual moral autonomy.[57]

In spite of these problems, one can still argue that having self-respect is a good because how others regard and treat us matters a great deal. Government can and should promote self-respect among its citizens by protecting human dignity. Those who are the least advantaged in society should not have to sacrifice dignity to receive help from society. When individuals seeking financial assistance are treated like people lost in a Kafka play, their sense of self-respect suffers because they are no longer being treated as ends in themselves.[58] Rawls is correct that self-respect would enhance social cooperation and lessen envy among citizens. Thus, one can accept that self-respect is rightfully placed as a primary good for all citizens in society.

Rawls wants to go beyond the primary goods, however, because what he proposes is to make all persons free and equal. This includes canceling out not only social, but also natural inequalities that people are born with so that they will have equal life prospects. Native endowments such as intelligence and imagination as well as good or ill fortune throughout the course of one's life are included in Rawls's calculations for a just society.[59] Since native endowments or ill fortune are morally arbitrary, meaning that individuals cannot be held morally responsible for their lack of native intelligence for example, but only how they may develop it throughout a lifetime, the difference principle aims to even out these inequalities. Those individuals who are born with greater natural endowments do not deserve greater advantages. Rawls is convinced that individuals who are fortunate would be willing to enjoy their advantages only when it also works to the benefit of those who are less fortunate. One could argue, however, that it is morally arbitrary to ask those with greater endowments to sacrifice for those who have less. The problem is that we know that human beings are neither free nor equal.[60] This is why Rawls appeals to social contract theory, but it is not clear that the contract is strong enough to make it work.

Rawls's position is correct, however, because certain social and natural goods are morally arbitrary. The problem is how to distinguish those arbitrary qualities that affect our lives from the choices that we make. It seems intuitively clear that we do want people to be responsible for their actions. At the same time, it is clear that individuals are not responsible for being born with disabilities, being born into dysfunctional families or having no family at all. Yet, what is not clear is how we separate the two. Rawls does not attempt to do this. In his scenario, the least advantaged who were born with chronic health problems are not compensated for those health problems. Rather, they may expect the same income as someone who was born with good health but who merely lacks ambition to develop his or her skills or to contribute to the common good based on his or her natural ability. It is true that the latter individual may have less material goods than if he or she were willing to earn them.[61]

There is also another side to this problem. Namely, if someone is born with tremendous talent, intelligence, and a good family, but she makes the decision not to work since she likes to watch television and do nothing productive, she is guaranteed the same standard of living as one who has none of her advantages. Contrary to seeming either just or fair, this appears to be patently unfair. It is these types of cases that make it difficult to draw a clear line between endowments and choices.[62] This problem plagued the American welfare system. On the one hand, some of the recipients were truly needy and the welfare benefits barely covered their basic expenses. Some may argue that it would be just for society to do more to help these individuals. On the other hand, one can assume that some of the recipients made bad decisions. Their receiving welfare had nothing to do with lack of natural endowments but more to do with bad decision-making. The difficulty is how does one put moral blame on those who make bad decisions? While those who make bad life decisions may appear to have sufficient talent and intelligence to cause one to think that they could be productive in a competitive market, perhaps they lack other skills necessary to do so. The idea of deserving and undeserving seems to lead down a morally ambiguous path that illustrates the complexity of attempting to solve the problem of poverty in liberal democracies. How does one define fairness for those who need help from others, and for those who supply the help? As we know, this is not a new problem. We saw how Locke and Tocqueville struggled with it. In addition, one may remember that this is precisely why John Stuart Mill thought that classifications such as deserving and undeserving were unjust. This goes to the heart of one of the most problematic features of Rawls's theory. Earlier, we saw that he rejects the idea of a social minimum as a safety net for the poor in society because he believes that the strains of commitment would be too great for the poor. In fact, the option for a social minimum is not considered in the original position. By asking us to imagine the worst-case scenario in the original position through a veil of ignorance, he is convinced that all would agree to his two principles of justice. As Seung points out, this amounts to a scare tactic to support his two principles of justice.[63] What is not clear, however, is why the strains of commitment would not be too great for those who are advantaged with greater native endowments and social positions. Rawls's moral psychology seems to dwell solely on those who are least advantaged. He does not take into consideration that the same feelings of envy and resentment may arise among the advantaged with native endowments and social positions in society. If one takes seriously the worries about the strain of commitment after the contract has been agreed to, one must think about it for all parties in society and not just the least advantaged. What is the motive for compliance once individuals leave the original position and the veil of ignorance is removed? Rawls relies on a sense of justice or a sense of fairness in all individuals that will trump the self-interested desires of the advantaged. Enlightened self-interest is the motive for all citizens to aim for fairness as found in the two principles of justice.

Rawls also fails to answer Marx's critique of liberal capitalism.[64] As we saw in the last chapter, Marx is concerned with the ownership of the means of production. This is more important than primary goods or the even distribution of those goods. Marx believes that the structure of capitalist production is the root of the problem and thus, equality can be achieved only when the proletariat is in charge of the means of production. In *Justice as Fairness*, Rawls says that the idea of worker-managed firms is fully compatible with a property-owning democracy.[65] He believes that the two principles of justice can be satisfied under a regime with private ownership of the means of production. If a liberal socialist regime can do better in realizing the two principles, then Rawls says that a case may be made for it from the standpoint of justice as fairness. That begs the question because it is unlikely that these two principles of justice would solve the structural and exploitative factors that contribute to the problem of poverty. After all, the difference principle can justify even gross inequalities as long as they are necessary for incentive and inducement. Thus, all of society benefits from these inequalities. In other words, without some incentive, the base payment for all would be lowered.[66] The problem is that Rawls seems not to take seriously the effect of economic inequalities on the political system or on political liberties.[67]

As Frank Michelman points out, justice as fairness does provide an adequate legal framework for welfare rights.[68] He says, "Thus the difference principle implies welfare rights in the elusive form of whatever is necessary to prevent the undermining of self-respect by relative deprivation."[69] Further, Michelman views the idea of the social minimum as an institutional feature linked specifically to the difference principle. He concludes that the entire theory reflects "a degree of risk aversion" which forces individuals in the original position to choose priorities that assure individuals that they will have their needs met. Most importantly, they will be able to maintain their self-respect.[70]

Rawls states at the beginning of *Justice as Fairness* that his work is "ideal theory." The normative concern is that the real world deviates in many ways from the conditions Rawls believes exist in a just, well-ordered society. So if one must accept the "ideal," what does Rawls contribute to solving the problem of poverty when the social forces and justice that he describes seem to be sorely lacking in the real world? For example, in *Political Liberalism*, he argues that people in contemporary democracies have what he calls "fully comprehensive doctrines" (FCDs). These FCDs include "conceptions of what is of value in human life, and ideals of personal character, as well as ideals of friendship and of familiar and associational relationships, and much else that is to inform our conduct, and in the limit to our life as a whole."[71] The problem is that few, if anyone in contemporary democracies have these FCDs. In fact, A. P. Martinich questions whether many people ever had them.[72] Martinich convincingly argues "that most people, including most reflective, educated people, operate with a poorly articulated, incomplete, highly contextualized, dynamic, and often inconsistent set of maxims."[73] This leads one to question Rawls's premise that an overlapping consensus of justice exists in spite of people's individual differences.[74] This is a significant point because it not only brings into question the helpfulness that ideal theory might bring to the problem of poverty in liberal democracies, but it also goes to the heart of the strains of commitment questions raised earlier. Professor Rawls is not unaware of the problem of poverty in America. On the back cover of *Justice as Fairness*, Erin Kelly, the editor, writes the following:

> Rawls is well aware that since the publication of *A Theory of Justice* in 1971, American society has moved farther away from the idea of justice as fairness. Yet his ideas retain their power and relevance to debates in a pluralistic society about the meaning and theoretical viability of liberalism. This book demonstrates that moral clarity can be achieved even when a collective commitment to justice is uncertain.

It is not clear, however, that moral clarity is achieved since Rawls's project hinges on the social contract and subsequent commitments made by citizens to the two principles under the veil of ignorance in the original position. Given that citizens make decisions based on their aversion to risk-taking, is that commitment strong enough to last once the veil is lifted? Is there a shared sense of justice that would sustain the commitment to the difference principle? It appears that the social contract move that Rawls makes to justify the obligation that we have to those who are less advantaged is weak at best.

What Rawls does accomplish, however, is significant. He forces us to confront the fact that many of the reasons that individuals find themselves in poverty have nothing to do with desert. Unlike Locke and Tocqueville, Rawls harkens back to Plato and Aristotle's acknowledgement of bad fortune and other morally arbitrary factors that affect one's place in society. His theory points to the complexities of the problem and illustrates that viable solutions are difficult to find. Government has a role to play in addressing the problem of poverty because without its intervention, according to Rawls, there is no chance that the plight of the poor will become easier in a liberal capitalist democracy. In contrast to Rawls, Robert Nozick thinks that the primary concern for political philosophers should be about justice for the individual. Not surprisingly, he rejects Rawls's preoccupation with the welfare of the least advantaged. The Rawlsian idea of justice as fairness, according to Nozick, is grossly unjust.

ROBERT NOZICK

In *Anarchy, State, and Utopia*, Robert Nozick restates John Locke's theories of the state, justice, and private property.[75] He begins from the individualistic position that there is no true political entity other than individuals and that, only individuals have rights.[76] He relies on a Kantian view of rights because he connects respecting private property ownership rights with respecting individuals as ends in themselves.[77] Nozick provides a defense of private property, accumulation, and social and political inequalities, not as things that are good in themselves, but as things, which can be removed only by violating the rights of individuals. He uses Locke to explain the principle of acquisition and the idea of self-ownership. In the end, Nozick argues for a minimal state. "At no point does *our* argument assume any background institutions more extensive than those of *the* minimal night-watchman state, a state limited to protecting persons against murder, assault, theft, fraud, and so forth."[78] Not only are there no provisions for equality of opportunity, but also the poor are left to fend for themselves because any government taxation or coercion to help them is unjust and amounts to theft.

Nozick's partial use of Locke and Kant's political theories is problematic. In the case of the Locke, Nozick uses a secularized version of his political philosophy. This interpretation fails because it is one that Locke would not recognize. Nozick applies the Kantian precept of treating people as ends in themselves to expose the injustice of government taxation to aid the poor. I argue there is textual support to show that Nozick's use of Kant's words is contrary to what Kant himself said about poverty. Providing public aid to the less fortunate, according to Kant, was government's responsibility. Moreover, he did not consider public aid to be charity, but a duty. To understand the implications of Nozick's theory for the poor in society, one must first investigate his theories of entitlement and self-ownership.

The entitlement theory, according to Nozick, explains how a just distribution of goods in society takes place. In brief, he says that if one assumes everyone is entitled to their possessions they currently own, then a just distribution is one of free exchange.[79] His theory has three categories to identify just ownership.

The first is the original acquisition of holdings or what he sometimes calls the principle of justice in acquisition.[80] A) What one produces belongs to him or her unless one sells, abandons, or gives it away. B) What individuals find belong to them as long as it does not belong to anyone else and they intentionally took control of it. This principle and principle two may be subject to the Lockean Proviso, which is stated by Locke in the *Second Treatise* as follows: "For this *Labour* being the unquestionable Property of the Labourer, no Man but he can have a right to what that is once joined to, at least where there is enough and as good left in common for others."[81]

Second, the just transfer of holdings specifies the processes by which individuals' entitlements may be legitimately transferred to another.[82] What one transfers to another individual belongs to that individual, provided that the initial acquisition was consistent with the first principle.

Finally, the principle of rectification identifies a procedure by which the effects of past injustices may be corrected. Thus, if one violates principle one, two, or both, then an injustice has occurred. Rectification means making an injustice right.[83]

Locke's notion of property ownership roughly states that mixing one's labor with something makes one the owner of it.[84] Michael Davis provides an interpretation of Locke's definition of acquisition in the following way:

Definition of "Produce" and "Find": (a) You produce an object if you make it what it is by physically changing the material of which it is made. (b) You produce an intangible insofar as what you do adds to the value of an already existing object without physically changing it. And (c) you find an object insofar as you take control of it without taking the object from another, physically changing it, or increasing its value.[85]

Nozick says that what Locke means is "that laboring on something improves it and makes it more valuable; and anyone is entitled to own a thing whose value he has created."[86] Historically, this is problematic since force is often involved in original acquisition of natural resources. Thus, if Q takes a plot of land from P and if Q has mixed his labor with the land to improve it, does this mean that Q's acquisition is legitimate or illegitimate. Either way, it does not matter, because if it is legitimate, then the government or someone else could also use force to take it away from Q and redistribute it. If it is illegitimate, then the government or someone else could take the land from Q and redistribute it.[87]

Nozick says that taking something by force makes the transaction illegitimate.[88] As a result, his principle of rectification kicks in and the land should be returned to P, its legitimate owner. The simple case of P and Q, however, do not illustrate the inherent, if not intractable difficulties in trying to decide whom the rightful owner is in many cases. Numerous examples come to mind, including the land used by Native Americans in North America, which was appropriated by the settlers. In fact, an argument could be made that Nozick's view supports returning much of New England to the Native Americans whose land was taken away.[89] How does one even start to trace original acquisition? Nozick asks a similar question, "How far back must one go in wiping clean the historical slate of injustices?"[90] He answers by saying that one should use history to unravel the actual course of events until one can make a "best estimate" of the information about what might have occurred.[91] The principle of rectification, according to Nozick, may cause a one-time redistribution of resources to wipe the slate clean. After that, however, his principles of entitlement would hold.[92]

Thus far all that has been covered is real property. What about natural talent, which cannot be separated from the person who possesses it? Of course, individuals may contract to sell their services, and that may in turn be described as property. The principle of self-ownership, according to Nozick, means that whatever natural talents one may be born with belong to that individual alone. He uses the Wilt Chamberlain example to make this point.[93] No matter how much profit Chamberlain may make from charging people an extra twenty-five cents to watch him play basketball, it is unjust for government to tax him to compensate others for their needs. He derives this claim from Locke's idea that persons have property in their own person. It is worth looking at Locke's own words about this.

> Though the Earth, and all inferior Creatures be common to all Men, yet every Man has a *Property* in his own *Person*. This no Body has any Right to but himself. The *Labour* of his body, and the *Work* of his Hands, we may say, are properly his. Whatsoever then removes out of the State that Nature hath provided and left it in, he hath mixed his Labour with, and joined to it something that is his own, and thereby makes it his *Property*. It being by him removed from the common state Nature placed it in, it hath by this *labour* something annexed to it, that excludes the common right of other Men, For this *Labour* being the unquestionable Property of the Labourer, no Man but he can have a right to what that is once joined to, at least where there is enough and as good left in common for others.[94]

From the above statement, Nozick concludes that Locke meant, "each person has a right to decide what would become of himself and what he would

do, and as having a right to reap the benefits of what he did."[95] It also provides a justification for the right to the market value of one's holding. Thus,
if one justly owns P, for example, one's natural talents, then one has a right to
the market value of one's holdings under a Lockean theory of ownership.
Moreover, it necessarily follows that one owns what anyone will voluntarily
compensate individuals for P.[96] Unlike Rawls, Nozick does not want to consider natural endowments, moral merit, or needs in his principle of distributive justice. "Whether or not people's natural assets are arbitrary from a moral
point of view, they are entitled to them, and to what flows from them."[97]

Nozick ties his interpretation of Locke's self-ownership with the Kantian
precept of treating people as ends in themselves because self-ownership protects individuals from being used as means to others' ends. Theories of justice that focus solely on recipients and their supposed rights, according to
him, ignore those who give and transfer their rights. Thus recipient-oriented
theories also ignore those who are producing wealth and their entitlement to
that wealth.[98] He concludes that taxation on individuals' earnings from their
labor is one kind of forced labor.[99] After all, no one would force unemployed
hippies to work to benefit the poor. If the latter policy example is illegitimate,
then it follows that a tax system that takes some of individuals' goods for the
needy would also be illegitimate.[100] Nozick directly connects these ideas to
Kant in the following passage:

> Why not *similarly* hold that some persons have to bear some costs that benefit
> other persons more, for the sake of the overall social good? But there is no *so-
> cial entity* with a good that undergoes some sacrifice for its own good. There are
> only individual people, different individual people, with their own individual
> lives. Using one of these people for the benefit of others, uses him and benefits
> the others. Nothing more. What happens is that something is done to him for the
> sake of others covers this up. (Intentionally?) To use a person in this way does
> not sufficiently respect and take account of the fact that he is a separate person
> and his is the only life he has. He does not get some overbalancing good from
> his overall sacrifice, and no one is entitled to force this upon him—least of all a
> state or government that claims his allegiance (as other individuals do not) and
> that therefore scrupulously must be *neutral* between its citizens.[101]

Nozick suggests that if we do not accept his position, then Kant's categorical imperative should be changed to state, "So act as to minimize the use of
humanity simply as a means."[102]

This is a problematic move for Nozick to make because of Kant's views on
how society ought to deal with the problem of poverty. In *The Metaphysics of
Morals*, Kant addresses this question directly. It is worth looking at Kant's

justification for why government and the wealthy are responsible to provide for the needs of the poor.

> The general will of the people has united itself into a society, which is to maintain itself perpetually; and for this end it has submitted itself to the internal authority of the state in order to maintain those members of the society who are unable to maintain themselves. For reasons of state the government is therefore authorized to constrain the wealthy to provide the means of sustenance to those who are unable to provide for even their most necessary natural needs. The wealthy have acquired an obligation to the commonwealth, since they owe their existence to an act of submitting to its protection and care, which they need in order live; on this obligation the state now bases its right to contribute what is theirs to maintaining their fellow citizens.[103]

Kant bases this obligation not on an appeal to benevolence but as an entreaty to the general will. Thus the protection against deprivation of primary needs is not cast in terms of charity but as what is justly due to the less privileged. To care for the poor, Kant suggests that taxes may be collected on property and commerce or the government may establish a fund and use the interest generated from it. He rejects devices such as lotteries to collect money for poor people because he says that lotteries simply produce more poor people.[104] In this respect, Rawls is in agreement with Kant because he believes that citizens understand that they must pay taxes as part of their obligation to society.[105]

As for Locke, even if one accepts Nozick's interpretations of the idea of self-ownership and the weak interpretation of the Lockean Proviso, there is still a problem that needs to be addressed. As we saw in chapter 3, Locke believes in natural law theory, which commands that no one perish from want of subsistence. After all, the rights to life and liberty precede the right to property in his political philosophy. As a result, Locke supported public aid along with the government apparatus to collect it. For all his harshness toward the poor, Locke believed that government had a fundamental duty to provide sustenance for them.

In response to Marxist ideas, Nozick says that for the most part, Marxist theory is obsolete. After a lengthy discussion about the problems inherent in Marx's labor theory of value, he declares that the idea of exploitation is a fraudulent one. Large segments of the American work force, according to Nozick, have cash reserves in personal property. Labor unions also have extensive cash reserves in union pension funds. As a result, he asks, why will these workers not use their money to establish worker-controlled factories? The answers he provides is that the workers lack the entrepreneurial spirit and it is simply too risky for them to do so. Any claims of exploitation by the workers are simply attempts to hide their own aversions to risk. The capitalist entrepreneurs who not only take risks, but also have the expertise to know how to make profits are entitled to sizeable shares of the product of their ventures. Do the ordinary people really have control over their pension funds?[106] This would come as a great surprise to former Enron employees who lost most of their retirement savings because the value of their 401Ks evaporated. Board members and other Enron executives, however, profited handsomely by selling their stock holdings months before the company collapsed.[107] Even if some workers could successfully pull together the necessary capital, it would be no more than a small minority who could take on such a task given the structural forces in place to prevent it from happening.[108] Nozick chooses to ignore certain social facts and by disregarding them, he makes things seem possible that are implausible in American society.[109] Moreover, he ignores Marx's claim that the ruling class controls not only wealth, but also the ideas and intellectual forces of society.[110]

In a direct attack on Marx, Nozick says that to think that the role of a theory of distributive justice is to fill in the blank "to each according to his _____" is to be predisposed to think that the other part of the equation, "from each according to his _____" is an entirely separate question. Nozick reformulates the famous quote from Marx in the following way: "From each as they choose, to each as they are chosen."[111]

The above quotation from Nozick succinctly sums up his philosophy. Throughout the entire work, he ignores any social or structural factors that may influence individuals' choices. Moreover, he offers nothing to those who are born with severe disabilities or other hindrances to leading a fulfilling life. Like Locke, Nozick ignores social and other empirical factors that contribute to the problem of poverty.

Nozick's political theory paints a chilling picture for a just society. Surely, few would want to live in his minimal state, which offers only limited protection for individuals and their property. Under his system, one can imagine the gap between wealthy and poor rising to heights that would surely threaten the security of everyone in that society. Without government intervention, or coercion, private charity would not sustain the poor. Nozick far surpasses the classical liberal idea of limited government because even Adam Smith acknowledged that no society could flourish or be happy when the greater part of its members are poor and miserable. Moreover, as we saw in chapter 4, Smith was not blind to the economic differences that existed in capitalist societies. He thought that taxation should be based on people's wealth and their ability to pay taxes and thus, advocated progressive taxation.[112] Smith also acknowledged the importance of public education as necessary for citizens and society to flourish. All these concerns are absent from Nozick's account of a just state. Likewise, Locke and Tocqueville's beliefs about the duty of others to promote self-preservation among all humanity are also absent. Nozick's picture of a just state is one that may be a bit more secure than the Hobbesean state of nature where life is "solitary, poor, nasty, brutish, and short."[113]

Unlike Nozick, Rawls acknowledges the many obstacles that poor people face in a democratic, capitalist state. By forcing us to consider just how contingent each individual's position is in society, Rawls's hypothetical situation in the original position drives home the meaning of the phrase, "there but by the grace of God go I." Moreover, he points to the natural and social benefits that some enjoy and he makes a strong case that those individuals *ought* or *will* be willing to sacrifice some material comforts for the sake of their fellow human beings. Both authors force readers to ask the question, do huge gaps in inequality of wealth matter in society?

For more than thirty years the gap between the wealthy and everyone else in the United States has been increasing. In fact, the level of inequality is higher in America than in any other industrialized nation.[114] Economists and other experts disagree about what significance this increasing gap may have for the country's future. For example, Martin Feldstein, a professor of economics at Harvard University and the former chair of President Reagan's Council of Economic Advisers, says that we should not worry "about the fact that some people on Wall Street and basketball players are making a lot of money."[115] He views inequality as a basic feature of the new high-tech economy. It is a natural consequence because capitalism rewards talent, skills, education, and entrepreneurial risk with increasing efficiency.[116] Another Harvard economist, Richard Freeman, disagrees with Feldstein. Freeman believes that something should be done. He says, "The question is whether you lean against the wind of the market to try to preserve decent living standards for working and poor people."[117] Other liberal economists agree with Freeman and think that Europe and Japan are doing just that.

Ronald Inglehart, a sociology professor at the University of Michigan, weighs in on the discussion because of his thirty years of research. He investigates what role levels of equality and inequality play in people's sense of satisfaction or dissatisfaction with their lot in life. Dr. Inglehart says, "Interestingly the levels of dissatisfaction are highest in the most equal countries in the world, the Communist countries or those that have just emerged from Communism, and also those with very high levels of inequality."[118] His research shows that total equality can only be achieved through coercion. This coercion makes individuals feel they have no control over their lives and no way to benefit from their labor. In other words, this group experiences some of the same feelings as those who are poor. High inequality in extremely stratified societies makes people feel crushed by the economic power of others and thus produces similar dissatisfaction. Thus neither situation is conducive to human flourishing since a loss of control takes a psychological toll and it matters little if it is a result of direct coercion or from living in a stratified society where some are wealthy while others are poor.

Feldstein insists that one should not be concerned with inequality because poverty is the problem.[119] He blames poverty on poor education, the breakdown of the family, and "low cognitive ability."[120] These are the critical factors that cause people to be poor. He adds that some poor people simply may choose not to work as hard as investment bankers working seventy hours a week, or to skip school, and thus earn less money. In other words, these individuals make choices and these choices contribute to their poverty.

Empirical data shows that children born to women in the bottom quarter of the income bracket or ones who grow up in single-parent households, will more than likely never attend college even if they have the same grades and test scores as those of their peers.[121] One thing that conservative and liberal economists agree on is that education is the key to rising out of poverty. Finishing high school increases an individual's income by 30 percent. Those who attend college may earn 60 percent more than those who have no higher education. James Heckman, a professor of economics at the University of Chicago who is also a self-proclaimed conservative and libertarian, made the following observation:

> Never has the accident of birth mattered more. If I am born to educated, supportive parents, my chances of doing well are totally different than if I were born to a single parent or abusive parents. I am a University of Chicago libertarian, but this is a case of market failure: children don't get to "buy" their parents, and so there has to be some kind of intervention to make up for these environmental differences.[122]

This last quotation goes to the heart of the difficulty that poverty creates for liberal political theorists like Rawls and Nozick. On the one hand, Rawls is trying to minimize, if not eliminate the negative effects that sometimes accompany the accident of birth since no one gets to choose his or her parents. On the other hand, Nozick believes it would be unjust to make any attempt to level the playing field given the sanctity of private property in his minimalist state. They provide two entirely different responses to resolve the dilemma. This is not surprising since trying to address the problem of poverty operating within liberal political theory is problematic, if not impossible.

Returning to the central question about the demands of justice, one can see that Nozick's theory of justice falls far short. Even if we granted all of his arguments about fairness for the individual based solely on just acquisition and property rights, a picture emerges of a state where individual dignity and worth are based on one's situation at birth or one's abilities to acquire property. Setting Nozick's political theory alongside Rawls's brings to the fore the question of moral equality. Do we think that by their nature alone, human beings are born morally equal? Yes, and at a minimum, justice demands that each individual is treated with dignity and respect by the virtue of his or her humanity alone. Since Nozick's social contract can accomplish nothing more than possibly the protection of one's property, he magnifies the individualistic nature of liberal theory and creates a state where there is no moral equality.

As a liberal theorist, Rawls wants to believe that we share certain values that commit us to care about justice and fairness for all individuals. The question then becomes; do we share those values? Certainly, most people would say that they want to be just and to treat individuals fairly. Of course, the problem is flushing out the ideas of justice and fairness. This is what Rawls's political theory attempts to do. At the beginning of this study, I said that the demands of justice necessarily entail that the political theorist engage with the problem of poverty with the goal being to suggest some thoughtful and reasonable approaches that might address the problem. Nozick fails to meet that standard while much, if not most, of Rawls's work aims to fulfill that goal.

NOTES

1. Myron Magnet's work is representative of this critique. See Magnet's, *The Dream and the Nightmare: The Sixties Legacy to the Underclass* (New York: Encounter Books, 1993).

2. Michael Sandel, *Liberalism and the Limits of Justice*, 2nd ed. (Cambridge: Cambridge University Press, 1998), 66.

3. John Rawls, *A Theory of Justice* (Cambridge: Harvard University Press, 1971). All references to this work are from this edition and hereafter cited as *TJ*.

4. For example, *Reading Rawls*, ed. Norman Daniels (Stanford University Press, 1989) is a critical study of *A Theory of Justice*. Brian Barry's book, the *Liberal Theory of Justice* (Oxford University Press, 1973) also offers a critical examination of *A Theory of Justice*. *Understanding Rawls* (Princeton University Press, 1977) by Robert Wolff provides a reconstruction and critique of Rawls's theory. Nozick's *Anarchy, State, and Utopia* (New York: Basic Books, 1974) is partially directed at refuting Rawls's difference principle. *Liberalism and the Limits of Justice* by Sandel (Cambridge University Press, 1982, 1998) is also an argument against Rawls's *Theory of Justice*.

5. John Rawls, *Justice as Fairness: A Restatement* (Cambridge: Harvard University Press, 2001). Hereafter cited as *JF*.

6. T. K. Seung, *Intuition and Construction: The Foundation of Normative Theory* (New Haven: Yale University Press, 1993), 38.

7. *JF*, 10.

8. Ibid., 139.

9. John Rawls, *Political Liberalism* (New York: Columbia University Press, 1996). Hereafter cited to as *PL*.

10. *PL*, 11–15.

11. *JF*, 29.

12. Ibid., 92.

13. Ibid., 32.

14. *TJ*, 15.

15. *JF*, 4.

16. Ibid., 8.

17. Ibid., 15.

18. Ibid., 42–43.

19. Ibid., 47.

20. Ibid., 44.

21. Seung, *Intuition and* Construction, 36.

22. *TJ*, 61.

23. *JF*, 43.

24. Ibid., 46.

25. Ibid., 44; *TJ*, 101, 107.

26. *JF*, 99.

27. Ibid., 60.

28. Ibid., 98.

29. Ibid., 64.

30. Ibid., 48.

31. Ibid., 316–17.

32. Seung, *Intuition and Construction*, 28.

33. Rawls, *TJ*, 317.

34. Seung, *Intuition and Construction*, 28.

35. Ibid., 28.

36. Rawls cites Jeremy Waldron's article "John Rawls and the Social Minimum," *Journal of Applied Philosophy* 3 (1986) for making him rethink his original reasons for rejecting the social minimum in *Theory of Justice*. Rawls says that he accepts Waldron's formulation of the social minimum as "a distinct idea of the minimum as that of meeting the basic human needs essential for a decent life" (*JF*, 127 n47).

37. *JF*, 130.

38. Ibid., 128–29.

39. Ibid., 130.

40. Ibid., 44, 58.

41. Ibid., 58–59

42. Ibid., 59.

43. Ibid., 63–64.

44. *TJ*, 440.

45. Ibid., 440–441.

46. *PL*, 203.

47. *TJ*, 178.

48. Ibid., 179.

49. Ibid., 534–35.

50. Ibid., 535.

51. Ibid., 531.

52. Ibid., 535.

53. Ibid., 536.

54. Ibid., 537–38.

55. Ibid., 544.

56. This is not the only area that is entangled with cultural relativism. As Seung points out, "Rawls's entire program becomes enchained to cultural relativism" (*Intuition and Construction*, 44).

57. *TJ*, 513.

58. Jonathan Kozel's descriptions of the bottomless bureaucratic trap that the homeless in America fall into provides a compelling account of the indignity and shame that people may have to endure while trying to survive. *Rachel and Her Children: Homeless Families in America* (New York; Facett Columbine, 1988).

59. *TJ*, 105; *JF*, 40.

60. Seung, *Intuition and Construction*, 39.

61. Will Kymlicka, *Contemporary Political Philosophy* (Oxford: Clarendon Press, 1990), 71–73.

62. Ibid., 73–74.

63. Seung, *Intuition and Construction*, 13.

64. Allan Bloom claims that not only does Rawls not address Marxist concerns in *A Theory of Justice*, but he also ignores issues raised by Nietzsche. "Justice: John Rawls vs. the Tradition of Political Philosophy," *The American Political Science Review* 69, no.2 (June 1975): 648.

65. *JF*, 178.

66. Seung, *Intuition and Construction*, 38.

67. Norman Daniels, "Equal Liberty and Unequal Worth of Liberty," in *Reading Rawls* (Stanford: Stanford University Press, 1989), 253–81.

68. Frank Michelman, "Constitutional Welfare Rights and *A Theory of Justice*," in *Reading Rawls* (Stanford: Stanford University Press, 1989), 319–47.

69. Ibid., 346.

70. Ibid., 347.

71. *PL*, 13.

72. A. P. Martinich, "Religion, Fanaticism, and Liberalism," *Pacific Philosophical Quarterly* 81 (2000): 409–25.

73. Ibid., 423.

74. *PL*, 11–15. This is what he later calls the idea of "reasonable pluralism" in *JF*, 92.

75. Robert Nozick, *Anarchy, State, and Utopia* (New York: Basic Books, Inc., 1974).

76. Ibid., 32–33.

77. Ibid., 30–33. Kant's categorical imperative states that one should "So act that you use humanity, whether in your own person or in the person of any other, always at the same time as an end, and never merely as a means." (Immanuel) Kant, *Groundwork of the Metaphysics of Morals*, trans, Mary Gregor (Cambridge: Cambridge University Press, 1997), 4: 429, 38.

78. *Anarchy, State, and Utopia*, 162.

79. Ibid., 51.

80. Ibid., 150.

81. Locke, *Second Treatise*, 27.

82. *Anarchy, State, and Utopia*, 150.

83. Ibid., 152–53.

84. Locke, *Second Treatise*, 27.

85. Michael Davis, Nozick's Argument *for* the Legitimacy of the Welfare State" in *Ethics* 97, no. 3 (April, 1987): 578.

86. *Anarchy, State, and Utopia*, 175.

87. G. A. Cohen, *History, Labour, and Freedom: Themes from Marx* (Oxford: Oxford University Press, 1988), 253–54.

88. *Anarchy, State, and Utopia* , 230–31.

89. D. Lyons, "The New Indian Claims and Original Rights to Land," in *Reading Nozick*, ed. J. Paul, (Totowas, NJ: Rowman and Littlefield, 1981), 198.

90. *Anarchy, State, and Utopia*, 152.

91. Ibid., 152.

92. Ibid., 153.

93. Ibid., 160–64.

94. Locke, *Second Treatise*, 27.

95. *Anarchy, State, and Utopia*, 171.

96. Ibid., 222.

97. Ibid., 226.

98. Ibid., 168.

99. Ibid., 169.

100. Ibid., 170.

101. Ibid., 32–33.

102. Ibid., 32.

103. Kant. *The Metaphysics of Morals*, 6:326, 101.

104. Ibid., 6: 327, 101.

105. *JF*, 52.

106. Milton Fisk, "Property and the State: A Discussion of Robert Nozick's *Anarchy, State, and Utopia*" in *Noüs* 14, no.1 1980): 105

107. Reed Abelson, "Enron Board Comes Under a Storm of Criticism," *The New York Times,* 16 December 2001: Business Section.

108. Fisk, "Property and the State," 106.

109. Ibid., 107.

110. Marx, *German Ideology*, 172.

111. *Anarchy, State, and Utopia*, 160.

112. Smith, *WN* II.v.ii: 350.

113. Thomas Hobbes, *Leviathan*, ed. Richard Tuck (Cambridge: Cambridge University Press, 1999), 189.

114. Alexander Stille, "Grounded by an Income Gap," *New York Times*, 15 December 2001: 15 (A).

115. Stille, "Grounded by an Income Gap," 15 (A).

116. Ibid., 15(A).

117. Ibid., 15(A).

118. Ibid., 15(A).

119. Ibid., 15(A).

120. Ibid., 15(A).

121. Ibid., 15(A).

122. Ibid., 15(A).

Chapter Eight

Conclusions

This study has explored the relationship between poverty and justice in society. At the outset, I said that at the core of this work is the claim that political theorists must engage with the problem of poverty and provide some thoughtful and reasonable approaches to address the problem. While some philosophers have clearly articulated theories of justice, others have ideas and statements throughout their works, which I have pieced together to bring clarity to their positions. We have seen that without exception each theorist is concerned with fairness and justice in the state. Unfortunately, we did not see the same uniformity in their treatments of poverty and its relationship to a just society. This is significant for several reasons. First, the number of people who live in poverty has always exceeded the numbers who do not, and thus it is reasonable to expect that engaging the relationship between the poor and the idea of a just state would be a prominent feature in any political theory. Second, the idea of justice is central to political philosophy and I argue that the idea of justice surely encompasses caring about others who are in need.

Each theorist's definition of human nature is central to his political theory and thus it may be tempting to think that their positive or negative views about human nature correspond to their beliefs about societal obligations to the poor or for that matter what justice demands societies ought to do about the problem. As I have shown, this would be a mistake. No one has a more positive view regarding the poor than Adam Smith, yet he does not believe that government has a moral obligation to help poor people. In fact, to do so would be unjust. Likewise, Locke's contempt for the poor does not prevent him from believing that government has a fundamental obligation to provide poor relief. To do otherwise would be unjust.

It is even more complicated than this since there is little agreement among the theorists about how one ought to define poverty or identify the poor. Thus, one must be clear that before any fruitful discussions about possible causes or solutions can proceed in any context, it is necessary to have some agreement about what constitutes poverty or perhaps, some agreement about human beings' needs to lead decent lives. As I have shown, each theorist's definition of poverty has significant implications for his political theory as well as his ideas about how the poor ought to be treated in the just state.

Discussions about poverty and the idea of justice require that one engage with the notion of distributive justice since how benefits and burdens are divided among individuals in society is fundamental. I have shown that while Plato and Aristotle never used that term, there was indeed a desire on their part to limit or in Plato's case, avoid the problem of poverty. This desire necessarily entailed redistribution of resources to help create a just state. Without a doubt, Aristotle and Plato had practical as well as moral concerns about the problem because they believed that poverty jeopardized the stability of society. While promoting societal stability was a critical concern, it was not their only one. Both Plato and Aristotle desired to create a just state and this meant that human well-being had to be part of that calculus. Perhaps, this latter point explains why the tone of their treatments is devoid of *ad hominem* attacks against the poor or the grinding of ideological axes. Aristotle, in particular takes a no-nonsense approach to his empirical investigation of the problem, which is followed with pragmatic policy proposals to help limit the incidence of poverty. The aims of their policies were twofold: to improve the impoverished individual's life and to promote the common good.

That justice demands some redistribution of resources in society is not surprising since as Rousseau said in the *Second Discourse*, there are two kinds of inequality, that is, natural and man-made. Since no one has control over the first kind, political theorists are forced to confront the second type of inequality. This leads to the question; are all human beings born morally equal? Moral equality simply means that by the virtue of one's humanity, she has intrinsic worth and that fact alone merits that she be treated with dignity and respect. We then have to ask if one believes that human beings are morally equal by the virtue of their humanity, what implications does that have for the construction of the just society? As one may imagine, it has profound implications because it means that the political theorist must take the problem of poverty as a serious threat to individual human worth and thus as a possible obstacle to creating a just state.

One problem that reappeared throughout this work was that poverty exposed inherent tensions in liberal theory. All of the liberal theorists—Locke, Rousseau, Smith, Tocqueville, Mill, Hegel, Rawls, and Nozick—confront this conflict among competing values. The sanctity of private property and the belief in individual accountability compete against beliefs about individual moral equality and societal responsibility for the poor. One approach to try to resolve this conflict was for the state to distinguish between the deserving and undeserving poor. My examination of Locke, Tocqueville, and Mill's treatments of poverty reveal the difficulty of this undertaking. That Locke, who was an empiricist, fails to take into account the economic circumstances of the 1690s in his Report, is telling. Just as revealing is Tocqueville and Mill's engagement with the devastating poverty in Ireland. In the latter cases, the empirical circumstances shape and to some degree, alter their beliefs about the poor and poverty. Mill is correct in thinking there is no substitution for individual responsibility. That being said, he, and Tocqueville are also right about the futility in trying to decide who is deserving or undeserving of public aid. For Mill it is a matter of justice since he thinks that it is both illogical and unjust for the state to provide the necessities for criminals while denying the poor those same essentials such as food, clothing, and shelter. His logical approach to confronting the problem of poverty reflects his rejection of intuition as a basis for making policy decisions. Void of logic, intuition leads to sentimentality and ineffective policies. Both Tocqueville and Mill rely on empirical evidence, reason, and logic. Their critical analyses provide two of the most thoughtful and substantive treatments of poverty.

While there is no substitute for personal responsibility that does not mean that market economies are not without fault in contributing to the problem of poverty and the exploitation of the poor. Marx was right in many of his critiques about the excesses of capitalism. The rampant exploitation that he along with Engels observed was based on individuals' economic insecurity and vulnerability. Marx never uses the word justice but as I have shown his passionate critique of capitalism indicates that his concern for the marginalized and exploited is indeed a matter of justice. For all of the shortcomings in Marx's theory, there is little doubt that his work was influential in curbing and correcting some of the excesses of capitalism. Government interventions to protect workers' safety and to limit the number of hours in a workday are two examples of the fruits of his critique. Moreover, he provides a significant challenge to Adam Smith's belief that relative poverty does not matter since the living conditions are vastly superior in capitalist societies when compared to those in non-market economies. Marx's reply to Smith was that relative poverty is directly connected to individuals' feelings of satisfaction in society and as a result, an individual's inequality is neither illusory nor superficial. This is true, Marx said, because many individual needs and desires are of a social nature, and thus one measures his or her personal satisfaction by society's standards rather than by some abstract concept. This leads one to ask: does relative poverty matter? It does matter but possibly for a different reason. The amount of control that individuals have over their lives directly contributes to their happiness. As empirical research has shown, high inequality in extremely stratified societies makes people feel crushed by the economic power of others, and this leads to dissatisfaction. History has shown that promoting total equality can only be achieved through coercion. This coercion makes individuals feel they have no control over their lives and no way to benefit from their labor. In other words, this latter group experiences some of the same feelings of dissatisfaction as those who are poor.[1] This points to the psychological toll that both poverty and coercion take on the individual since the ideas of autonomy and freedom are fundamental to human happiness.

It is not surprising if one lays bare the fundamental disagreements about justice and poverty that well-intentioned individuals have, there appears to be in an intractable debate about what the causes and possible solutions are to the problem of poverty. One might reasonably think that if progress toward understanding the problem and finding possible solutions to alleviate it, we must aim toward a time when dialogues about solving the problem of poverty start with candid and sincere discussions about who the poor are, why they are poor, and what implications having a large number of poor may have for society. In the United States, the dialogue about poverty is dominated with quantitative social scientific literature, yet poverty has actually increased in recent years. In her remarkable work, *Poverty Knowledge*, Alice O'Connor argues that the way we think about the poverty problem and how social programs affect the poor is inadequate.[2] This must change if we are to be successful in attacking the problem of poverty in the United States. She says that in spite of all the empirical data resulting from myriad studies,

> contemporary poverty knowledge does not define itself as an inquiry into the political economy and culture of late twentieth century capitalism; it is knowledge about the characteristics and behavior and, especially in recent years, about the welfare status of the poor. Nor does it countenance knowledge honed in direct action or everyday experience, whether generated from activism or from living poor in the United States. Historically devalued as "impressionistic, "feminized," or "ideological," this kind of knowledge simply does not translate into the measurable variables that are the common currency of "objective," "scientific," and hence authoritative poverty research.[3]

O'Connor makes a persuasive argument that policy makers take as given post-industrial capitalism and thus, focus on the behavior of the poor and evaluating poverty programs.[4]

This is not surprising since one looks to empirical evidence to understand social phenomena. I suggest that just as critical is an acknowledgment of the basic values and tenants of liberalism that provide the theoretical underpinning for discussions about justice in Western political thought. Most individuals would say that they want to live in a just society and that human beings have a right to lead a dignified life. What the tradition of Western political philosophy tells us is that justice demands that societies thoughtfully examine the problem and take steps to alleviate poverty because doing so is both an intrinsic and consequential good. It is an intrinsic good because having the necessities to live a dignified life is like having good health. It is also of great consequence because we should take seriously the warnings provided throughout the Great tradition of Western political thought from Plato to Rawls. Surely no society can flourish where there is great poverty. Moreover, even more ominous are their predictions about the dire consequences for ignoring the problem. It is thus not only necessary for the poor, but it is also necessary for the good of all society. This means that the question is not if governments have a moral obligation to try to alleviate poverty but instead, what that obligation entails in a just society. I have shown how some of the most significant theorists in the Great tradition of Western political theory provide some provocative answers to the latter question. Nozick and Rawls's competing visions for what a just society might look like are symptomatic of a failure to move beyond two extremes. Moreover, these types of ideological battles along with all the social scientific studies may actually constrain political actors from thinking creatively about the problem and from implementing sound policies that benefit the poor and thus all of society.

Without a doubt, the problem of poverty will continue to pose one of the most difficult challenges for political theorists, economists, politicians, and societies. With a world divided between rich and poor countries and the countries themselves becoming more economically stratified, political theorists must continue to search for ways to promote greater equality and concern for how poverty negatively affects not only the impoverished but also potentially the political stability among nations. There is a direct connection between justice and the treatment of poverty. Plato said, "The community which has neither poverty nor riches will always have the noblest principles; in it there is no insolence or injustice, nor again are there any contentions or envyings."[5] Justice demands that political theorists continue the search for those noble principles that may provide new possibilities for confronting and alleviating the problem of poverty.

NOTES

1. Stille, "Grounded by an Income Gap," A17.

2. Alice O'Connor, *Poverty Knowledge: Social Science, Social Policy, and the Poor in Twentieth-Century U.S. History* (Princeton: Princeton University Press, 2001), 4.

3. Ibid., 4.

4. Ibid., 16.

5. Plato, *Laws*, trans. Benjamin Jowett (New York: Prometheus Books, May 2000), 679b.

Appendix: List of Abbreviations

CPC	*Constitutional Project for Corsica*
CGP	"Critique of the Gotha Program"
DPE	*Discourse on Political Economy*
ELN	*Essays on the Laws of Nature*
Essay	*An Essay Concerning Human Understanding*
GP	*Government of Poland*
JF	*Justice as Fairness: A Restatement*
Lectures	*Philosophie des Rechts: die Vorlesung von 1819/20 in eigner Nachschrift*
MP	*Memoir on Pauperism*
Manuscripts 1844	*Economic and Philosophic Manuscripts of 1844*
OSC	*On The Social Contract*
PL	*Political Liberalism*
PPE	*Principles of Political Economy*
PR	*Elements of the Philosophy of Right*
Report	"Report to the Board of Trade to the Lords Justices 1697, Respecting the Relief and Unemployment of the Poor"
SMP	*Second Mémoire Sur Le Paupérisme*
TJ	*A Theory of Justice*
TMS	*The Theory of Moral Sentiments*
WLC	"Wages, Labour and Capital"
WN	*An Inquiry into the Nature and Causes of The Wealth of Nations*

Bibliography

Abelson, Reed, "Enron Board Comes Under a Storm of Criticism," *The New York Times* 16 (December 2001): Business Section.

Appleby, Andrew, "Grain Prices and Subsistence Crises in England and France, 1590–1740," *Journal of Economic History* 39, no.12 (December 1979): 865–87.

Aristophanes, *The Clouds*, trans. Peter Meineck. Indianapolis: Hackett Publishing Company Publishing Company, 1988.

Aristotle, *Nicomachean Ethics*, trans. Terence Irwin. Indianapolis: Hackett Publishing Company Publishing Company, 1985.

——. *The Politics of Aristotle*, ed. and trans. Ernest Barker. Oxford: Oxford University Press, 1958.

——. *Politics*, trans. C. D. C. Reeve. Indianapolis: Hackett Publishing Company Publishing Company, 1998.

——. *Rhetoric* in *Aristotle Selections*, trans. Terence Irwin and Gail Fine. Indianapolis: Hackett Publishing Company, 1995.

Ashcraft, Richard, "Liberalism and the Problem of Poverty," *Critical Review*, 6, no.4 (1992): 493–516.

Avineri, Shlomo, *Hegel's Theory of the Modern State*. Cambridge: Cambridge University Press, 1972.

Banfield, Edward, *The Unheavenly City*. Boston: Little, Brown, 1968.

Barry, Brian, *Liberal Theory of Justice*. Oxford: Oxford University Press, 1973.

Beier, A. L., "'Utter Strangers to Industry, Morality and Religion': John Locke on the Poor," *Eighteenth Century Life* 12, no.3 (November 1988): 28–41.

Blaug, Mark, *Economic Theory in Retrospect*. Oxford: Oxford University Press, 1978.

Bloom, Allan, "Justice: John Rawls vs. The Tradition of Political Philosophy," *The American Political Science Review* 69, no.2 (June 1975): 648–52.

Buchanan, Allen, *Marx and Justice*. New Jersey: Rowman & Allanheld, 1982.

Campbell, William F, "Adam Smith's Theory of Justice, Prudence, and Beneficence," *The American Economic Review* 57, no.2. Papers and proceedings of the Seventy-ninth Annual Meeting of the American Economic Association (May 1967): 571–77.

Chappell, Vere, ed., *The Cambridge Companion to Locke*. Cambridge: Cambridge University Press, 1994.

Cicero, *The Republic*, in *Readings in Classical Political Thought*, ed. Peter J. Steinberger. Indianapolis: Hackett Publishing Co., Inc., 2000.

Coeyman, Marjorie, "Lost in the Shuffle," *The Christian Science Monitor* 24 (April 2001): 13.

Cohen, G. A., *History, Labour, and Freedom: Themes from Marx*. Oxford: Oxford University Press, 1988.

———. "The Labor Theory of Value and the Concept of Exploitation," *Philosophy and Public Affairs* 8 (1979): 339–60.

Cooper, John, "Aristotle on the Goods of Fortune," *The Philosophical Review* (April 1985): 173–97.

Copeland, E., "The Institutional Setting of Plato's *Republic*," *International Journal of Ethics* 34, no.3 (April 1924): 228–42.

Cranston, Maurice, *The Early Life and Work of Jean-Jacques 1712–1754*. New York: W.W. Norton and Company, 1982.

Damrosch, Leo, *Jean Jacques Rousseau: Restless Genius*. New York: Houghton Mifflin Company, 2005.

Danford, John, "Adam Smith and Equality," *American Journal of Political Science* 24, no.4 (November 1980): 674–95.

Daniels, Norman, "Equal Liberty and Unequal Worth of Liberty," *Reading Rawls* Stanford: Stanford University Press, 1989: 253–81.

———, ed. *Reading Rawls*. Stanford: Stanford University Press, 1989.

Darwall, S., "Sympathetic Liberalism: Recent Works on Adam Smith," *Philosophy and Public Affairs* 28, no.2, Spring 1999: 139–64.

Daunton, M. J., *Progress and Poverty: An Economic and Social History of Britain, 1700–1850*. Oxford: Oxford University Press, 1995.

Davis, Michael, "Nozick's Argument for the Legitimacy of the Welfare State," *Ethics* 97, no.3 (April 1987): 576–94.

DiNitto, Diana, *Social Welfare: Politics and Public Policy*. Boston: Allyn and Bacon, 2000.

Douglass, R. Bruce, ed., *Liberalism and the Good*. New York: Routledge, 1990.

Dunn, John, *The Political Thought of John Locke*. Cambridge: Cambridge University Press, 1969.

Elshtain, Jean Bethke, *Public Man, Private Woman*, Princeton: Princeton University Press, 1982.

Finley, M. I., *Politics in the Ancient World*. Cambridge: Harvard University Press, 1983.

Fisk, Milton, "Property and the State: A Discussion of Robert Nozick's *Anarchy, State, and Utopia*," *Noŭs* 14, no.1 (1980): 99–108.

Fitzgibbons, Athol, *Adam Smith's System of Liberty, Wealth, and Virtue*. Oxford: Clarendon Press, 1995.

Fleischacker, Samuel, *A Short History of Distributive Justice*. Cambridge: Harvard University Press, 2004.

Fridén, Bertril, *Rousseau's Economic Philosophy*. Dordrecht, The Netherlands: Kluwer Academic Publishers, 1998.

Friedlander, Eli, "Chambery, 12 June 1754: Rousseau's Writing on Inequality," *Political Theory* 28, no.2 (April 2000): 254–72.

Fuks, Alexander, "Plato and the Social Question: The Problem of Poverty and Riches in the Republic," *Ancient Society* 8 (1977): 49–83.

———. "Plato and the Social Question: The Problem of Poverty and Riches in the *Laws*," *Ancient Society* 10 (1979): 33–78.

Goodenough, Erwin R., "The Ethical Teaching of Jesus," *The Jewish Quarterly Review*, New Ser. 57, The Seventy-Fifth Anniversary Volume of the Jewish Quarterly Review (1967), 265.

Griswold, Charles, Jr., *Adam Smith and the Virtues of Enlightenment*. Cambridge: Cambridge University Press, 1994.

Hegel, G. W. F., *Elements of the Philosophy of Right*. Ed. Allen Wood, Trans. H. B. Nisbet. Cambridge: Cambridge University Press, 1991.

———. *Philosophie des Rechts: die Vorlesung von 1819/20 in eigner Nachschrift*, ed., Dieter Henrich. Frankfurt am Man: Suhrkamp, 1983. Trans. Shlomo Avineri, "The Discovery of Hegel's Early Lectures on the Philosophy of Right" *The Owl of Minerva* 16, no.2 (Spring 1985): 199–208.

Hill, Christopher, *Puritanism and Revolution: Studies in the English Revolution of the 17th Century*. New York: Palagrave Macmillan, 1997.

Himmelfarb, Gertrude, *The Idea of Poverty: England in the Early Industrial Age*. New York: Alfred A Knopf, 1984.

Hobbes, Thomas, *Leviathan*. Ed. Richard Tuck. Cambridge: Cambridge University Press, 1999.

Hont, Istvan and Michael Ignatieff, "Needs and Justice in the *Wealth of Nations*," In *Wealth and Virtue: The Shaping of Political Economy in the Scottish Enlightenment*. Ed. Istvan Hont and Michael Ignatieff. Cambridge: Cambridge University Press, 1983.

Horne, Thomas, *Property Rights and Poverty: Political Arguments in Britain, 1605–1834*. Chapel Hill: The University of North Carolina Press, 1990.

Hundert, E. J., "The Making of Homo Faber: John Locke Between Ideology and History," *Journal of the History of Ideas* 33 (1972): 3–22.

Husami, Ziyad, "Marx on Distributive Justice," *Philosophy and Public Affairs* 8 (1978): 27–64.

Inwood, Michael, *A Hegel Dictionary*. Oxford: Blackwell Publishers, Ltd., 1998.

Irwin, Terence, "Aristotle's Defense of Private Property," in *A Companion to Aristotle's Politics*, ed. David Keyt and Fred Miller, Jr., Oxford: Oxford University Press, 1991.

Johnston, David Clay, "The Very Rich, It Now Appears Give Their Share and Even More," *The New York Times*, January 1, 2004.

Kahan, Alan S., *Aristocratic Liberalism*. New York: Oxford University Press, 1992.

Kant, Immanuel, *Groundwork of the Metaphysics of Morals*. Trans. Mary Gregor. Cambridge: Cambridge University Press, 1997.

——. *The Metaphysics of Morals*. Trans. Mary Gregor. Cambridge: Cambridge University Press, 1996.

Kateb, George, "Aspects of Rousseau's Political Thought," *Political Science Quarterly* 76, no.4 (December 1961): 519–43.

Kinzer, Bruce L., *England's Disgrace?: J. S. Mill and the Irish Question*. Toronto: University of Toronto Press, Inc., 2001.

Kozel, Jonathan, *Rachel and Her Children: Homeless Families in America*. New York: Facett Columbine, 1988.

Kymlicka, Will, *Contemporary Political Philosophy*. Oxford: Clarendon Press, 1990.

Lamb, Robert, "The Political Economy of Alienation, Karl Marx and Adam Smith," *Oxford Economic Papers* 25, no.2, (July 1973): 276

Lees, Lynn Hollen, *The Solidarities of Strangers: The English Poor Laws and the People, 1700–1946*. Cambridge: Cambridge University Press, 1998.

Levine, Donald J., "Adam Smith and the Problem of Justice," *The Journal of Legal Studies* 6, no.2 (June 1977): 399–409.

Locke, John, *An Essay Concerning Human Understanding,* ed. Peter Nidditch Oxford: Oxford University Press, 1975.

——. Nine essays in Latin reprinted as "Essays on the Laws of Nature," In *Locke: Political Essays*, ed. Mark Goldie, 2nd ed. Cambridge: Cambridge University Press, 1999: 79–133.

——. "Report to the Board of Trade to the Lords Justices 1697, Respecting the Relief and Unemployment of the Poor," reprinted as "An Essay on the Poor Law," in *Locke: Political Essays*, ed. Mark Goldie, 2nd ed., Cambridge: Cambridge University Press, 1999: 183–98.

——. *Two Treatises of Government*, ed. Peter Laslett, 3rd ed. Cambridge: Cambridge University Press, 1988.

——. "Venditio," in *Locke: Political Essays*, ed. Mark Goldie, 2nd ed. Cambridge: Cambridge University Press, 1997: 339–43.

Lötter, H. P. P., "The Significance of Poverty and Wealth in Plato's Republic," *South African Journal of Philosophy* 22, no.3 (2004): 189–206.

Lyall, Sarah, "Past as Prologue: Blair Faults Britain in Irish Potato Blight," *New York Times*, June 3, 1997, 3(A).

Lyons, D., "The New Indian Claims and Original Rights to Land," in *Reading Nozick*. Ed. J. Paul, Totowas, NJ: Rowman and Littlefield, 1981.

MacPherson, C. B., *The Political Theory of Possessive Individualism*. Oxford: Oxford University Press, 1962.

Magnet, Myron, *The Dream and the Nightmare: The Sixties Legacy to the Underclass*. New York: Encounter Books, 1993.

Malthus, Thomas R., *An Essay on the Principle of Population*. New York: Oxford University Press, 1999.

Mandeville, Bernard de, *The Fable of the Bees and Other Writings*. Abridged and ed. E. J. Hundert. Indianapolis: Hackett Publishing Company, Inc., 1997.

Martinich, A. P., "Religion, Fanaticism, and Liberalism," *Pacific Philosophical Quarterly* 81 (2000): 409–25.

———. "The Interpretation of Covenants" in *Leviathan after 350 Years*, eds. Tom Sorrell and Luc Foisneau. Oxford: Clarendon Press, 2004.

Marx, Karl, "Alienation and Social Classes." *The Marx Engels Reader*, 2nd ed., ed. Robert Tucker. New York: W. W. Norton & Company, Inc., 1978: 133–35.

———. *Capital*, vol. 1, trans. Ben Fowkes. New York: Vintage Books, 1977.

———. "Contribution to the Critique of Hegel's *Philosophy of Right*: Introduction," *The Marx Engels Reader*, 2nd ed., ed. Robert Tucker. New York: W. W. Norton & Company, Inc., 1978: 53–65.

———. "Critique of the Gotha Program," *The Marx Engels Reader*, 2nd ed., ed. Robert Tucker. New York: W. W. Norton & Company, Inc., 1978: 525–41.

———. *Economic and Philosophic Manuscripts of 1844*. *The Marx-Engels Reader*, 2nd ed., ed. Robert Tucker. New York: W. W. Norton & Company, Inc., 1978: 66–125.

———. *The German Ideology*. *The Marx-Engels Reader*, 2nd ed., ed. Robert Tucker. New York: W. W. Norton & Company, Inc., 1978: 146–200.

———. Letter to P. W. Annekov. 28 December 1846. *The Marx-Engels Reader*, 2nd ed., ed. Robert Tucker. New York: W. W. Norton & Company, Inc., 1978: 136–42.

———. "Manifesto of the Communist Party," *The Marx-Engels Reader*, 2nd ed., ed. Robert Tucker. New York: W.W. Norton & Company, Inc., 1978: 473–500.

———. "After the Revolution: Marx Debates Bakunin," *The Marx-Engels Reader*, 2nd ed., ed. Robert Tucker. New York: W.W. Norton & Company, Inc., 1978: 542–48

———. "Theses on Feuerbach," *The Marx-Engels Reader*, 2nd ed., ed. Robert Tucker. New York: W. W. Norton & Company, Inc., 1978: 143–45.

———. "Wages, Labour and Capital," *Karl Marx and Frederick Engels Selected Works, Volume I*. Moscow: Foreign Languages Publishing House, 1958: 203–17.

Mason, M. G., "John Locke's Proposals for Work-House Schools," *Durham Research Review* 4 (1962): 8–16.

Masters, Roger, *The Political Philosophy of Rousseau*. Princeton: Princeton University Press, 1976.

Mathis, Thomas R., *An Essay on the Principle of Population*, Introduction by Geoffrey Gilbert. New York: Oxford University Press, Reissue Edition, 1999.

McClendon, Michael, "Tocqueville, Jansenism, and the Psychology of Freedom," *American Journal of Political Science* 50, no.3 (July 2006): 664–75.

Melling, Elizabeth, *Kentish Sources IV: The Poor*. Maidstone, England: Kent County Council, 1964.

Melzer, Arthur M., *The Natural Goodness of Man*. Chicago: University of Chicago-Press, 1990.

Michelman, Frank, "Constitutional Welfare Rights and *a Theory of Justice*," in *Reading Rawls*. Stanford: Stanford University Press, 1989: 319–47.

Mill, John Stuart, *Autobiography of John Stuart Mill*. Preface by John Jacob Cuss. New York: Columbia University Press, 1944.

———. *Essays on England, Ireland, and the Empire*, ed., John Robson with introduction by Joseph Hamburger. Toronto: University of Toronto Press, 1982.

——. *Principles of Political Economy with Some of Their Applications to Social Philosophy* (1848). New York: Prometheus Books, 2004.

——. *Utilitarianism*. In *Collected Works of John Stuart Mill, Essays on Ethics, Religion, and Society*, vol. 10, ed. J. M. Robson. Indianapolis: Liberty Fund, Inc., 2006.

Miller, Fred, Jr., *Nature, Justice and Rights in Aristotle's Politics*. Oxford: Oxford University Press, 1995.

Miller, Richard W., "Social and Political Theory: Class, State, Revolution," *The Cambridge Companion to Marx*. Cambridge: Cambridge University Press, 1991: 55–105.

Mokyr, Joel, ed., *The Economics of the Industrial Revolution*. London: George Allen & Unwin, 1985.

Morrow, Glenn, *Plato's Cretan City*. Princeton: Princeton University Press, 1993.

Mulgan, Richard, "Was Aristotle an Aristotelian Social Democrat?" *Ethics* 111 (October 2000): 79–108.

Muller, Jerry, *Adam Smith in His Time and Ours: Designing the Decent Society*. New York: The Free Press, 1993.

Nathanson, Stephen, "Editor's Introduction" to *Principles of Political Economy with Some of Their Applications to Social Philosophy*. Abridged Edition. Indianapolis: Hackett Publishing, Inc., 2004: ix–xxxv.

Nozick, Robert, *Anarchy, State, and Utopia*. New York: Basic Books, Inc., 1974.

Nussbaum, Martha, "Nature, Function, and Capability: Aristotle on Political Distribution," *Oxford Studies in Ancient Philosophy*, suppl. (1988): 145–84.

——. "Aristotle, Politics, and Human Capabilities: A Response to Antony, Arneson, Charlesworth and Mulgan," *Ethics* 11, no.1 (October 2000): 102–40.

——. "Aristotelian Social Democracy," in *Liberalism and the Public Good*. Edited by R. Bruce Douglas, et al. New York: Routledge, 1990.

O'Connor, Alice, *Poverty Knowledge: Social Science, Social Policy, and the Poor in Twentieth-Century U.S. History*. Princeton: Princeton University Press, 2001.

Okin, Susan Moller, *Women in Western Political Thought*. Princeton: Princeton University Press, 1979.

Pickard, Liza, *Dr. Johnson's London*. New York: St. Martin's Griffin, 2000.

Plato. *Republic*. Trans. G. M. A. Grube, Rev. C. D. C. Reeve. *Plato Complete Works*, Ed. John M. Cooper and D. S. Hutchinson. Indianapolis: Hackett Publishing Company, 1997: 971–1223.

——. *Laws*. Trans. Benjamin Jowett. New York: Prometheus Books, May 200.

——. *Laws*. Trans. Trevor J. Saunders. *Plato Complete Works*. Ed. John M. Cooper and D.S. Hutchinson. Indianapolis: Hackett Publishing Company, 1997: 1318–1616.

Plutarch, *Plutarch's Lives Volume I*. The Dryden Translation, edited with Notes and Preface by Arthur Hugh Clough. Reprint. New York: Modern Library Paperback Edition, 2001.

Price, Richard, *British Society 1680–1880*. Cambridge: Cambridge University Press, 1999).

Raphael, D. O., *Adam Smith*. Oxford: Oxford University Press, 1985.

Rashid, Salim, "The Politics of *Laissez-Faire* During Scarcities," in *The Economic Journal* 90, no.359 (September 1980): 493–503.

Rauhut, Daniel, "Adam Smith—Champion for the Poor!" in *Economists and Poverty: From Adam Smith to Amartya Sen*. Editors, Daniel Rauhut, Neelambar Hatti and Carl-Axel Olsson. New Delhi: Vedams Pvt. Ltd., 2005: 21–40.

———. "Saving the Poor: J. S. Mill on Poverty!" in *Economists and Poverty: From Adam Smith to Amartya Sen*. Editors, Daniel Rauhut, Neelambar Hatti and Carl-Axel Olsson. New Delhi: Vedams Pvt. Ltd., 2005: 56–76.

Rawls, John, *A Theory of Justice*. Cambridge: Harvard University Press, 1971.

———. *Justice as Fairness: A Restatement*. Cambridge: Harvard University Press, 2001.

———. *Lectures on the History of Political Philosophy*, ed. Samuel Freeman, Cambridge: The Belknap Press of Harvard University Press, 2007.

———. *Political Liberalism*. New York: Columbia University Press, 1996.

Rees, Albert, "Compensating Wage Differentials," In *Essays on Adam Smith*, ed. Andrew Skinner and Thomas Wilson. Oxford: Oxford University Press, 1976: 336–49.

Reisman, David, *Adam Smith's Sociological Economics*. London: Croom Helm Ltd., 1976.

Roll, Eric, *A History of Economic Thought*. England: Farber and Farber, 1992.

Rothschild, Emma, *Economic Sentiments: Adam Smith, Condorcet, and the Enlightenment*. Cambridge: Harvard University Press, 2001.

Rousseau, Jean-Jacques, *Confessions*. Translated by Angela Scholar and edited by Patrick Coleman. Oxford: Oxford University Press, 2000.

———. "Constitutional Project for Corsica," (CPC) in *Jean-Jacques Rousseau Political Writings*, trans. and ed. by Frederick Watkins with foreword by Patrick Riley. Madison: University of Wisconsin Press, 1986.

———. "Discourse on Political Economy," (DPE) in *Jean-Jacques Rousseau: The Basic Political Writings*, trans. Donald A. Cress. Indianapolis: Hackett Publishing, 1987.

———. "Discourse on the Origin and Foundations of Inequality Among Men," (Second Discourse) in *Jean-Jacques Rousseau: The Basic Political Writings*, trans. Donald A. Cress. Indianapolis: Hackett Publishing, 1987.

———. "Discourse on the Sciences and the Arts," (First Discourse) in *Rousseau's Political Writings*, trans. Julia Bondanella, eds. Allen Ritter and Julia Bondanella. New York: W. W. Norton, 1998.

———. "Discourse on the Sciences and the Arts," (First Discourse) in *Jean-Jacques Rousseau: The Basic Political Writings*, trans. Donald A. Cress. Indianapolis: Hackett Publishing, 1987.

———. *Reveries of the Solitary Walker*, (Reveries) trans. Charles Butterworth. Indianapolis: Hackett Publishing Company, 1992.

———. *The Government of Poland*, (GP) trans. Wilmoore Kendall. Indianapolis: Hackett Publishing Company, Inc., 1985.

Ryan, Alan, "Liberalism," in *A Companion to Contemporary Political Philosophy*. eds. Robert E. Goodin and Philip Pettit, 2nd ed. New York: Oxford University Press, 1995: 291–311.

Salter, John, "Sympathy with the Poor: Theories of Punishment in Hugo Grotius and Adam Smith," *History of Political Thought* 20, no.2 (Summer 1999): 205–24.

Sandel, Michael, *Liberalism and the Limits of Justice*, 2nd ed. Cambridge: Cambridge University Press, 1998.

Schneewind, J. B., "Locke's Moral Philosophy," in *The Cambridge Companion to Locke*, ed. Vere Chappell. Cambridge: Cambridge University Press, 1994: 199–225.

Schumpeter, Joseph, *History of Economic Analysis*. New York: Oxford University Press, 1954.

Sen, Amartya, *On Ethics and Economics*. Gateshead: Blackwell Publishing, 1997.

Seung, T. K., *Intuition and Construction: The Foundation of Normative Theory*. New Haven: Yale University Press, 1993.

Sheasgreen, W. J., "John Locke and the Charity School Movement," *History of Education* 15 (1986): 63–79.

Shklar, Judith, "Jean-Jacques Rousseau and Equality," in *Rousseau's Political Writings*, Norton Critical Edition, ed. Alan Ritter and Julia Bondanella. New York: W. W. Norton & Company, Inc., 1988: 274.

Singer. Peter, *Marx: A Very Short Introduction*. Oxford: Oxford University Press, 2000.

Smith, Adam, *An Inquiry into the Nature and Causes of The Wealth of Nations*, (WN) ed. Edwin Cannan. Chicago: University of Chicago Press, 1976.

——. *Lectures on Justice, Policy, Revenue and Arms*, ed. Edwin Cannan. 1896, 158. Quoted in West, 114.

——. "Letter to the Edinburgh Review," in *Essays on Philosophical Subjects*, edited by W. D. Wrightman. Indianapolis: Liberty Fund, Inc. 1982: 250–56.

——. [1759] *The Theory of Moral Sentiments*, (TMS). New York: Prometheus Books, 2000.

Sowell, Thomas, *Classical Economics Reconsidered*. Princeton: Princeton University Press, 1974.

Stalley, R. F., "Aristotle's Criticism of Plato's Republic," In *A Companion to Aristotle's Politics*. Ed. David Keyt and Fred Miller, Jr. Oxford: Oxford University Press, 1991: 182–99.

Stille, Alexander, "Grounded by an Income Gap," *New York Times* 15, December 2001: 15 (A).

Stone, Lawrence, *The Family, Sex and Marriage in England 1500–1800*. New York: Harper & Row, 1979.

Strauss, Leo, *Natural Right and History*. Chicago: Chicago University Press, 1953.

Teichgraeber, Richard, "Hegel on Property and Poverty," *Journal of the History of Ideas* 38 (1977): 47–64.

Thomas, Paul, "Critical Reception: Marx Then and Now," in *The Cambridge Companion to Marx*, ed. Terrell Carver. Cambridge: Cambridge University Press, 1991: 23–54.

Tocqueville, *Alexis de Tocqueville's Journey to Ireland*, ed., trans. and with introduction by Emmet Larkin. Washington, D.C.: Catholic University Press, 1990.

———. Alexis de, *Journeys to England and Ireland*, trans. George Lawrence and K. P. Mayer, ed. J. P. Mayer. London: 1958.

———. "Memoir on Pauperism," trans. Seymour Drescher. Chicago: Ivan Re. Dee, 1997.

———. "*Second Mémoire Sur Le Paupérisme*," in *Oeuvres Complètes, Tome* XVI, ed. J. P. Mayer. Paris: 1990: 140–57.

Tully, James, *An Approach to Political Philosophy: Locke in Context*. Cambridge: Cambridge University Press, 1993.

U.S. Census Bureau, 2005 American Community Survey http://factfinder.census.gov/ (accessed July 15, 007).

Waldron, Jeremy, "John Rawls and the Social Minimum," *Journal of Applied Philosophy 3* (1986): 21–33.

Walzer, Michael, *The Revolution of the Saints*. Cambridge: Cambridge University Press, 1965.

Welles, C. Bradford, "The Economic Background of Plato's Communism," *The Journal of Economic History* Suppl. No.8 (1948): 110–14.

Werhane, Patricia, *Adam Smith and His Legacy for Modern Capitalism*. Oxford: Oxford University Press, 1991.

West, E. G., "Adam Smith and Alienation: A Rejoinder," *Oxford Economic Papers*, 27, no.2 (July 1975): 296

———. "Adam Smith's Philosophy of Riches," *Philosophy* 44, no.168 (April 1969): 101–15.

———. "Adam Smith and Rousseau's *Discourse on Inequality*: Inspiration or Provocation?" *Journal of Economic Issues* 5 (1971): 56–70.

Westphal, Kenneth, "The Basic Context and Structure of Hegel's *Philosophy of Right*," in *The Cambridge Companion to Hegel*, ed. Frederick C. Beiser. Cambridge: Cambridge University Press, 1993: 234–69.

Wheeler, M., "Self-Sufficiency and the Greek City," *Journal of the History of Ideas* 16 (June 1955): 416–20.

Williams, David L., "Justice and the General Will: Affirming Rousseau's Ancient Orientation," *Journal of the History of Ideas* 6, no.3 (July 2005): 383–411.

———. *Rousseau's Platonic Enlightenment*. University Park: Pennsylvania State University Press, 2007.

Wokler, Robert, *Rousseau: A Very Short Introduction*. Oxford: Oxford University Press, 2001.

Wolff, Robert, *Understanding Rawls*. Princeton: Princeton University Press, 1977.

Wooten, David, "Rousseau, the Enlightenment, and the Age of Reason," in *Modern Political Thought: Readings from Machiavelli to Nietzsche*, ed. David Wooten. Indianapolis: Hackett Publishing Company, 1996: 397–403.

Index

absolute poverty: Aristotle on, 23–24; capitalism and, 56; deprivation and, 4; government and, 23–24; happiness and, 23–24; Locke on, 49, 55–56, 75–76; Marx on, 152–53; Mill on, 131–32; natural law and, 55–56, 75–76; overview of, 4; Plato on, 19–20, 21–22; property and, 56; Smith on, 84, 87–88, 152–53; Tocqueville on, 112, 121, 131–32; virtue and, 88

agriculture: government assistance and, 107, 111; health and, 118–19; Hegel on, 144–45; population and, 106; property and, 118, 119–20; Rousseau on, 77, 78, 79; society and, 144–45; Tocqueville on, 111, 118–20

alcohol, 52

alienation (of laborers), 90–93, 152

alienation (of property), 30

"An Essay on the Poor Law" (Locke), 49, 51–59

aristocracy, 16

Aristophanes, 13

Aristotle: on absolute poverty, 23–24; on autonomy, 34–35; on charity, 23, 31; on circumstantial poverty, 37, 123–24; on citizenship, 23, 24–26; on civil war, 36, 120–21; on communism, 26–29; on crime, 32; on deprivation, 23–24; on desert, 25–26, 28, 29, 31–32, 37; on distributive justice, 25–26, 29, 32–34; on education, 28, 32, 36; on equality, 25, 26–29, 33; on fortune, 34–38; on friendship, 27, 30, 36; on golden mean, 26, 83; on goods, 34–38; on government, 22–26, 32–34, 36–38; on government assistance, 9, 23, 33–34; on greed, 28, 32, 36, 172; on happiness, 23–24, 27, 33, 34–36, 37; historical context of, 24–25; on human nature, 24, 27–28, 36, 172; on justice, 3, 25–26, 29, 37–38, 192; on laborers, 24–25, 36–37; on need, 29, 31–32, 37; on the poor, 37, 38; on population, 23, 32; on poverty generally, 3, 9–10, 22–23; on property, 23, 26–32, 33, 36; on redistributive justice, 9–10, 29, 38, 192; on slaves, 24–25, 36–37; on social class, 23, 33; on virtue, 23–24, 25, 26, 29–32, 33, 34–36; on wealth, 34–36; on women, 24–25, 36–37

Ashcraft, Richard, 57, 60n. 11, 60n. 13

Athenian Stranger, 17–18, 19, 20, 21

Augustine, Saint, 45
autonomy, 6, 34–35, 68, 194. *See also* freedom
Avineri, Shlomo, 148

Bakunin, Mikhail, 155–56
Banfield, Edward, 60n. 21
Beier, A. L., 57
Blair, Tony, 106–7
Bloom, Allan, 187n. 64
Buchanan, Allen, 162n. 125
Burnet, John, 26

Calvinism, 50–51
Campbell, William F., 93
capitalism: absolute poverty and, 56; equality and, 64, 88–89, 152–53; exploitation and, 5; government assistance and, 112, 115; Hegel on, 139, 147, 156; human nature and, 140–41; justice and, 141–42, 153; laborers and, 111, 117, 148–51; Locke on, 56, 59; Marx on, 5, 140–42, 148–54, 175, 193–94; Mill on, 131; natural law and, 56, 59; the poor and, 151–52; property and, 117; Rawls on, 175; relative poverty and, 4, 84, 87–90; rise of, 46; Smith on, 4, 80, 84, 87–90, 105, 182–83; social class and, 148–52; society and, 139, 148; Tocqueville on, 111–12, 115, 117
Cephalus, 12–13, 34
Chamberlain, Wilt, 179
charity: Aristotle on, 23, 31; desert and, 116, 129; government and, 84; Hegel on, 147; Locke and, 57–58; Mill on, 108, 128–29, 132–33; need and, 129; property and, 31; Smith on, 84; Tocqueville on, 108, 109, 115–16, 119, 128–29, 132–33; women and, 129. *See also* government assistance
children: circumstantial poverty and, 6; education and, 5, 52, 77; employment and, 54–55; equality

and, 77; Hegel on, 143; Locke on, 52, 54–55; Plato on, 66; poor laws and, 52, 54–55; relative poverty and, 4; religion and, 55; Rousseau and, 66–67, 77; Smith on, 90; society and, 143. *See also* family; population
Christianity, 45–46, 50–51, 59. *See also* God; religion
Cicero, 45–46, 92
circumstantial poverty: Aristotle on, 37, 123–24; children and, 6; education and, 6; employment and, 6; equality and, 173–74; health and, 6; Hegel on, 146–47; Locke and, 58; Mill on, 123–24, 131–32; Nozick on, 182; overview of, 6; Rawls on, 37, 173–74, 184; Rousseau on, 65, 93–94; Smith on, 93–94; society and, 165–66
citizenship, 23, 24–26, 67–68, 81, 146, 166–67
civil war: Aristotle on, 36, 120–21; government and, 15–17; justice and, 10; Plato on, 9, 10, 15–17, 19, 36, 74, 120–21; Tocqueville on, 120–21; wealth and, 10, 15–17, 19
The Clouds (Aristophanes), 13
Coleman, Patrick, 66
colonialism, 130, 147–48, 156
communism: Aristotle on, 26–29; desert and, 28; equality and, 26–29; freedom and, 130–31; friendship and, 27, 30; government assistance compared, 123–24; happiness and, 27; human nature and, 27–28, 155–56, 157; justice and, 155, 193–94; Marx on, 154–56; Mill on, 123–24, 130–31; Nozick on, 181–82; Plato on, 14–15, 17–21, 27, 28; power and, 155–56; property and, 14–15, 18–20, 26–29; society and, 154–56; wealth and, 14–15, 17–21
Constitutional Project for Corsica (Rousseau), 79–80
Cooper, John, 35

Copeland, Edith, 13
corporations, 145–46
Corsica, 79–80
Cranston, Maurice, 66, 73
crime, 32
Cromwell, Oliver, 48
culture, 5, 69–70, 71
Cyrus, King, 70

Damrosch, Leo, 66
Davis, Michael, 178
democracy, 17, 24, 33, 165
deprivation, 4, 19–20, 21–22, 23–24
desert: Aristotle on, 25–26, 28, 29,
    31–32, 37; charity and, 116, 129;
    citizenship and, 25–26; communism
    and, 28; distributive justice and,
    25–26, 29; government and, 25–26;
    government assistance and, 113;
    human nature and, 28; justice and,
    21, 25–26, 29, 37; Marx on, 21; Mill
    on, 129; overview of, 3; Plato on, 21;
    property and, 28, 31–32; Rawls on,
    174–75, 176–77; redistributive
    justice and, 29; Tocqueville on, 113,
    116
dialogue, 3
difference principle, 166–68, 170, 175
Discourse on Political Economy
    (Rousseau), 67, 69, 75–78
discrimination, 4, 5. *See also* equality
distributive justice: Aristotle on, 25–26,
    29, 32–34; desert and, 25–26, 29;
    equality and, 33; government and,
    32–34; Locke on, 55–56, 59; natural
    law and, 55–56; need and, 29,
    31–32; Nozick on, 178–79; social
    class, 33. *See also* redistributive
    justice
Dunn, John, 50–51, 57

economy: equality and, 64; government
    and, 13–17, 89–90; importance of
    generally, 2; Mill on, 126–27,
    130–31; Plato on, 13–21; Rawls on,

165; relative poverty and, 89–90;
    Rousseau on, 63–64; self-discipline
    and, 126–27; Smith on, 63–64,
    89–90; social class and, 13–17;
    virtue and, 63–64; wealth and,
    13–21, 126–27. *See also* capitalism;
    communism
education: Aristotle on, 28, 32, 36;
    children and, 5, 52, 77;
    circumstantial poverty and, 6; crime
    and, 32; discrimination and, 5;
    equality and, 77, 80, 167, 184;
    freedom and, 167; government and,
    89; greed and, 28, 32; happiness and,
    20; justice and, 167; laborers and,
    91; Locke on, 52; Mill and, 106, 121,
    126, 129–30; Plato on, 20, 32, 36;
    poor laws and, 52; population and,
    106; property and, 28; Rawls on,
    167; relative poverty and, 20;
    Rousseau on, 77, 80; self-discipline
    and, 129–30; Smith on, 84, 89, 91,
    182–83; society and, 167; women
    and, 5
Elshtain, Jean Bethke, 25
employment: children and, 54–55;
    circumstantial poverty and, 6;
    government assistance and, 113–14,
    147; Hegel on, 147; human nature
    and, 80, 113–14; Locke on, 52–55,
    58–59; Mill on, 124–25; Plato on,
    13; poor laws and, 52–55, 105–6;
    population and, 124–25; Rousseau
    on, 80; self-discipline and, 124–25;
    Smith on, 84, 90; social class and,
    13; Tocqueville on, 111–12, 113–14,
    116; women and, 54. *See also*
    laborers
Engels, Freidrich, 141
England. *See* poor laws
entitlement, 178–79
equality: Aristotle on, 25, 26–29, 33;
    capitalism and, 64, 88–89, 152–53;
    children and, 77; circumstantial
    poverty and, 173–74; citizenship and,

67–68; communism and, 26–29; culture and, 70; discrimination and, 4; distributive justice and, 33; economy and, 64; education and, 77, 80, 167, 184; freedom and, 47–48, 69, 75–76, 108–9, 167; the good and, 75–78; government and, 33, 74, 75–78; happiness and, 110; human nature and, 71–75; justice and, 25, 68–69, 93, 108–9, 166–71, 182–85, 192, 195; laborers and, 73–74, 92–93; liberalism and, 47–48; Marx on, 152–53; Mill on, 131; natural law and, 70–71; Nozick on, 182–85; overview of, 3; population and, 77; power and, 68–69; property and, 26–29, 33, 73, 75–76, 84–85, 109–11, 131; Rawls on, 166–71, 173–75, 183; relative poverty and, 4, 84–85, 88–89, 110; Rousseau on, 67–68, 68–69, 70–81, 88, 192; Smith on, 64, 84–85, 88–89, 92–93, 121, 152–53; society and, 70, 71–75, 109–11, 166–71, 182–85; taxes and, 77–78; Tocqueville on, 108–9, 109–11; virtue and, 70, 192; wealth and, 68–69; will and, 75–76

An Essay on the Principle of Population (Malthus), 106

exploitation, 5, 148–52, 181–82

The Fable of the Bees (Mandeville), 63–64

family, 14–15, 143–44. *See also* children; population

Feldstein, Martin, 183, 184

Finley, M. I., 13

First Discourse (Rousseau), 69–70

Fleishchacker, Samuel: on Aristotle, 9–10, 29; on distributive justice generally, 3; on Locke, 56; on Mill, 128; on Plato, 9–10, 21–22; on Rousseau, 67–68, 73, 75, 78, 81; on Smith, 82

food. *See* agriculture

fortune, 34–38. *See also* goods

freedom: autonomy and, 6; communism and, 130–31; education and, 167; equality and, 47–48, 69, 75–76, 108–9, 167; government and, 146; Hegel on, 139–40, 143, 146; justice and, 69, 93, 108–9, 139–40, 157; liberalism and, 47–48, 59; Marx on, 157; Mill on, 130–31; overview of, 6; property and, 75–76; Rawls on, 167; Rousseau on, 66, 68, 69, 75–76; Smith on, 93; society and, 143, 146, 167; Tocqueville on, 108–9; wealth and, 66. *See also* autonomy

Freeman, Richard, 183

Fridén, Bertril, 98n. 89

friendship, 27, 30, 36. *See also* love

Fuks, Alexander, 10, 16, 19, 20

globalization, 163–64

God, 45–46, 56, 59, 110–11. *See also* Christianity; religion

golden mean, 26, 83

the good, 11, 49–50, 68–69, 75–78, 80. *See also* goods; virtue

goods, 34–38. *See also* the good

government: absolute poverty and, 23–24; Aristotle on, 22–26, 32–34, 36–38; charity and, 84; citizenship and, 24–26; civil war and, 15–17; desert and, 25–26; distributive justice and, 32–34; economy and, 13–17, 89–90; education and, 89; equality and, 33, 74, 75–78; freedom and, 146; the good and, 75–78; happiness and, 23–24, 146; Hegel on, 144, 145, 146; justice and, 16, 25–26, 84; Nozick on, 177; Plato on, 13–17, 19–21, 24; property and, 33, 85; Rawls on, 165; reason and, 146; relative poverty and, 89–90; Rousseau on, 74, 75–78; Smith on, 84, 85, 89–90; social class and, 13–17, 33; society and, 144, 146; virtue and, 23–24; wealth and,

13–17, 19–21; will and, 75–76. *See also* citizenship; government assistance

government assistance: agriculture and, 107, 111; Aristotle on, 9, 23, 33–34; capitalism and, 112, 115; communism compared, 123–24; culture and, 5; desert and, 113; distributive justice and, 33–34; employment and, 113–14, 147; globalization and, 163–64; Hegel on, 147; human nature and, 117–18; justice and, 11, 93, 132; liberalism and, 6–7, 59, 163–64; Locke on, 7, 49, 52–53, 55–56, 58–59, 75–76, 181; Mill on, 7, 107–8, 123–24, 128, 130, 132; natural law and, 55–56; Nozick on, 7, 177, 180–81, 184; overview of, 6–7; Plato on, 9, 11, 19; the poor and, 114–15; poor laws and, 52–53, 55–56, 58–59, 105–6; population and, 128; property and, 6–7, 121, 130; psychology of, 112–13; Rawls on, 7; reason and, 128; relative poverty and, 89; Smith on, 7, 84, 89, 93, 121; Tocqueville on, 7, 107–8, 109, 111, 112–15, 117–18, 121; virtue and, 114–16. *See also* charity; redistributive justice

The Government of Poland (Rousseau), 79, 80

greed, 15, 17–19, 28, 32, 36, 172

happiness: absolute poverty and, 23–24; Aristotle on, 23–24, 27, 33, 34–36, 37; autonomy and, 34–35; communism and, 27; education and, 20; equality and, 110; goods and, 34–36; government and, 23–24, 146; Hegel on, 146; human nature and, 49; justice and, 37, 122; Locke on, 49; Marx on, 156; Mill on, 122; Plato on, 12–13, 20; the poor and, 49; property and, 27, 73, 110, 111; relative poverty and, 20; Rousseau

on, 65–66, 68, 73, 110, 111; Smith on, 85–86; society and, 85–86, 110, 146; Tocqueville on, 110, 111; virtue and, 23–24, 33, 34–36; wealth and, 12–13, 34–36, 65–66

health: agriculture and, 118–19; circumstantial poverty and, 6; justice and, 92–93; Marx on, 156; Mill on, 125; population and, 125; Rousseau on, 70, 72; society and, 70, 72; Tocqueville on, 118–19; virtue and, 70; wealth and, 70; women and, 125. *See also* psychology

Hegel, G. W.: on agriculture, 144–45; on capitalism, 139, 147, 156; on charity, 147; on children, 143; on circumstantial poverty, 146–47; on citizenship, 146; on colonialism, 147–48, 156; on corporations, 145–46; on culture, 5; on employment, 147; on family, 143–44; on freedom, 139–40, 143, 146; on government, 144, 145, 146; on government assistance, 147; on happiness, 146; historical context of, 139, 147–48; on human nature, 147; on institutions, 140, 143; on justice, 139–40, 145, 148, 156, 157; on laborers, 144–45; on police power, 145; on the poor, 142–43, 146; on poverty generally, 133; on property, 143, 145; on reason, 142–43, 146; on redistributive justice, 147; on society, 139–40, 142–46; on taxes, 147

Himmelfarb, Gertrude, 124

historical context: of Aristotle's thought, 24–25; of Hegel's thought, 139, 147–48; importance of generally, 2, 7–8; of Locke's thought, 45–47, 48–49, 57–58; of Marx's thought, 139; of Mill's thought, 105–7; of Plato's thought, 13–14; of Tocqueville's thought, 105–7

Hobbes, Thomas, 70–71, 73, 74

Horne, Thomas, 57

human nature: Aristotle on, 24, 27–28, 36, 172; capitalism and, 140–41; communism and, 27–28, 155–56, 157; desert and, 28; employment and, 80, 113–14; equality and, 71–75; the good and, 49–50; government assistance and, 117–18; happiness and, 49; Hegel on, 147; justice and, 191; Locke on, 49–51, 58–59, 121; Marx on, 140–41, 155–56, 157; Mill on, 107–8; Plato on, 12, 15, 172; the poor and, 49–51, 58–59, 64, 73, 75, 81, 117–18, 121, 191; property and, 27–28; Rawls on, 169–73; Rousseau on, 64, 71–75, 80, 81, 87, 111, 134n. 31; self-respect and, 169–73; Smith on, 64, 80, 85–87, 121, 134n. 31; society and, 71–75; Tocqueville on, 107–8, 111–12, 113–14, 117–18, 121; wealth and, 15, 86–87, 108. *See also* greed; psychology; self-discipline
Husami, Ziyad, 162n. 125

inequality. *See* equality
Inglehart, Ronald, 183–84
institutions, 5, 140, 143, 164–65
Ireland, 118–21, 127, 131–32
Irwin, Terrence, 31

Jesus Christ, 45
justice: Aristotle on, 3, 25–26, 29, 37–38, 192; capitalism and, 141–42, 153; citizenship and, 25–26; civil war and, 10; communism and, 155, 193–94; desert and, 21, 25–26, 29, 37; education and, 167; equality and, 25, 68–69, 93, 108–9, 166–71, 182–85, 192, 195; freedom and, 69, 93, 108–9, 139–40, 157; as a good, 11; the good and, 68–69; government and, 16, 25–26, 84; government assistance and, 11, 93, 132; happiness and, 37, 122; health and, 92–93; Hegel on, 139–40, 145, 148,

156, 157; human nature and, 191; institutions and, 140, 164–65; liberalism and, 193–95; Locke on, 46, 47–48, 59, 164; love and, 12; Marx on, 141–42, 153, 155, 156–57; Mill on, 122, 131–33; natural law and, 46, 47–48; need and, 37; Nozick on, 2, 164, 182–85, 195; Plato on, 3, 10–13, 16, 22, 69, 192; poverty and, 1–3, 7–8, 12–13, 22, 37–38, 59, 64–65, 121, 131–33, 140, 148, 156–57, 163–64, 184–85, 191–95; power and, 68–69; property and, 92, 145; psychology and, 12, 82–83; Rawls on, 2, 68, 122, 164–71, 174–77, 195; relative poverty and, 193–94; Rousseau on, 3, 64–65, 68–69; Smith on, 3, 64–65, 69, 82–84, 92–93; social class and, 11–12; society and, 139–40, 145, 164–71, 182–85; soul and, 12; Tocqueville on, 108–9, 121, 131–33; utility and, 122; virtue and, 25, 192; wealth and, 10–11, 12–13, 68–69; will and, 68–69. *See also* distributive justice; redistributive justice

Kahan, Alan, 107
Kant, Immanuel, 3, 6, 31, 164, 177, 180–81
Kateb, George, 68
Kelly, Erin, 176
Kelly, Thomas, 119–20
Kinzer, Bruce L., 127
Kozel, Jonathan, 187n. 58
Kroger, Alan, 82

laborers: alienation of, 90–93, 152; Aristotle on, 24–25, 36–37; capitalism and, 111, 117, 148–51; citizenship and, 24–25; education and, 91; equality and, 73–74, 92–93; Hegel on, 144–45; Marx on, 91–92, 148–51; property and, 117, 179–80; relative poverty and, 92; Rousseau on, 73–74, 91; Smith on, 90–93; society and, 73–74, 144–45; Tocqueville on, 111, 117; virtue and, 92. *See also* employment

Lamb, Robert, 91

Larkin, Emmet, 118

Laslett, Peter, 60n. 13

laws. *See* government; poor laws

Laws (Plato), 10–11, 17–22

Lees, Lynn, 56

Le Vasseur, Thérèse, 67

Levine, Daniel, 84

liberalism: definition of, 61n. 38; equality and, 47–48; freedom and, 47–48, 59; government assistance and, 6–7, 59, 163–64; justice and, 193–95; Locke and, 47–48, 163, 193; Mill and, 107–8, 193; Nozick and, 164; Rawls and, 164; Tocqueville and, 107–8, 121, 163, 193

liberty. *See* freedom

Locke, John: on absolute poverty, 49, 55–56, 75–76; on alcohol, 52; on capitalism, 56, 59; charity and, 57–58; on children, 52, 54–55; circumstantial poverty and, 58; on culture, 5; on distributive justice, 55–56, 59; on education, 52; on employment, 52–55, 58–59; on the good, 49–50; on government assistance, 7, 49, 52–53, 55–56, 58–59, 75–76, 181; on happiness, 49; historical context of, 45–47, 48–49, 57–58; on human nature, 49–51, 58–59, 121; on justice, 46, 47–48, 59, 164; liberalism and, 47–48, 163, 193; on movement, 53, 89; on natural law, 46, 47–48, 55–56, 59, 75–76, 121, 181; on the poor, 47, 49–51, 58–59, 75, 121, 191; on poor laws, 46, 49, 51–59; on poverty generally, 3, 7, 46–48; on property, 56, 59, 75–76, 177, 178, 181; on psychology, 6; on punitive measures, 49–50, 51–55; on redistributive

justice, 56, 59; on religion, 55; on settlement, 47; on the social contract, 71, 74; on the state of nature, 70–71, 73; on women, 53–54

Lötter, H. P. P., 10

love, 12, 14, 15, 76, 80. *See also* friendship

Lycurgus, 14, 76

MacPherson, C. B., 50–51, 57

Malthus, Thomas R., 106, 124

Mandeville, Bernard, 63–64, 71, 73, 92

Martinich, A. P., 176

Marx, Karl: on absolute poverty, 152–53; on capitalism, 5, 140–42, 148–54, 175, 193–94; on communism, 154–56; on culture, 71; on desert, 21; on equality, 152–53; on exploitation, 5, 148–52; on freedom, 157; on happiness, 156; on health, 156; historical context of, 139; on human nature, 140–41, 155–56, 157; on justice, 141–42, 153, 155, 156–57; on laborers, 91–92, 148–51; on the poor, 151–52; on poverty generally, 3, 133; on relative poverty, 4, 152–53, 157, 193–94; Rousseau influences, 81; on social class, 17, 148–52; on society, 71, 148, 154–56; on wages, 149–50, 153

Masters, Roger, 96n. 39, 97n. 72

McClendon, Michael, 134n. 29

mean. *See* golden mean

Memoirs on Pauperism (Tocqueville), 108–18

Michelman, Frank, 175

Mill, John Stuart: on absolute poverty, 131–32; on autonomy, 6; on capitalism, 131; on charity, 108, 128–29, 132–33; on circumstantial poverty, 123–24, 131–32; on colonialism, 130; on communism, 123–24, 130–31; on desert, 129; on economy, 126–27, 130–31; on education, 106, 126, 129–30; education of, 121; on employment, 124–25; on equality, 131; on exploitation, 5; on freedom, 130–31; on government assistance, 7, 107–8, 123–24, 128, 130, 132; on happiness, 122; on health, 125; historical context of, 105–7; on human nature, 107–8; on justice, 122, 131–33; liberalism and, 107–8, 193; on need, 129; on poor laws, 128; on population, 106, 124–25, 128, 129, 130; on poverty generally, 105–8, 123–24; on property, 108, 126–27, 130, 131; on reason, 108, 121–22, 125, 128, 133; on religion, 125; on self-discipline, 107–8, 123–27, 129–30; on taxes, 126, 127; on utility, 122; on virtue, 107–8, 126; on wages, 124–25; on wealth, 108, 126–27; on women, 106, 125, 129

Mill, James, 121, 127

Miller, Fred, Jr., 31–32, 34

money, 79–80. *See also* wealth

morality. *See* virtue

movement, 53, 89, 116

Mulgan, Richard, 24–25

Muller, Jerry, 88

Murphy, William, 119

Nathanson, Stephen, 131

natural law: absolute poverty and, 55–56, 75–76; capitalism and, 56, 59; distributive justice and, 55–56; equality and, 70–71; God and, 45–46, 56, 59; government assistance, 55–56; justice and, 46, 47–48; Locke on, 46, 47–48, 55–56, 59, 75–76, 121, 181; property and, 56, 59; Rousseau on, 70–71, 74; theory of generally, 45–46; Tocqueville on, 121. *See also* the state of nature

need, 29, 31–32, 37, 111–12, 129

Nolan, Edward, 120

Nozick: on circumstantial poverty, 182; on communism, 181–82; on distributive justice, 178–79; on entitlement, 178–79; on equality, 182–85; on exploitation, 181–82; on government, 177; on government assistance, 7, 177, 180–81, 184; on justice, 2, 164, 182–85, 195; liberalism and, 164; on poverty generally, 3; on property, 164, 177–81, 184; on self-ownership, 179–80; on society, 182–85; on taxes, 164, 180

Nussbaum, Martha, 25, 31, 36–37, 92–93

O'Connor, Alice, 194–95

Okin, Susan Moller, 25

oligarchy, 16–17, 33

philosophy, 3

Plato: on absolute poverty, 19–20, 21–22; on autonomy, 6; on children, 66; on civil war, 9, 10, 15–17, 19, 36, 74, 120–21; on communism, 14–15, 17–21, 27, 28; on deprivation, 21–22; on desert, 21; on economy, 13–21; on education, 20, 32, 36; on employment, 13; on family, 14–15; on friendship, 36; on good, 11; on government, 13–17, 19–21, 24; on government assistance, 9, 11, 19; on greed, 15, 17–19, 32, 172; on happiness, 12–13, 20; historical context of, 13–14; on human nature, 12, 15, 172; on justice, 3, 10–13, 16, 22, 69, 192; on love, 12, 15, 76; on the poor, 22, 37, 38; on population, 15; on poverty generally, 3, 7, 9–11, 195; on property, 14–15, 18–20, 28, 36; on psychology, 12; on redistributive justice, 9–10, 38, 192; on relative poverty, 20; on self-discipline, 12; on social class, 11–12, 13–17, 27; on soul, 12, 123; on virtue, 12, 15, 18–19; on wealth, 10–11, 12–21, 195

Plutarch, 13–14

Poland, 79, 80

police power, 145

politics. *See* citizenship; government

the poor: Aristotle on, 37, 38; capitalism and, 151–52; citizenship and, 81; the good and, 49–50; government assistance and, 114–15; happiness and, 49; Hegel on, 142–43, 146; human nature and, 49–51, 58–59, 64, 73, 75, 81, 117–18, 121, 191; Locke on, 47, 49–51, 58–59, 75, 121, 191; Marx on, 151–52; Plato on, 22, 37, 38; as rabble, 142–43, 146; reason and, 142–43; Rousseau on, 64, 73, 77–78, 81, 93–94; Smith on, 64, 81–82, 84, 86, 93–94, 121, 191; taxes and, 77–78; Tocqueville on, 114–15, 117–18, 120, 121; virtue and, 114–15, 120

poor laws: children and, 52, 54–55; education and, 52; employment and, 52–55, 105–6; government assistance and, 52–53, 55–56, 58–59, 105–6; Locke on, 46, 49, 51–59; Mill on, 128; religion and, 55; Smith on, 89; Tocqueville on, 113–14, 116; women and, 53–54

population: agriculture and, 106; Aristotle on, 23, 32; crime and, 32; education and, 106; employment and, 124–25; equality and, 77; government assistance and, 128; health and, 125; Malthus on, 106; Mill on, 106, 124–25, 128, 129, 130; Plato on, 15; reason and, 125; religion and, 125; Rousseau on, 77; self-discipline and, 124–25; wages and, 124–25; women and, 106, 125, 129. *See also* children

poverty: Aristotle on generally, 3, 9–10, 22–23; causes of, 5–7, 32, 36, 46–47, 49–52, 57–59, 73–75, 76–77, 107–8, 111–15, 120, 123–27, 146–47, 149–52; defining, 3–4, 192; Hegel on generally, 133; justice and, 1–3, 7–8, 12–13, 22, 37–38, 59, 64–65, 121, 131–33, 140, 148, 156–57, 163–64, 184–85, 191–95; limiting, 9, 22–23, 32, 33–34, 36, 37–38; Locke on generally, 3, 7, 46–48; Marx on generally, 3, 133; Mill on generally, 105–8, 123–24; Nozick on generally, 3; Plato on generally, 3, 7, 9–11, 195; preventing, 9, 14–15, 19–21, 21–22, 76–77; Rawls on generally, 3; of Rousseau, 65–66; Rousseau on generally, 3, 59, 64–65, 67–68, 93–95; Smith on generally, 3, 59, 64–65, 81–82, 93–95; solutions for, 52–56, 75–78, 115–18, 123, 129–33, 147–48, 154–57; Tocqueville on generally, 105–8. *See also* absolute poverty; circumstantial poverty; relative poverty; the poor

power, 68–69, 155–56

property: absolute poverty and, 56; agriculture and, 118, 119–20; alienation of, 30; Aristotle on, 23, 26–32, 33, 36; capitalism and, 117; charity and, 31; colonialism and, 130; communism and, 14–15, 18–20, 26–29; desert and, 28, 31–32; education and, 28; equality and, 26–29, 33, 73, 75–76, 84–85, 109–11, 131; family and, 143; freedom and, 75–76; friendship and, 27, 30; government and, 33, 85; government assistance and, 6–7, 121, 130; happiness and, 27, 73, 110, 111; Hegel on, 143, 145; human nature and, 27–28; justice and, 92, 145; Kant on, 31; laborers and, 117, 179–80; Locke on, 56, 59, 75–76, 177, 178, 181; Mill on, 108, 126–27, 130, 131; natural law and, 56, 59; Nozick on, 164, 177–81, 184; Plato on, 14–15, 18–20, 28, 36; Rawls on,

164, 165; relative poverty and, 84,
110; Rousseau on, 64, 67, 68, 73,
75–76, 86, 111; self-discipline and,
126–27; Smith on, 64, 84–85; social
class and, 23; society and, 73,
109–12, 143, 145, 165; Tocqueville
on, 108, 109–12, 117, 118, 119–20,
121; use of, 29–32; virtue and,
29–32; wealth and, 14–15, 18–20.
See also communism
psychology, 6, 12, 20, 82–83, 112–13,
169–73. *See also* human nature
punitive measures, 49–50, 51–55

Raphael, D. O., 89
Rauhut, Daniel, 82, 123
Rawls: on capitalism, 175; on
circumstantial poverty, 37, 173–74,
184; on citizenship, 166–67; on
desert, 174–75, 176–77; on
difference principle, 166–68, 170,
175; on economy, 165; on education,
167; on equality, 166–71, 173–75,
183; on freedom, 167; on
government, 165; on government
assistance, 7; on human nature,
169–73; on institutions, 164–65; on
justice, 2, 68, 122, 164–71, 174–77,
195; liberalism and, 164; on poverty
generally, 3; on property, 164, 165;
on self-respect, 169–73; on the social
contract, 165–68, 176; on society,
164–71; on taxes, 181; on utility, 122
reason: government and, 146;
government assistance and, 128;
Hegel on, 142–43, 146; Mill on, 108,
121–22, 125, 128, 133; the poor and,
142–43; population and, 125;
religion and, 125; society and, 146;
Tocqueville on, 108, 133
redistributive justice: Aristotle on, 9–10,
29, 38, 192; desert and, 29; Hegel
on, 147; Locke on, 56, 59; of
Lycurgus, 14; overview of, 3; Plato

on, 9–10, 21–22, 38, 192; of Solon,
14. *See also* distributive justice;
government assistance
Reeve, C. D. C., 30
Reisman, David, 91
relative poverty: autonomy and, 194;
capitalism and, 4, 84, 87–90;
children and, 4; discrimination and,
4; economy and, 89–90; education
and, 20; equality and, 4, 84–85,
88–89, 110; government and, 89–90;
government assistance and, 89;
happiness and, 20; justice and,
193–94; laborers and, 92; Marx on,
4, 152–53, 157, 193–94; overview
of, 4; Plato on, 20; property and, 84,
110; psychology and, 20; Rousseau
on, 64; Smith on, 4, 64, 84, 87–90,
92, 94, 152–53, 193–94; society and,
110; Tocqueville on, 110, 112;
women and, 4
religion, 55, 63–64, 112, 125, 134n. 29.
See also Christianity; God
Republic (Plato), 10–17
the rich. *See* wealth
Rothschild, Emma, 81–82
Rousseau, Jean Jacques: on agriculture,
77, 78, 79; on autonomy, 68;
children and, 66–67, 77; on
circumstantial poverty, 65, 93–94;
on citizenship, 67–68, 81; on
culture, 69–70; on economy, 63–64;
on education, 77, 80; on
employment, 80; on equality, 67–68,
68–69, 70–81, 88, 192; on freedom,
66, 68, 69, 75–76; on the good,
68–69, 75–78, 80; on government,
74, 75–78; on happiness, 65–66, 68,
73, 110, 111; on health, 70, 72; on
human nature, 64, 71–75, 80, 81,
87, 111, 134n. 31; on justice, 3,
64–65, 68–69; on laborers, 73–74,
91; on love, 76, 80; on money,
79–80; on natural law, 70–71, 74;

on the poor, 64, 73, 77–78, 81, 93–94; on population, 77; on poverty generally, 3, 59, 64–65, 67–68, 93–95; poverty of, 65–66; on power, 68–69; on property, 64, 67, 68, 73, 75–76, 86, 111; on psychology, 6; on relative poverty, 64; on the social contract, 74; on society, 69–70, 71–75, 91; on the state of nature, 71–73, 75, 87, 91; on taxes, 64, 68, 77–78, 86; on virtue, 63–64, 69–70, 192; on wealth, 65–66, 68–69, 70; on will, 75–76, 80

Sandel, Michael, 164
Schneewind, J. B., 49
Second Discourse (Rousseau), 70–75
self-discipline, 12, 85, 92, 107–8, 123–27, 129–30, 131–32
self-ownership, 179–80
self-respect, 169–73
settlement, 47
Seung, T. K., 11, 12, 13, 168, 174, 187n. 56
Shklar, Judith, 81
Singer, Peter, 140, 155, 157, 162n. 125
slavery, 24–25, 36–37
Smith, Adam: on absolute poverty, 84, 87–88, 152–53; on alcohol, 61n. 34; on capitalism, 4, 80, 84, 87–90, 105, 182–83; on charity, 84; on children, 90; on circumstantial poverty, 93–94; on economy, 63–64, 89–90; on education, 84, 89, 91, 182–83; on employment, 84, 90; on equality, 64, 84–85, 88–89, 92–93, 121, 152–53; on freedom, 93; on government, 84, 85, 89–90; on government assistance, 7, 84, 89, 93, 121; on happiness, 85–86; on human nature, 64, 80, 85–87, 121, 134n. 31; on justice, 3, 64–65, 69, 82–84, 92–93; on laborers, 90–93; on movement, 53,

89; on the poor, 64, 81–82, 84, 86, 93–94, 121, 191; on poor laws, 89; on poverty generally, 3, 59, 64–65, 81–82, 93–95; on property, 64, 84–85; on psychology, 82–83, 171–72; on relative poverty, 4, 64, 84, 87–90, 92, 94, 152–53, 193–94; on self-discipline, 85, 92; on society, 85–86, 144; on taxes, 64, 68, 77, 84, 89–90, 182–83; on virtue, 63–64, 88, 92; on wages, 90; on wealth, 86–87
social class, 11–12, 13–17, 23, 27, 33, 148–52. *See also* citizenship
the social contract, 71, 74, 165–68, 176. *See also* society
social services. *See* charity; government assistance
society: agriculture and, 144–45; capitalism and, 139, 148; children and, 143; circumstantial poverty and, 165–66; communism and, 154–56; culture in, 69–70; education and, 167; equality and, 70, 71–75, 109–11, 166–71, 182–85; family and, 143–44; freedom and, 143, 146, 167; God and, 110–11; government and, 144, 146; happiness and, 85–86, 110, 146; health and, 70, 72; Hegel on, 139–40, 142–46; human nature and, 71–75; institutions and, 140, 143, 164–65; justice and, 139–40, 145, 164–71, 182–85; laborers and, 73–74, 144–45; Marx on, 71, 148, 154–56; Nozick on, 182–85; property and, 73, 109–12, 143, 145, 165; Rawls on, 164–71; reason and, 146; relative poverty and, 110; Rousseau on, 69–70, 71–75, 91; Smith on, 85–86, 144; Tocqueville on, 109–11; virtue and, 69–70; wealth and, 70. *See also* the social contract
Socrates, 12–13, 15, 16
Solon, 13–14, 33

soul, 12, 123. *See also* human nature
spectator, 82–83
Stalley, R. F., 27
state. *See* citizenship; government
the state of nature, 70–71, 71–73, 75,
    87, 91, 109. *See also* natural law
Strauss, Leo, 96n. 39, 97n. 72

taxes: equality and, 77–78; Hegel on,
    147; Mill on, 126, 127; Nozick on,
    164, 180; the poor and, 77–78;
    Rawls on, 181; Rousseau on, 64, 68,
    77–78, 86; Smith on, 64, 68, 77, 84,
    89–90, 182–83
Taylor, Harriet, 131
Thomas Aquinas, Saint, 45, 46
timocracy, 16
Tocqueville: on absolute poverty, 112,
    121, 131–32; on agriculture, 111,
    118–20; on capitalism, 111–12, 115,
    117; on charity, 108, 109, 115–16,
    119, 128–29, 132–33; on civil war,
    120–21; on culture, 5; on desert, 113,
    116; on employment, 111–12,
    113–14, 116; on equality, 108–9,
    109–11; on exploitation, 5; on
    freedom, 108–9; on God, 110–11; on
    government assistance, 7, 107–8,
    109, 111, 112–15, 117–18, 121; on
    happiness, 110, 111; on health,
    118–19; historical context of, 105–7;
    on human nature, 107–8, 111–12,
    113–14, 117–18, 121; on justice,
    108–9, 121, 131–33; on laborers,
    111, 117; liberalism and, 107–8, 121,
    163, 193; on movement, 53, 116; on
    natural law, 121; on need, 111–12;
    on the poor, 114–15, 117–18, 120,
    121; on poor laws, 113–14, 116; on
    poverty generally, 105–8; on
    property, 108, 109–12, 117, 118,
    119–20, 121; on psychology, 112; on
    reason, 108, 133; on relative poverty,
    110, 112; on religion, 112, 125,

134n. 29; on self-discipline, 107–8;
    on society, 109–11; on the state of
    nature, 109; on virtue, 107–8,
    114–16, 120; on wealth, 108, 120
Tully, James, 57
tyranny, 17

utility, 122

virtue: absolute poverty and, 88;
    Aristotle on, 23–24, 25, 26, 29–32,
    33, 34–36; autonomy and, 34–35;
    culture and, 69–70; economy and,
    63–64; equality and, 70, 192; golden
    mean in, 26; goods and, 34–36;
    government and, 23–24; government
    assistance and, 114–16; happiness
    and, 23–24, 33, 34–36; health and,
    70; justice and, 25, 192; laborers
    and, 92; Mill on, 107–8, 126; Plato
    on, 12, 15, 18–19; the poor and,
    114–15, 120; property and, 29–32;
    religion and, 63–64; Rousseau on,
    63–64, 69–70, 192; Smith on, 63–64,
    88, 92; society and, 69–70;
    Tocqueville on, 107–8, 114–16, 120;
    wealth and, 15, 18–19, 34–36, 70,
    108, 120, 126. *See also* the good

wages, 90, 124–25, 149–50, 153
Waldron, Jeremy, 186n. 36
wealth: Aristotle on, 34–36; autonomy
    and, 34–35; civil war and, 10, 15–17,
    19; communism and, 14–15, 17–21;
    culture and, 70; economy and, 13–21,
    126–27; equality and, 68–69; family
    and, 14–15; freedom and, 66;
    government and, 13–17, 19–21;
    happiness and, 12–13, 34–36, 65–66;
    health and, 70; human nature and, 15,
    86–87, 108; justice and, 10–11,
    12–13, 68–69; Mill on, 108, 126–27;
    Plato on, 10–11, 12–21, 195; property
    and, 14–15, 18–20; Rousseau on,

65–66, 68–69, 70; self-discipline and, 126–27, 131–32; Smith on, 86–87; social class and, 13–17; society and, 70; Tocqueville on, 108, 120; virtue and, 15, 18–19, 34–36, 70, 108, 120, 126. *See also* money

Wealth of Nations (Smith), 87–93

Werhane, Patricia, 91–92

West, E. G., 88, 91

Westphal, Kenneth, 145–46

will, 68–69, 75–76, 80

Williams, David, 69, 98n. 72

Wokler, Robert, 68

women: Aristotle on, 24–25, 36–37; charity and, 129; citizenship and, 24–25; education and, 5; employment and, 54; health and, 125; Locke on, 53–54; Mill on, 106, 125, 129; poor laws and, 53–54; population and, 106, 125, 129; relative poverty and, 4

Wooten, David, 68